What's the Middle Class?

Rick Smith's journey to teach his kids what none of us learned in school

Pat LaMarche

CHARLES BRUCE FOUNDATION
CARLISLE, PA

©2014, Pat LaMarche
ISBN: 978-0-9913082-1-7
Daddy, What's The Middle Class?
Pat LaMarche
All Rights Reserved

Book design: Chad Bruce
Cover illustration: Chris Mackie

Preliminary Edition
Printed and bound in the United States
Published by the Charles Bruce Foundation

No part of this book may be reproduced in any manner without written permission from the author.

For Claire Welch
She's got spunk and I love spunk!

Table of Contents

Dedication	III
Time Line	VIII
Forward	XI
Introduction	XV
Map	XVIII
1. New York	1
2. LAWCHA	3
3. It Only Took 18 Minutes	7
4. Still Getting Burned	17
5. The World's a Small Place When Corporations Want to Hide	21
6. Load 'er Up, Move 'er Out	25
7. A Sign of the Times	29
8. It's All About the Regress	35
9. Daddy, Why Does That Man Have a Gun?	39
10. Largest Episode of Class War in U.S. History	45
11. Jesus and the Faithless Economy	49
12. Rosa Parks Boot Camp	51
13. Walkin' in Memphis	55
14. A Tale of Two Johnsons	61
15. Guns in the Workplace But No Living Wage	67
16. Little Rock Nine	71
17. Yes Virginia, There is a Middle Class	77
18. Dealey Plaza	81
19. Governor Bush's Presidential Library	85
20. I'm Busted	91

21.	The Ups and Downs of Gender in the Workplace	95
22.	Bruce Scabbit	99
23.	The Grand Canyon Between the Rich and the Poor	103
24	The Chinese and the Irish Built America's Railroads	107
25	Women Laborers and the Servant Class	111
26	$240 Million Tribute to Military Incompetence	115
27	Las Vegas' Biggest Gamble: Working for the State	119
28	Sombody's Getting Jumped	123
29	Well, Do Ya, Punk?	127
30	The Banditelli Brothers	131
31	A Day Off	133
32	Our Little Detour	137
33	Don't Mourn, Organize	141
34	Sammi's the Star	145
35	Cowboy Cuisine	149
36	The American Nightmare	151
37	Massacres R U$	155
38	Have You Seen What You're Driving?	161
39	I Like Ike	165
40	The Myth of Henry Ford	169
41	Fighting for Today's Low Wage Workers	175
42	"You Got Spunk. I Hate Spunk."	177
43	The Garment District	181
44	"The Buck Stops Here"	185
45	Miners Died: Worker's Comp Was Born	189
46	Working Men to Arms	193
47	The Teamsters	201
48	Detroit Destroyed	205
49	Put Ford on Trial	209
50	Ball-Busting "Patriots" offshore the Middle Class	213
	Epilogue by Rick Smith	219
	Appendix	225

Middle Class

Texas Annexed	**1845**
Mexican Territory Annexed	**1848**
Confederates Destroy WV Railroad	**1861**
Sand Creek Massacre	**1864**
John Wesley Powell Explores Colorado River	**1869**
Transcontinental Railroad Completed	**1869**
Nation's Largest Railroad Strike	**1877**
Chinese Exclusion Act	**1885**
McCormick Reaper Strike	**1886**
Illinois Murders Haymarket Martyrs	**1887**
22,000 Railroad Worker Casualties	**1889**
Plessy v. Ferguson	**1896**
Cripple Creek War	**1904**
Triangle Shirt Waist Factory Strike	**1909**
Cherry Mine Fire	**1909**
Sand Creek Massacre Scalps Donated	**1911**
Triangle Shirt Waist Factory Fire	**1911**
Ludlow Massacre	**1914**
Ford Offers Workers $5 per Day	**1914**
Utah Murders Joe Hill	**1915**
National Parks Service Founded	**1916**
Bisbee Deportation	**1917**
Grand Canyon becomes National Park	**1919**
Battle of Blair Mountain	**1920**
Doud Eisenhower Dies of Scarlet Fever	**1921**
Columbine Mine Massacre	**1927**
James Adams Coins "The American Dream"	**1931**
Highlander School Founded	**1932**
Aldous Huxley Writes Brave New World	**1932**
Boulder Dam Completed	**1935**
National Labor Relations Act	**1935**
San Francisco-Oakland Bay Bridge Opens	**1936**

Time Line

1937 Ford Winchester Plant Sit Down Strike
1937 Battle of the Overpass
1945 Franklin Delano Roosevelt Dies
1947 Boulder Dam Renamed Hoover Dam
1947 Ed Asner Graduates from High School
1947 Taft-Hartley Act
1948 UAW Pension Drive
1954 Brown v. Board of Education
1955 Presidential Libraries Act
1956 Federal Aid Highway Act
1957 Japanese Car Imports Begin
1957 Arkansas Ordered to Desegregate
1963 President John F. Kennedy Murdered
1964 Civil Rights Act
1964 National Master Freight Agreement
1967 Race Riots
1968 Memphis Sanitation Strike
1968 Martin Luther King, Jr. Murdered
1978 Presidential Records Act
1981 President Ronald Reagan Busts Patco
1983 Clifton Morenci Strike
1987 Hoover Dam Expense Paid in Full
1989 Arturo DiModica gifts "Charging Bull"
1999 Gas Explosion Ford Rouge Plant
1999 Columbine High School Massacre
2000 NYU Graduate Students Organize
2004 Pat Tillman Killed by Friendly Fire
2004 NYU Busts Graduate Student Union
2010 O'Callaghan-Tillman Bypass Completed
2012 Aurora, Colorado Movieplex Massacre
2013 Dkaha Bangladesh Factory Collapses
2013 West Fertilizer Company Explodes

Foreword

I've had passing knowledge of Rick Smith for a number of years. I used to work at a Central Pennsylvania homeless shelter and Rick was one of the good guys in the area who used their broadcast pulpit to help us when we needed some publicity. He did a little more than most though; Rick also used to chip in some of his own money to help us help the down trodden.

Because of this passing knowledge, I wasn't all that surprised when Rick broached the subject of taking a nationwide trip to check out the history of the labor movement. He clearly gave a damn, and in a much more *hands on way* then most broadcasters. I'm glad there are broadcasters like Rick, the world has way too many Rush Limbaughs and Sean Hannities. And I felt a kindred spirit to the guy. I'd spent the bulk of my broadcast career giving a damn too. In fact during the days of my favorite radio gig, from 1998 until 2004 when I used the pseudonym Genny Judge, I took to the streets weekly – often daily – to rub elbows with the listeners.

That gig ended when I ran for Vice-President of the United States. That's also when my understanding of community and the scale of my approach to helping folks around me changed enormously.

I've spent the last decade traveling the nation regularly. I immersed myself in poverty issues and I got into writing as well. I traveled for the campaign and continued when the election was over. 2004 was the very beginning of blogging and most of the stories written about that year were news stories by others. The following year I wrote a book and landed a gig writing political columns for newspapers. I continued working with the common man and through my writing, I tried to take the reader with me. Still, even after far-flung trips around the U.S. and in other parts of the world, I knew that I wanted a more immediate way to bring the average person into contact with other average people. I wanted an opportunity to broadcast from my experiences. Nine years later, Rick Smith offered me a chance to take the listener on the road in a big way: in a way I'd really hoped to be able to do for a long time.

In the winter of 2013, Rick wrote me an email and invited me to lunch. I was curious what he might have on his mind. I had relocated to central PA after doing a bit of radio in my home state of Maine. Rick's award winning progressive talk show had grown during the year and a half I was gone. It was no longer a part time local effort by a hardworking Teamster truck driver. It was now his full time gig, broadcasting five nights a week out of Harrisburg, the nearby PA capitol city.

I figured if he knew I was back in town, he might want someone to cover his show when he took a night off. I was working very part time, so I was psyched to get my freelance writer's butt over to our lunch appointment and see what he had in mind.

I sat down in the restaurant next to Rick and the guy was just so likable and easy to talk to, it seemed as though I'd known him for years. Maybe that's why I wasn't so surprised when he told me that he wanted a whole lot more than my input on his show. And yeah, he did want me to cover for him when he was away. But, he really wanted to know if I'd be interested in taking a month long trip around the U.S. and write a book about labor history in the United States.

I had just finished a cross country trip with homeless advocate, Diane Nilan. We went skulking around the poorest parts of the desert southwest, going from ghost towns to homeless shelters to prisons. Still, this trip sounded really different and I was interested in what he was planning.

Rick's idea was simple. He had identified several important labor history sites around the country and he wanted to go to them. He wanted to interview local historians, labor leaders, union members and their families. He knew that the trip wouldn't be some comprehensive history of the entire labor movement, but he didn't feel like it needed to be. He just wanted to pique the interest of his listener, stir the consciousness of the average American, and plant the seed in the minds of children that what the middle class worker takes as a regular working condition was the result of hard work and courage on the part of an awful lot of nameless, faceless workers. And he wanted to meet some of the people who are still fighting.

Rick's plan was even more ambitious than anything I had participated in before, but it was what I had hoped I'd do for a very long time. While away, we wouldn't just gather the information needed for the book he wanted written – this book – we would also produce his nightly radio show from the road. You bet I wanted to do radio from the road, but I'm no radio producer and neither is Rick. When I mentioned that I couldn't do any of that production work, Rick said, "You won't have to, we're bringing Brett along."

Brett Banditelli, Rick's producer, is in his late 20's and has worked for years doing PR for labor organizations. Brett both intellectually and viscerally gets what's going on nationwide in the labor movement. He knows what is happening to labor contracts. He knows that both business owners and governments have broken promises with their employees, even though they made those promises years ago. Really, Brett should've written this book. He's got more labor history knowledge in his little finger than I had – at least when I started – in my whole head. And while I've never asked Brett why he doesn't write an authoritative resource on the history of the labor movement, I can guess why. Brett's the master of the 140-character message. He loves the speed with which the electronic age can deliver a stunning photograph. Brett and his social media colleagues – for better or for worse – have left literary dinosaurs like books and their authors way behind.

As for Rick writing the book? He, like Brett, has a baseline knowledge of the subject matter that would have taken 90 percent of the research time out of the task. But writing it would have been one chore too many for this already over taxed multi-tasker. Rick was already working as fundraiser, broadcaster, anchor of the show, clothing outfitter, itinerary planner, RV driver and dad. Yep, that's right, along with Rick, Brett and me in an eight person camper were Rick's wife Carol and their three children, Sam, Alex and Aly. Oh and if you've been in an RV that small then you know that when they say eight persons, they mean eight persons who love each other an awful lot.

When I think back to Rick's proposal that Brett and I jump into an RV with his family and travel nearly 10,000 miles to record and write an incomplete history which would be added to countless other incomplete histories, I wonder why I jumped at the chance. But jump I did.

Daddy, What's the Middle Class? is the result of that journey. In many ways that trip was the toughest thing I've ever elected to do. I've done individual things that were more difficult but they didn't last anywhere near as long.

The trip was – as an old army veteran once said – "like drinking out of a fire hydrant, because you miss so much more than you take in." Is *Daddy, What's the Middle Class?* the history of the U.S. labor movement? No, but it's everything Rick Smith said he wanted to accomplish.

Daddy, What's the Middle Class? is the story of a good dad and a good mom wanting to show their children a United States of America they could be proud to call home. It's a radio show stretching the limits of affordable technology to bring the voices of elevator mechanics, sanitation workers, train engineers, coal miners and so many other average American laborers to the ears of anyone who is eager to learn the true identities of those who built this country. And it's the summer vacation of some really lovable kids who after eight or nine hours driving through the desert or over mountains still had the energy to ask, "does this place have a pool," at literally every RV park we visited.

Daddy, What's the Middle Class? is a chance to learn a little about some well-known historic events and it's a chance to learn a lot about some lesser-known ones. Lastly, *Daddy, What's the Middle Class?* is an opportunity to decide if middle class jobs, 40 hour work weeks, factories that don't blow up and retirements that are still there when you retire aren't just so adorably – yet irretrievably – 20th century.

13 August 2013
Carlisle, PA

Introduction

Carol Smith moved from the west coast to the east coast when she was just a kid. Those transitions are never easy for kids, but her parents tried to make some sense of the bi-coastal move by driving cross-country and letting the kids develop some perspective for their relocation. Carol was 10 at the time and her little brother, David, was 8. Her fond memories from camping along the way with her folks and her recollections of some pretty amazing parts of the U.S. made her want to take her own kids on a similar trip, someday.

When her husband, award winning talk radio host Rick Smith, came to her with an idea to travel the country and visit many of the nation's labor history sites, Carol told him that she loved the idea and that she and the kids would like to come along.

What kind of a guy loads his wife and three kids – aged 4, 7, and 11 – into an RV with his radio show producer and a total stranger? The same kind of guy who learns that a person's always wanted to dine in an old pub where George Washington strategized to beat the British and immediately takes that person there.

Rick's a benevolent dictator – or at least he was on the trip. Somebody's got to be in charge, and that position is never as enviable as it looks. Still Rick listened carefully to the needs and wants of the people who tagged along on his journey and whenever possible he blended his vision for the trip with each individual desire or side bar.

I've already mentioned the kids' penchant for swimming pools. Even though we conducted dozens of interviews, produced 16 radio shows, and traveled nearly 10,000 miles, playgrounds and other amusements were considered essential as well.

At the very end of the journey "Despicable Me 2" hit the movie theaters and we broke from our breakneck route to take a movie pit stop.

Heck, the very timing of the trip was because producer, Brett Banditelli, wanted to go to Netroots Nation. The event in San Jose, California began on the 20th of June and was billed as – at least according to the event website – "one of the most powerful political events of the year..." And Brett agreed. Brett viewed Netroots Nation as a chance to commune with like-minded activists and recharge his rebellion batteries.

Netroots Nation wasn't just a progressive conference Brett wanted to attend; it was a conference center full of Brett Banditellis. So Rick planned the trip to begin when the kids got out of school for summer break and he planned a route along the southern states that would land us in San Jose in time for the conference.

All along the way, as interviews and locations were fitted into place; Rick took into consideration the things each of us wanted to do personally as well as professionally. Brett's desire to be at Netroots was a mix of both. While my request to stop at the new George W. Bush presidential library was professional, my desire to see my son in Indianapolis was purely personal. Rick weighted them equally when planning our trip.

Most cross-country trips include the Grand Canyon – but ours only allowed for three hours there. When we got to the RV Park the night before and learned that there was a train ride to the natural wonder, Rick sprung for the tickets and we all got to go. When you get to the chapters on northern Arizona you'll see that the railroad, and who built it, and what it represents of the nation's labor history made it a perfect fit for the show. But that's not why we got to go. We got to go because Rick saw how excited we all were at the prospect of chugging along to the canyon's rim the way folks did a hundred years ago. Rick was all about making this a trip we enjoyed. And that was at least as important to him as making it a trip to find the lost truth about who built this country.

With the exception of Ed Asner you probably won't recognize the name of a single character we met along the way. And maybe that's what will make this book important to read. To me, the people who built this country are like the people who built the pyramids. They are nameless and faceless and pretty much forgotten even though their work was remarkable and essential and someone else invariably got credit for it.

When Rick watched the History Channel's "The Men Who Built America" he bristled at the pro-robber baron spin the show put on the nation's birth and adolescence. He can't remember during which episode he hatched the plan to tell the real story. But that program cemented Rick's desire to prove that it wasn't Henry Ford who built America; it was thousands upon thousands of automotive workers and their wives and children. It wasn't Cornelius Vanderbilt who built America; but thousands upon thousands of railroad men and miners and their wives and children. It wasn't Andrew Carnegie who built America; it was thousands upon thousands of steel workers and their wives and children. It wasn't... well, you get the picture.

And what matters at least as much as those manufacturers of wealth and their families, were the civil servants – and their families – who rounded out the communities in which they all toiled. The teachers, fire fighters, sanitation workers, social workers, policemen and women and countless others who built our social fiber and preserve generation after generation of American dreams.

Our little road trip to right the wrongs done all through American History by lionizing the robber barons and trivializing the workers was set to begin on June 8th. But we had one side trip to make first. We could not begin "The People's Tour for America" until we spent a few days in New York City rubbing elbows with corporately controlled radio talk hosts at the 2013 Talkers Convention. Before we could head off to our first stop in the mountains of West Virginia we went to the nation's largest concrete jungle. The Big Apple literally exemplifies the myths and the realities of a nation built by the masses and owned by the few. And what better place to start than surrounded by the mouthpieces who earn their living perpetuating the lie of equity in the American way of life.

Oh yeah, and then there's Wall Street too. We stayed in Lower Manhattan: home of the Fraunces Tavern where George Washington strategized to beat the British and home of the U.S. Stock Exchange where the average workers' wages are a liability when counted against the growth of individual wealth.

Turn the page and join us as we embark on "The People's Tour for America."

λ λ

Middle Class

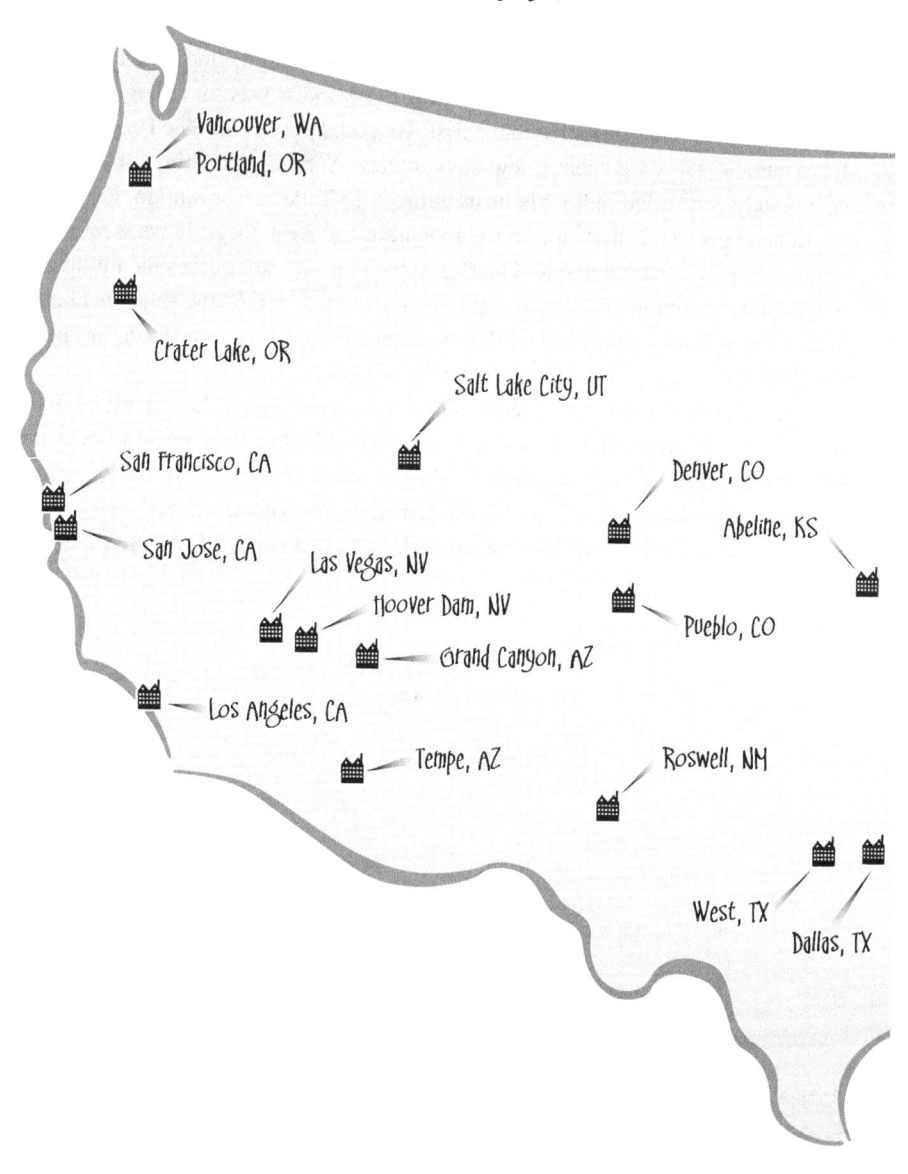

Vancouver, WA
Portland, OR
Crater Lake, OR
Salt Lake City, UT
San Francisco, CA
Denver, CO
San Jose, CA
Abeline, KS
Las Vegas, NV
Hoover Dam, NV
Pueblo, CO
Grand Canyon, AZ
Los Angeles, CA
Tempe, AZ
Roswell, NM
West, TX
Dallas, TX

Motor Route

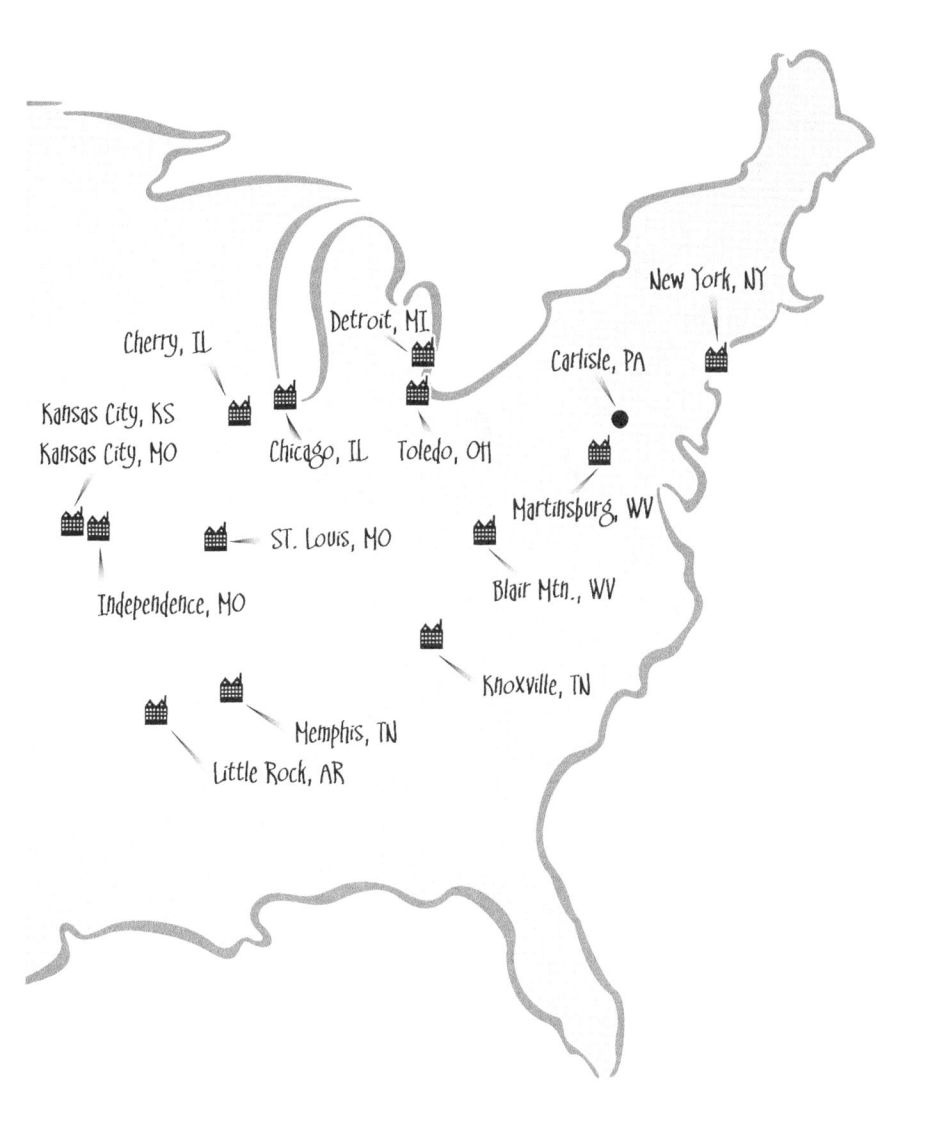

Cherry, IL
Kansas City, KS
Kansas City, MO
Detroit, MI
Chicago, IL
Toledo, OH
Carlisle, PA
New York, NY
Martinsburg, WV
St. Louis, MO
Independence, MO
Blair Mtn., WV
Knoxville, TN
Memphis, TN
Little Rock, AR

Chapter 1 New York
λ λλ

There's a bull on Broadway in lower Manhattan. Most people think of it as the Merrill Lynch Bull. Maybe that 's because it has a sack, not a Goldman Sach, a genuine sack: as in genitals. You can't miss them. There's a giant set of bronze balls hanging under the Wall Street icon. And they're polished to a high shine because – quite frankly – passersby continually rub them.

But the bull actually has nothing to do with Merrill Lynch. And it's not a sign of grotesque wealth, Wall Street indulgence or over-arching greed. At least not according to the artist's web page.

In 1989 Italian artist Arturo Di Modica assembled the 3½ ton sculpture "Charging Bull" as a tribute to the "can-do spirit of America and especially New York, where people from all over [sic] the world could come regardless of their origin or circumstances, and through determination and hard work overcome every obstacle to become successful." The website goes on to explain that, "It's this symbol of virility and courage…" Well, we can stop there. Virility explains the big balls.

And when you think about Wall Street tycoons like Merrill Lynch CEO, Stanley O'Neill, and Goldman Sach's CEO, Lloyd Blankfein, whose mortgage bubble crashed the U.S. economy, you realize that the Charging Bull's cojones really aren't anywhere large enough to stand for the hubris exhibited by centuries of Wall Street tycoons.

Still, the best thing about Di Modica's sculpture is about as unknown as the origin of the statue itself, and that's that it was unwelcome. The artist plopped it down under cover of darkness like so many occupy movement members who would appear on Wall Street a generation later. Sneaking his artwork into the financial district, Di Modica timed his conveyance very carefully so that the regular patrol officer who walks that beat would not catch him delivering his gift. With fewer than five minutes to work, Di Modica dropped off his modern day Statue of Liberty. Much like Lady Liberty's creator Frédéric Auguste Bartholdi, Di Modica wished to demonstrate his respect for those who lived and worked in the U.S. because they were seeking a better life for themselves and their families. And while Bartholdi entitled his work, "Liberty Enlightening the World," underscoring how essential freedom is to personal success, Di Modica's *Charging Bull* paid tribute to the gusto required once freedom had been achieved.

Di Modica mistakenly determined that the New York Stock Exchange was the home of American ferocity and tenacity. Consequently Di Modica dropped it off on "Broad Street, right in front of the New York Stock Exchange" (NYSE), but by the end of the day, the fat cats at the NYSE, who wanted nothing to do with the sculptor's gift, had it removed.

The Charging Bull is now in a much more fitting place, Bowling Green, which commemorates the founding of New York and with the exception of a few million dead or displaced Native Americans and a few million more African Slaves, it can be seen as tribute to the voluntary construct of the American Dream.

Radio host Rick Smith, his producer Brett Banditelli and I began our "People's Tour For America" across the street from – and staring at – the bronze bovine sculpture. When we got there June 6th we were ignorant of the true origin of the Charging Bull. We called it the Merrill Lynch Bull and no one corrected us. We were – like so many others – horrified by the symbolism of the giant golden idol because we thought it was a tribute to the greed, excess, and calamity of unbridled capitalism. And we stood slack-jawed as we tried to figure the expense to the taxpayer of the Charging Bull's round the clock NYPD protective detail.

We hadn't yet picked up the RV-camper we would call home for the next month, and we hadn't yet begun to travel with Rick's wife, Carol, and their kids. But we had two conferences to attend in the Big Apple and they fitted nicely into our plan. We were off to witness what we could of modern day middle class labor issues and to ferret out as many historical landmarks as we could along our way. Rick and Brett had spent months reaching out to local union members and their leadership, to history professors, and to members of the media who might help us round out a real time excursion into the history of America's middle class. We wanted to do this trip, broadcast the interviews and write a book including some of the people who made America great.

With hindsight we came to understand how prophetical it was that we started our trip at the Charging Bull. It wasn't a symbol of avarice as much as it was a symbol of rewritten history. We thought it a craven idol dedicated to a legacy of stealing wealth from the people who created it. But it was, in fact, a tribute to those hard working men and women who undauntedly built this country with their own grit and gristle. If we could use our trip to debunk the lies of American Corporate Exceptionalism and replace it with the true stories of natives, slaves, immigrants, migrants and the underclass that built this nation, we might one day get the folks on Broadway to know the truth about their bull.

Chapter 2 LAWCHA
λ

We pulled into lower Manhattan, dropped Brett off at 25 Broadway, and went to check into our hotel. Our 200 mile ride up from Carlisle, PA to NYC that morning had been relatively uneventful – unless you count a serious game of possum Rick played with a limousine driver as we approached the Holland Tunnel. Not surprisingly, Rick – old Teamster that he is – won. And we got a one fingered wave that is always most elegant when performed out the window of a limo.

Rick and I stood at the front desk of our swank hotel. The gentleman behind the counter asked our last name. Rick said "Smith" and I blushed just for the fun of it. As we walked over to City University of New York (CUNY) building where we had dropped Brett to get our booth set up, Rick asked if I wanted some lunch. We ducked into Fraunces Tavern. Earlier, while we looked for a place to park, I had remarked that I'd always wanted to eat there. See, legend has it that George Washington and his crew supped there often while they fomented and executed their sedition and revolution. And I really wanted to go.

Sup and foment revolution now, and everyone from the NSA to the neighborhood preacher will condemn you as a bad American – if you get off that easily. Gitmo's full of people with a whole lot less on their conscience than our first president, but such is the role of power and legacy in our historic perspective.

I was beyond excited to go to Fraunces and really delighted that Rick made that happen. I surmised while sitting there, that every part of all worthwhile American history is about overcoming those more powerful to make the nation a better place.

And even though ole aristocratic General Washington and his high brow buddies overthrowing the king was more about the former's thirst for power and land than about the latter's tax policies, somewhere along the way, the little guy would benefit. Yeah, overthrowing the king would definitely lead to a better way of life for the peasant. At least that was the plan. That was what the Constitution allegedly promised. And when it failed to deliver, it was amended to compensate for its deficiencies.

We sat in that revolutionary tavern and fortified ourselves so we could begin the "People's Tour for America." It was a very poetic beginning to our trip. We started where revolution started. We were out to chronicle the great changes in the American human condition. And we would be revealing a story about the creation and subsequent decline of America's middle class.

Rick and Brett spent months preparing for the People's Tour for America. Before the tour had a name or a schedule, they approached would-be sponsors and other allies who could make the project happen. They extended an invitation to anyone and everyone that they could think of: including me. Rick and Brett knew they could pull off a month-long radio show. But they wanted to write a book about it too, and for that they wanted help.

Perhaps the biggest challenge to trying something new and as yet undone is first understanding the concept and then conveying that concept to others. It's not like you could just roll tape on when this had all happened before. Here's where I had the advantage. I had done more than a few of these cross-country trips. Traveling along at the ground level of society – gathering information – is not like any other kind of travel. The fact-finder needs to prioritize locations, line up authorities, eye witnesses and interviews, and strategize the correct time and place to get there. And because you're collecting previously unknown data, you may have some idea of what you'll learn but you have no way of knowing if your assumptions are correct.

I had done a number of cross-country trips – and smaller multistate jaunts – to detail homelessness and poverty in the U.S. My familiarity with traveling and interviewing people who think of themselves as too ordinary, without any real information to share, meant that I already knew most people wouldn't talk to us until we got in their faces. I knew that we would have to be flexible and patient as regular folks who never thought their opinions or experiences mattered came to understand that they were the authorities – the absolute experts – we were after, and we wanted them to share their knowledge. They had no idea that the common ordinary nature of their lives made them valuable because they represented so many others just like them all across the country.

We set out to chronicle the lives of those who made America great: Not those who stole greatness from the millions who created it. There were already plenty of books and radio and television shows about the robber barons and virtually nothing about the worker.

My understanding of the complexity and fluidity required to make this trip a success is where my experiential advantage stopped.

I had devoted my career to interviewing and defining the impoverished. I didn't know too much about the middle class. My familiarity with middle class experiences, the benefit of union jobs when it came to building a middle class, and the role government and education played in securing a continued middle class rested entirely on anecdotal information I got by growing up in a middle class family.

Like Rick Smith who grew up in poverty in a Cleveland, Ohio housing project, I started my life in a Housing Project. As a little kid I lived in Chad Brown Housing Project in Providence, RI. But my family's climb out of poverty was very different from Rick's. My family moved out of the projects when my dad finished getting his education. An education paid for by the taxpayers, through the G.I. Bill.

Rick moved out of poverty when his mom died.

Rick went to live with his grandparents when he was only 13. His granddad was a Teamster. He worked hard driving a truck and consequently, he and Rick's grandma owned their own home.

So while I assured Rick and Brett that "things" would come together on the road, they tutored me on what it meant to be part of the labor movement. I was on an intense learning curve and the boys were hoping to bring me up to speed in time to write this book.

None of us worried about the radio gigs. Anyone who is any good at broadcasting can interview a person they don't know, about things they don't understand. Just like any self-help book will tell you, admitting you don't know is the first step.

Through the joint process of interviewing and sharing experiences with our guests, our nightly radio show helped me better understand the labor movement and labor's ongoing struggle. That alone might not have been enough to help me get a grip on labor movements present, past and future. Luckily, that wasn't all we had.

One of the reasons we went to New York City before we headed west for our trip was the LAWCHA conference being held at the Brooklyn College Graduate Center for Worker Education – in a building right across from the *Charging Bull*.

LAWCHA stands for the Labor And Working Class History Association and because of the conference, some of the nation's most dedicated archivists and historians gathered in lower Manhattan. We scored a few interesting interviews which have been archived with all the others from our trip at our People's Tour Website – www.peoplestourforamerica.com. And we met a handful of labor history gurus who invited us to stop by when we passed through their home states while others suggested websites and literature to augment our understanding.

Still, LAWCHA wasn't all back slaps and networking. We also learned a little something about current events that the mainstream media had neglected to report adequately – if they reported on it at all. In fact, in some cases it wasn't that the media failed to report, it was that they told boldfaced lies. And the LAWCHA offered us a real opportunity to see the truth with our own eyes.

Super Storm Sandy ravaged the Mid-Atlantic States. According to the AFL-CIO website, 1/3 of all union firefighters lived in the path of the storm. The first responders were among the first victims. One of the most interesting and important messages delivered at the LAWCHA conference was the story of brave men and women who worked day and night to rescue their neighbors and restore necessities to millions of storm victims.

Exhibitors at the conference produced a photo essay showing the intense beating taken from the wind and the water, and then showing the response from workers up and down the impact area. The exhibit they created is a traveling show, and it is available to others who would like to debunk the notion that civil servants and other government employees are non-essential. It also underscores the necessity for well-trained organized professionals to repair and build our nation's infrastructure. Once that infrastructure is demolished, volunteer and unskilled labor cannot replace it.

If not for the LAWCHA conference, I would never have known how important unions and union labor was to Sandy's recovery. I don't know whose job it is to tell these stories or whose job it is to correct the lies. It isn't the mass-market media's anymore. That sad reality is all too obvious. Perhaps the only way to tell America what really happens in this country is to raise the money to start new broadcast entities, to write new newspapers, to support the few honest and honorable agencies that currently exist. It appears that labor will have to start telling the truth about labor history and labor current events for themselves and to a much larger more diverse group than the one assembled June 6th at 25 Broadway.

But it was definitely a good place to start. And it turned us onto the reality of Super Storm Sandy's clean up.

One thing is for certain: being abandoned by the media is a crime and a theft of the public trust and the public airwaves. It should be the role of the media to tell the truth, to provide a thorough and accurate account of events. But the media doesn't do their job anymore. I feel comfortable telling you that, because I'm a member of the media. So is Rick. And as such we headed across town at the Talkers' convention when we left the LAWCHA conference.

At Talkers' New York 2013, we sat down with those most responsible for misleading the American public. The on-air personnel, the producers, the advertising sales people, and the management; they were all getting together to talk about themselves, and to talk about talk radio, and to talk about how to make more money. But nobody was going to talk about personal integrity, ethical broadcasting, or telling the truth. Oh well, if you can't beat them, the least you can do is learn their tricks, so we went uptown to learn how the bad guys keep winning.

Chapter 3   It Only Took 18 Minutes
λ λ

"Everyone that jumped was on fire."
~Joseph Granick, Fabric Cutter, 8th floor.

In his survivor interview, Granick went on to describe how he, "saw a number of firemen crying as they witnessed victims of the fire killed as they broke through the nets."

Cornell University's website has transcriptions of the eyewitness accounts from survivors, passersby and a firefighter at the scene of the horrific Triangle Shirt Waist Factory Fire. Reading these accounts is like sitting in the room with the victims. They are chilling and frightening and they relate a horror that would be unimaginable without these testimonies.

The building where that factory burned, March 25, 1911, is now a part of New York University (NYU). It took about 18 minutes for us to get from Lower Manhattan to its Greenwich Village location. That's about the same amount of time it took for 146 young men and women to burn to death, to be asphyxiated, or to die on the street below.

I first learned about the fire in a college history course. The class was an upper level elective when I was a history major at Boston College. The story ran a few paragraphs in the textbook and we spent part of a day discussing it. There were no graphic details and no real discussion of the fire itself. We mostly spoke about the plight of labor in the big picture of U.S. history. And I never added it to my mental list of historic landmarks I'd like to visit. I guess I assumed the factory had been torn down because damage accompanying such rapid carnage must have destroyed the building as well.

I'm sure I figured there'd be a plaque somewhere paying tribute to the tragedy, maybe even a park. And there is a plaque, but it's on the side of the NYU laboratory the factory has become.

While we were staffing our booth at the LAWCHA conference, I got tipped off that the Asch building was still standing. Yeah, that was the name of it: the Asch building – pronounced ash. I chatted with the guy staffing the booth next to ours and I mentioned that I always wondered what happened to the factory. He turned out to be an NYU student and he said that the old deathtrap had been donated to the university a few years after the fire. As soon as I heard that, I hopped on the phone and called the number listed on line for NYU's public relations department. They agreed to take us on a tour of the floors where the Triangle Factory was housed. I mentioned it to Rick and he said, "Let's go."

Wandering the building today, you'd never guess how over crowded and treacherous the conditions were on the 8th and 9th floors of the building at the corner of Greene Street by Washington Square East. The rib cage high lab tables are about twice as far apart as the sewing machines and the cutting tables were on the day of the fire. In complete contradiction to the way things were in 1911, there are emergency stations and exit markings, even signs that say not to block the exits and that the exit doors must not be locked.

The brightly lit rooms have the same stone window casings that were there when the fire victims leapt – or were pushed – to their deaths. Fire Captain, Joe Rabino, one of the first responders, explained that people didn't mean to shove each other out the windows, "they were being pushed by those in back of them who were being burned by the fire. That was not panic - there was nothing else they could do but go out the window."

I stood in the windows on the corner looking down at the concrete sidewalk below. I couldn't imagine falling from that great height.

When the first survivors got to the sidewalk they didn't understand that the people lying there had fallen. Josephine Nicolosi explained, "When we came downstairs, the firemen were not there yet but the first thing we saw were girls lying on the sidewalk. We thought they had fainted and one of my girl friends said, 'Thank God we are not like them, we're alright.' She went over to one of the girls lying on the sidewalk and bent over her and she was hit by another falling body and killed."

The oral histories describe the building's interior, including the comfortable lofty corner where we stood. It's very different from the congested factory corner it was that day. That part of the 8th floor is now a lounge. Eyewitnesses spoke of a young woman who had climbed the length of the ledge to get to that corner. She was on fire. She stayed on the ledge and held on as long as the flames and her pain would let her. When she finally fell, she descended fully engulfed to the pavement.

The Triangle Company only occupied the top 3 floors. The factory workers were on the 8th and 9th floors and the 10th floor housed the company's administrative offices. There were doors and elevators at the front and the back of the workspace. Both accesses were open in the morning when the workers came in, but the front space was locked tight after the day's shift began so that no one could leave without being searched. The owners, Isaac Harris and Max Blanc, were convinced that the workers would steal fabric or lace from the company, if they were not searched every night. To save money, they only hired one set of security guards, so the workers were only allowed to exit on one side of the building.

Mary Domsky-Abrams recalled, "In the morning, when we were going up to work, both elevators (front and back) would be operating. But on leaving, only the one in the back was allowed to run. This was because the company directed a watchman to search the girls' pocketbooks, in which we used to carry our lunches. As the bosses wanted to save the expense of having another watchman at the front, they allowed only one exit to be used for all three floors."

Domsky-Abrams didn't know how anyone could be afraid of the workers stealing, there were too many checks in place at their workstations, "The fact was that, even if the workers had wanted to steal anything, it would have been impossible, because when bundles of work were distributed, every item was counted and listed on the tickets. And when the work was completed, everything was counted again."

While it's a tribute to the greed of the employers, it is even more blatantly evidence of the subjugation of the workers – security guards included – that the watchmen continued to search bags, even as the workers fled the fire. When her account of the locked doors was challenged by the attorneys for Blanc and Harris, Domsky-Abrams got angry, "The bosses' [sic] lawyers made all sorts of excuses, attempting to defend the employers on keeping the door locked, in face of another girl's [sic] testimony that even when the fire already had broken out, and she was among the first to reach the elevator, she had to show the watchman the contents of her pocketbook..."

With the doors securely locked at one side of the building, escape could only be made by the other set of industrial elevators, the adjoining flight of stairs and the fire escape. When the survivors were asked why they did not use the fire escape they said they didn't know the building had one. This is one of the reasons they survived. The rusted escape was so rickety that it collapsed under the weight of those who did use it, and everyone on it perished in the fall.

The 1901 neo-renaissance building's stone façade had a wooden infrastructure. The floors were soaked in oil. Barrels of machine oil were intermittently placed throughout the factory and in the stairwells. Rows of sewing machines were positioned so close together that it was difficult to move between them. When the fire broke out, eyewitness explained that many women climbed across the machines as their only means of escape.

Each seamstress sat with a straw basket loaded with cloth pieces on either side of her. One side had items to be stitched and the finished products were on the other. On the cutting floor – which was above the sewing room – long tables were stacked with a hundred or more layers of cloth to be cut. Holes were cut in the tables to throw the cut away scraps through. When the fire broke out on the 8th floor these openings acted as flues to wick the fire up through the cutting room full of fabric.

The entire factory was fuel or accelerant. The sewing rooms were strung from one side to the other with cord upon which the workers would hang their finished blouses. Captain Rubino said that this network of hanging clothes helped the fire to spread: a fire that scarcely needed the help.

Water buckets hung from the walls in the corners by the windows – like the corner where Rick, Brett and I stood gazing down and from whence the burning women had fallen. In her account, Domsky-Abrams revealed that the buckets were empty and she remembered thinking about that on the morning of the fire: "On that particular morning, the day of the tragedy, I remarked to my colleagues that the buckets were empty, and that if anything were to happen, they would be of no use." Domsky-Abrams recalled one of her friends mentioning this to the manager, "'Mr. Bonstein, why is there no water in the buckets? In case of a fire, there would be nothing with which to fight it,' He became enraged at our group of price committee members (the union had members that represented the workers on issues of price, working conditions, etc. Domsky-Abrams had participated in the 1909 Triangle Strike and was on one of these committees), and with inhuman anger replied: 'If you'll burn, there'll be something to put out the fire.'"

Mr. Bonstein's plan to have the women burn as a firebreak may have worked to his advantage. Bonstein survived the fire.

On our tour we walked from the old Ashe Building, now known as the Brown Building, through a narrow stairwell to the adjacent Silver Building. On the day of the fire these buildings were not connected. We could see from our tour that the buildings appeared to have been about 15 to 20 feet apart. This gap between the buildings was a scene of great courage.

Domsky-Abrams recalled, "A group of men made a human ladder of themselves in an attempt to make it possible for girls hunched in fear at the windows not yet on fire to cross over to the next building, to which there was a small bridge (or passage.) But all the men, about 10 of them, fell down, not being able to bear up under the weight, and were killed together with those who tried to save themselves. We were all deeply moved by the heroism and tried to kiss their bodies as they were being removed to the morgue."

Most of the surviving workers had no idea how they survived. Most of the survivors interviewed didn't know there was a fire escape or an available stairway. They ran for elevators that often were too full or locked away from them. Many fell down the elevator shafts or tried to hang onto an elevator cable to slide down. It's easy enough to understand that if the survivors didn't know where the stairways and fire escapes were, that those who died didn't know either. Those victims likely had the same knowledge but far worse luck.

The old industrial elevators had cables that went through the center. While the front elevator was locked away from the workers, the back elevator managed to make a few trips up to the 9th floor – the 8th floor burned too quickly – it would have been suicide to open the elevator door or linger on that floor. After one or two trips, no one was willing to stay in the elevator to run the cables and bring it back to the top. Without anyone to operate the elevator, it sat at the bottom of the Ashe building and a number of workers wrapped cloth on their hands and slid down the cables. Some made it to the bottom. Some let go. For others the friction wore through the fabric and tore their wrapped hands. In the end people hoping to escape the flames inadvertently threw other workers down the shaft, and some may have jumped. Consequently, bodies piled up on top of the car on the ground floor.

Sarah Friedman Dworetz was one of the lucky few who managed to make it down the elevator. Dworetz remembered, "It was the old style elevator – cable elevator – to make it go down, you pulled the cable from the floor up. That cable was at the side of the elevator shaft. I reached out and grabbed it. I remember sliding all the way down. I was the first one to slide down the shaft. I ended up on top of the elevator and then I lost consciousness. Others must have landed on top of me. When the rescue workers came to the shaft they pulled me out and laid me out on the street. I had a broken leg, broken arm. My skull had been injured. One of my hands had been burned by friction."

The rescue teams laid Sarah on the street along with the rest of the dead from the elevator shaft. When they realized she was alive, she was sent to the hospital and treated for her injuries.

Dora Appel Skalka took the stairs down. As she went down, she noticed the barrels of machine oil. Dora believed the building was a bomb waiting to explode. When she got to the ground floor, she tried to run out of the building to safety on the street. But the rescuers would not let her leave, "There were maybe 20 or 30 people in the lobby. Some were crying and hysterical but they would not let us out. When we finally got out of the lobby into the street I could see why - because there, smashed on the sidewalk, were the beautiful faces of those who were my neighbors at the machines."

Just as Domsky-Abrams told many stories of young women falling to their death, bystanders came forward to do the same. They remembered when the recent factory strike brought these women out to the streets. Those who had been part of the strike of 1909 recounted that the company hired prostitutes to serve as strike breakers. That was because men couldn't hassle the women on the picket line, but other women could.

In 1909 the workers struck for better wages, conditions, and oversight of the subcontractors who brought recent immigrants in to work and learn a trade. But even after their hard-won victories from 1909, children were still being smuggled in to work at the Triangle Shirtwaist Factory. Many of the survivors recalled the inspectors walking through the plant and the supervisors hiding the children in the wicker baskets or the rest room because they were too young. Ida Kornweiser was one of those children, "I worked about 4-5 weeks without pay, then I began to make about $3 or $4 a week from the inside contractor who took me up. I must have been a child at that time because I remember that when the inspector used to come they would push me into the toilet to hide."

The youngest casualty of the fire was a 14 year old who died on Greene Street.

Many of the victims draped themselves in cloth to try and keep their own clothes and hair from catching fire. Domsky-Abrams remembered some girls who chose an especially ironic drapery, "In the panic of the fire, I recall that three girls wrapped themselves in the American flag and jumped out the window together. They landed on the glass manhole cover on the sidewalk and broke through it. Their bodies were found later buried in the deep."

Most urban centers have flat basement covers in the sidewalk in front of the buildings. In a more rural setting these would be bulkhead doors that slant up to the side of structure. Because sidewalks are a necessary part of each city block, inner cities use access covers that are flush with the pavement, better accommodating pedestrian traffic. Many of the women who fell to their death crashed through these horizontal bulkheads.

Captain Rubino explained that the burning bodies falling to the ground only spread the fire more, "While we were upstairs, we had others who were fighting another fire in the cellar. Some of the falling bodies crashed through the dead lights and went into the cellar which was stored with rabbits' fur and set that on fire. We had to lay out lines in the cellar."

Firefighters' resources weren't just trained on the building and its basement, they also had fires to extinguish on the sidewalk. Again, Rubino explained, "Those bodies were coming down with the force of 1 1/2 tons by the time they hit the sidewalk. They were coming down with hair and clothes burning - you know the girls at that time wore long hair. When the bodies didn't crash through the deadlights, they lay there on the sidewalk three or four high, burning, and we had to play the hoses on them."

Joe Flecher was the office manager. He agreed to an interview with Leon Stein. You can read 19 of Stein's interviews at Cornell University's website.

Joe blamed the police and Joe blamed the fire departments for the deaths at the factory. And even though he couldn't get out of the building either, he remained loyal to the company in his court testimony and 46 years later in his living room when Stein recorded his eyewitness account.

Joe had been lucky enough to be on the 10th floor when the fire began. Only one person from the 10th floor died. Joe went up onto the roof. He crawled across to another building. He was followed by workers along the fragile catwalk Joe used, the catwalk collapsed under their weight. They were killed.

Joe said that the hoses didn't have enough pressure. He said that the ladders were too short and he said that the nets were too weak. He never once said that oil-soaked floorboards and oil drums in the stairwells exacerbated the carnage. He never said that empty water buckets and locked doors gave the fire means and opportunity to kill more than a hundred people. Joe didn't explain why the workers didn't know about the fire escapes or why the fire escapes weren't better maintained.

Why would Joe be so loyal to the end? It might have been that he identified with the company's owners more than he did the workers – although that would have been wishful thinking at best. It also might have been a one thousand dollar gift made to anyone who agreed to testify in favor of Max Blanc, Isaac Harris, and the company.

There is no proof that Joe was offered or accepted a payoff. Certainly, if anyone did sell out to the company, they didn't admit it. The only survivor who mentioned a bribe was Josephine Nicolosi, she said that her employer Max Blanc, "offered me $1,000 to change my testimony. He said to me, 'Come here you. Why you say the door's locked.' I said to him, 'That is the truth.' He said, 'How much do you want.' I screamed to the police, 'He wants me to cheat my friends.'"

Nicolosi was doubly repulsed by the offer because she believed that the company would have paid her with the money from her dead co-workers, "You know the company held back one week's pay all the time. That is why after the fire we had to go to an empty store - I don't remember where - to collect the pay the company held back." If 146 dead people didn't collect their pay, and countless others of the 500 employees were too traumatized to, Harris and Blanc had an awful lot of someone else's money with which to bargain.

18 minutes. It only took 18 minutes. 146 persons roasting and smothering and smashing on the sidewalk, and it was over in 18 minutes.

No cause was ever attributed to the fire. Some conjectured it was a cigarette or a match used to light one. Others believed that management deliberately set the fire. Domsky-Abrams said, "A judge or a lawyer, I don't remember which asked me whether I thought the fire was started by the company, I replied … that this wasn't the first, but the third fire at the company, which could be verified very easily."

That answer – and the confidence with which survivor after survivor testified against the company – infuriated the defense. "The company lawyer jumped up, interrupting me, and started to shout that I wasn't telling the truth, that I had deliberately come to court in a black dress with a white collar in order to impress the jury."

Domsky-Abrams' reply was concise and accurate; "I told him that no deeper impression was needed than the 147 innocent, young victims of the Triangle Company, the locked door, and the refusal of the bosses to recognize even their indirect responsibility for what had happened." Domsky-Abrams counted an extra casualty because a grief stricken loved one died of a heart attack when told about the fire.

Fearful that testimony like Domsky-Abrams' was actually impacting the trial, the company lawyers had her barred from the proceedings, "In the following days of the trial, we survivors of the fire no longer were allowed in court."

Domsky-Abrams summed up the verdict, "The Triangle Company bosses went free. 'Justice' found them not guilty. In those days – and also today – there was no proper measure of justice for lives of workers."

Less than three weeks after our visit to the old Asch Building in New York, Rick and his daughter Sammi, Brett and I would wander the exploded streets of West, Texas where a fertilizer plant fire killed those at work at the time and 11 of the first responders who were called to the blaze. Domsky-Abrams is still right, "and also today – there was no proper measure of justice for lives of workers."

The trial ended, the owners went free. Once relocated Blanc and Harris reopened their factory and went back into operation. On various occasions Blanc and Harris were sited for safety violations, they shrugged the fines off and continued to exploit their workers and the work place.

Some survivors longed for revenge. Some even said they plotted revenge for a while. But none followed through with their fantasy.

Without the benefit of mass media outlets and real time news reporting, some of the women got in trouble with their traditional immigrant parents for getting home late from work. Ethel Monick Feigen was punished, "The night of the fire I got home late. I got a licking from my father. He called me a 'bummike' and my mother stood in the corner shivering. I kept hollering, 'But Pa' but he would not listen…He wouldn't listen about the fire."

Countless survivors felt guilty for surviving and struggled to comfort the family members of those who did not.

"We had a 'lanslady' -- I was very friendly with her daughter who was their only child and who worked in Triangle. When the 'lanslady' heard that I had been saved she came yelling into our house and in her sorrow began to wave her hands at me and berate me why I had not saved her daughter." Rose Hauser continued, "The poor woman -- she lost her mind. My mother pleaded with her and tried to calm her. For a long time after that I was afraid to walk on the block where she lived. I was afraid to meet her."

And of course there were final good-byes. And on that, Mary Domsky-Abrams shall have the last words: "Choked sobs were heard all around. The people were crying, the streets were crying – and the skies also were crying that day. Just as if heaven and earth were taking part in the tragedy, on that day of the funeral it was a pouring rain. You could touch the sorrow in the air."

Chapter 4 Still Getting Burned

ʎ

> "I kept saying to myself what all the greenhorns used to say, that in America they don't allow one to burn."
> ~Rose Indursky, Sleeve setter, 9th floor.

Rick, Brett and I weathered a downpour to get back to the LAWCHA conference after our tour of the old Triangle Shirt Waist Factory. As we ran across the street to shelter under a construction overhang built around the building next door, Brett said. "That's so crazy. I'm pretty sure that's one of the NYU labs that had their union busted."

"What?" I yelped. It's fun to hang out with Brett and Rick. Their knowledge of union issues and union activities is so enormous – especially when compared to mine.

Brett went on, "Yeah, you can look it up. But NYU was like the first private university to allow collective bargaining for their grad students. Well, allow is a funny word I guess, the NLRB forced them to, but then when Bush became president, the board changed and NYU was able to beat the union back down. I think they were part of a transportation union or something. Look it up."

Brett's favorite form of language is the initialism. Initialisms are like acronyms only you say all the letters. An acronym is a word made from word beginnings like "scuba" but an initialism is a new word still pronounced by its individual letters like "FBI." Consequently, every one of Brett's sentences is like a bowl of alphabet soup. So the first think I looked up was NLRB. The National Labor Relations Board, according to their website, "has five Members and primarily acts as a quasi-judicial body in deciding cases on the basis of formal records in administrative proceedings. Board Members are appointed by the President to 5-year terms, with Senate consent, the term of one Member expiring each year."

After I understood that, I looked up their rulings on collective bargaining for university students and sure enough, Brett was right. NYU had been the first private university with collective bargaining for their graduate students. Brett was also right that NYU had been forced to allow a graduate student union; they had not willingly come to the table with them. Their compulsory participation in negotiations with their researchers made me wonder how many other "safety measures" in place at NYU – or at any public building – were only in place because laws required them.

A lot had changed in the old Ashe building; a lot that had been mandated by municipal, state and federal regulation, and much of it because of the unnecessary loss of 146 lives right there in that same building.

The changes were evident to us when we stood in the hallway waiting for admission to the labs on the 8th and 9th floors of what NYU now calls the Brown Building. We photographed signs that cautioned against locked doors and blocked exits. But I saw no sign that said, "A union would provide a safer work place and better pay." No that lesson was obviously not carried forward after the disaster. After I learned about the union forced on NYU and then busted by NYU, I wondered if the university would have active fire extinguishers and escape routes if the various levels of government mandating such things, ceased to require them.

When I did as Brett directed and started "looking up" what happened to fair wages and collective bargaining for graduate students, I was amazed by the power of the NLRB to shape the way laws are administered, interpreted and consequently, how workers are treated. I guess I never thought that there'd be a system in place to interfere in a bargain struck between workers and their employer. But I forgot that some workers aren't considered workers and some classifications of workers – like agricultural workers – aren't protected with a minimum wage or maximum hours in a workweek. This People's Tour would strip away most, if not all, of my naiveté when it came to workers having the right to stand up for themselves.

See there are public universities where the graduate students can bargain for their wages. But private institutions for some reason – cost savings they insist – don't see them as employees. Places like NYU and Brown University – the university that eventually won the case that NYU used to eliminate the union – see them as merely students.

So what was at the heart of the dispute was whether graduate students are students or employees. When NYU's graduate students brought their case before the NLRB in 2000, the board – heavily weighted with President Clinton's appointees – ruled that they were workers and as such could strike. The students formed the Graduate Students Organizing Committee (GSOC), an affiliate of United Auto Workers (UAW) Local 2110.

The GSOC negotiated with NYU and began working under a contract. But in 2004, Brown University and some other Ivy League schools went back to the

NLRB with the argument that graduate students weren't workers and had no right to strike and this time the board – loaded with Geo. W. Bush appointees – agreed with them. After the reversal, NYU didn't have to union bust, but they did.

The union busting had dire consequences. Graduate students were threatened with expulsion from their programs if they attempted a strike. For foreign students, expulsion also meant deportation. Still the GSOC and the UAW tried to keep up the fight, a former Yale University undergraduate and union activist, Josh Eidelson, writing for Salon noted, "Union members alleged that they were interrogated about their union activism by their supervisors. 20 strikers were fired."

Triangle Shirtwaist Factory owners, Isaac Harris and Max Blanc, would be so proud.

λ

Chapter 5   The World's a Small Place When Corporations Want to Hide

Earlier in 2013 – before we went on our People's Tour – Rick, Brett, a volunteer named Jake and I held an action at a number of power retailers in Harrisburg. A factory collapse in Dhaka, Bangladesh, killed 1127 workers. As I type this in late September 2013 the Washington Post reports, "Nearly five months after the deadliest incident in garment manufacturing history, the suffering is far from over for the victims, their relatives and the rescue workers. Many families have received only part of their promised financial compensation."

In May, we went to Macy's, Target, J.C. Penney and Footlocker distributing leaflets with information that these and other retailers – most notably Wal*Mart – refused to sign onto a safety agreement with the factories in Bangladesh. We did so with the hope that consumers would motivate these multi-national corporations to care about worker safety. An AFl-CIO website explaining the reluctance of some retailers to sign the international workplace safety agreement postulated that Wal*Mart and The Gap wanted to make their own agreements with workers that "probably won't be of a legally-binding nature."

International agreements of a legally binding nature just aren't in keeping with the corporate imperative to increase profits no matter what. And without an international governing body that can hold multi-national corporations liable for injuries occurring to workers in foreign countries – meaning countries other than the host nation that licensed the corporation – the Wal*Marts of the world can buy from manufacturers that oppress and endanger workers. Worker exploitation and endangerment without consequence is a major reason – if not the reason – companies move manufacturing overseas.

For the most part, the U.S. consumer has lost his or her stomach for images of workers being crushed when factories collapse or burning women falling to their deaths, as was the case in the Triangle Shirtwaist Factory Fire. Consequently, unscrupulous companies choose to purchase from factories located far from the critical gaze of the American consumer.

It's not just workplace safety that suffers when multi-national jurisdictions pass differing regulations, have lax enforcement, neglect to inspect for workplace hazards or refuse to respect global impact of local actions. Consequently, international governance and enforcement – for any reason – is extremely limited in the 21st century.

When "Operation Iraqi Freedom" began, U.N. Secretary General Kofi Annan accused the U.S. and the United Kingdom of violating their U.N. Charter by invading Iraq. The U.S. and the U.K. argued that Resolution 1441 – legislation that the leadership of both nations rammed through the general assembly – justified it. And what ensued is arguably the greatest unprovoked invasion and occupation since WW II.

As for the perpetrators – the U.S. and the U.K. – a lack of genuine international oversight meant that there were no consequences and no war crimes trials.

When individuals in the U.S. – and around the world – decried the lack of deference the Bush and Blair Administrations showed to U.N. authority, our conservative counterparts in talk radio took aim with renewed vigor at the United Nations and their attempts to regulate these super powers.

Talk radio hosts from Sean Hannity to Rush Limbaugh vacillated from American apologist to War Hawk demanding blood. The last thing I would have expected any conservative host to do was voluntarily broadcast from the United Nations compound on Manhattan's east side.

Yet there we were, Rick, Brett, and I, in New York City, touring labor history locations, rubbing elbows with labor historians from across the country and then running across town to switch gears and join the 2013 NYC Talkers Convention attendees at Talk Radio Day United Nations.

Fortunately for us, the LAWCHA and Talkers conferences were held the same week in the same city. And part of the festivities planned by our Talkers Conference hosts was their annual visit to the U.N.

Michael Harrison, publisher of Talkers Magazine, couldn't quite remember how long his company had been facilitating broadcasts from the United Nations Compound for radio hosts, but he'd guessed that it was at least seven years. I asked Harrison why he would bring so many broadcasters who so clearly despised the U.N. to interview international specialists and diplomats. I gave him an example of what I meant by despised. At the event, I overheard one of the conservative hosts – after interviewing an envoy – tell his listeners, "Well, that guy really put the ass in ambassador." After a brief chuckle Harrison replied, "When we invite radio hosts to broadcast, nobody's told they have to say nice things about the U.N.

and nobody's told they have to say bad things about the U.N., basically we're opening up the world to America's media."

But it's not America's media, it's America's talk radio media: A far more agenda driven group than the media is supposed to be in general. Harrison thinks that's ok though, "American media needs to remember the lines between philosophies are blurred at best."

Harrison didn't acknowledge that conservative talk radio, a billion plus dollar industry, does the bidding of their wealthy corporate sponsors. And in that role they purposefully leave out part of the story.

Still, on the morning of the broadcast we – both liberal and conservative hosts – shared the same guests and those guest were exemplary. I heard many a U.N. spokesperson make mincemeat out of their conservative interviewer, and Harrison says that's really the value of talk radio. If Talkers can put the world's movers and shakers a few inches from the nation's microphones, then it's up to the globe's diplomatic personnel to get their point across.

While I heard a few snippets of other talk shows, we were incredibly busy interviewing undersecretaries, scientists, and humanitarian aid activists. For the most part we were way too busy to really listen in on the interviews our peers were conducting. But there was one woman parked at a conference table so close to ours that we just couldn't help but overhear her.

I don't know her name or what radio market she was from and I have resisted the urge to correct my own ignorance: but really only for her sake. She was clearly conflicted, fluctuating between professional woman and middle school teenybopper in seconds. Every time this middle-aged broadcaster cracked open the mic to speak to her audience, she oozed contempt for the U.N. and its mission. That was until Paul Heslop sat down across from her. One of the people we had available to us for interviews, Heslop is the U.N. Mine Action Program Management Chief.

Heslop, a handsome rugged 40-something himself, had all the charm one would expect from a British military officer, all the courageous swagger one would expect from someone who dug up land mines for a living, and all the celebrity a small time star who was Princess Diana's land mine escort could amass by association. And when he sat down with the ante-menopausal conservative contrarian talk host to my left, she devolved back into her totally juvenile flirtatious shtick. And Heslop artfully used her guile against her.

An hour later Rick and I interviewed Heslop. We asked him about land mines, their locations, and whether or not the U.S. was still producing and placing them in war zones. And just before our interview was through, I asked him about our adolescent counterpart who had spoken with him earlier. Heslop said he speaks with folks like her rather frequently. He said that most folks find it darn hard to endorse land mines and they can't in good conscience talk trash about an agency that removes them. But, that doesn't stop U.N. detractors from struggling against accepting the U.N. as an agency. Heslop said they simply ignore the good work that's done by various U.N. departments, like his.

Heslop would like talk hosts to take a step back, get a bigger picture in their minds of what is done when nations cooperate. But in lieu of that, he does every interview hoping to drive home the notion that the U.N. does vital work for the people of the world – and that includes folks living in the U.S.

Michael Harrison thinks that whether it's the U.N., the U.S., or some local organization in a talk host's hometown, he wants broadcasters to make remind their listeners, "All organizations of human beings are potentially equally dangerous." Harrison emphasizes that these groups are, "Not necessarily dangerous, but they are potentially dangerous." And he continued, "Somebody's going to be kept outside." Harrison feels that this exclusion keeps the potentially dangerous groups from being exposed. That's where radio, television, the Internet and individuals are essential. Harrison concluded, "The First Amendment is the prime remedy to this potential abuse, to the dangerous abuse of the individual by the group."

Harrison and I disagree as to whether or not talk radio is the wheelhouse of these protections. The medium seems to cause more regression then progression on most topics. But, during our time at the U.N., and when we got to speak to some of the courageous world players who not only clear land mines but preserve drinking water, stop human trafficking, and struggle to defend world peace, Rick, Brett and I totally appreciated Harrison and the rest of the Talkers' staff who connect talk radio's listeners with these diplomats and activists.

ʎ

Chapter 6 Load 'er Up, Move 'er Out
ʎ ʎʎ

Rick and Brett returned to Carlisle from New York City via New Jersey. I had taken the train back the night before and they got up early Saturday morning following the United Nations Broadcast to drive down and pick up the Recreational Vehicle (RV) Rick had rented for our journey. Rick went through quite an ordeal to locate an RV that would hold 4 adults and 3 children – especially 'cause he wanted one that wasn't plastered with the corporate logos of some national rental company.

The rig he decided on had a semi-private room in the back. That meant that an accordion door closed it off from the rest of the vehicle. Rick's kids Sammi (11), Alex (7), and Aly (4) shared its double bed. Just next to that room we had a shower and a small lavatory. Rick made the only attempt to shower in the RV. After the report he gave, the rest of us decided we were better off washing up at rest areas and RV parks.

Forward of the rear bedroom and bath facilities was a small kitchenette. Carol had worked for weeks in advance of our trip shopping, pre-cooking meals, chopping vegetables, and putting together snack packs for the kids. We literally had half a month's food with us at the outset of our trip – or so we thought – driving all day works up an appetite none of us could explain and scarcely could control.

The side exit door was right next to the fridge. And further along that wall towards the driver's cab was a fold down couch. That's where Brett slept at night and because of his crazy late night hours uploading shows; he often slept there during the day. Across from Brett's couch was a café style table and benches. The table collapsed level with the benches. I slept on the table. Forward of all that was the driver's cab, above which, was a double bed where Rick and Carol slept.

The camper with seven people would have been a snug fit for a family like ours on vacation. Because this RV doubled as our traveling radio, sound, and recording studio – as well as activist workshop – we had computers, soundboards, recording equipment, even a six-foot folding table in Rick and Carol's bed. Every sliver of space was used, we stuffed rolled up banners into the few open spaces under and behind the camper's cupboards and furnishings.

Every night when Rick and Carol went to bed, they had to pull the table and sound equipment from atop their bed and stow it in other parts of the camper. The folding table was removed to the shower area and everyone who wanted to move from one end of our living space to the other had to cleverly dance around it.

Some additional awkwardly placed items took on new roles. The ice chests filled with soda and water doubled as Brett's workbench when Rick and I broadcast from the road. With the mixing board on the bench beside the dinette table, Brett could sit on the cooler in the aisle and feed the microphones through the open space into the cockpit. While Rick drove to our next destination, he and I would tape the segue segments that went between interviews in each night's show. Brett would open his laptop on the table and don his headphones to make sure our sound levels were good. His headphones also kept out road noise and the sound of the kids playing up back. Brett would give us our in and out cues and let us know the proper times for our segments. As efficient as it was chaotic, we absolutely had to do these taping sessions on the fly if we wanted to produce show content for work every night we were gone.

Brett and Rick pulled into Carlisle with the RV midday Saturday and Rick shot me a text. We were ready to roll. I'd done a number of these trips and each time I felt as though I had packed too much. This time I went for a true combination of austerity and idiosyncratic necessity. I brought along a French press coffee maker because I was the only passenger with a coffee addiction. Everyone else satisfied their caffeine jones with carbonated beverages.

In my luggage I also had two pounds of coffee, six Rick Smith Show shirts – all the adults had enough show shirts to do public appearances every day and not need to do laundry for a week – shorts, undergarments, a swimsuit, some sunscreen and three notebooks.

I also brought lots of stamps and a hundred blank post cards so the kids and I could draw on them and send them out to folks as we went along. Oh, and I had my laptop. Not only was I planning to do research along the way, I thought I could write from the journey as well.

The last time I did a cross-country tour, I spent five weeks on a tour of the nation's poorest neighborhoods and wrote 17 stories from the road. This tour was so much more grueling and hectic, I wrote only one story. I had completely underestimated how time consuming the radio broadcasts would be and how distracting traveling with children was. When I finally accepted that I would not be able to write, I doubled down on the radio work and really got into hanging out with the kids.

Rick and Sammi picked me up at my house in the pace car. Pace car's what I called it. Truth be told, our punishing pace was really kept by the teamster at the camper's helm. But we needed an extra vehicle and Rick's insurance wouldn't allow us to tow a car, so Carol volunteered to drive the family mini-van. Rick wanted a vehicle along so we wouldn't have to take the RV on short jaunts and so that Carol could take off with the kids when we were facing a long day of interviews or detours from the main route.

Oh yeah, and we needed a car to send Carol off with the kids when the "Friends of Coal" showed up at a few of our miner interviews toting side arms. But I'm getting ahead of myself – I'll have more on that in the chapter about Blair Mountain titled, "Daddy, Why Does That Man Have a Gun?"

When Rick, Sammi and I got back to Rick's house, Carol finished buttoning up the house for a month away and we set out for Martinsburg, West Virginia.

λ

Chapter 7 A Sign of the Times
ƛƛ

There's an historical marker in Martinsburg, West Virginia. The marker's prophetic, really. It tells the tale of modern history in general and tells the story of modern labor history in specific. See, the sign's got two sides. It's got one side that's visible from the street and sidewalk and all the public areas near the historic railroad yard. And the other side of the sign, the side you have to risk life and limb to read – by either standing on the active rail road tracks or climbing on a six foot stone wall – is the deeper darker truer "rest" of the story.

Seemingly sleepy little Martinsburg, in the upper eastern panhandle section of West Virginia, has been a conflicted mess pretty much since it was founded. The powerful have often fought to control its residents or struggled to shrug off their duty to the people there and abandon the town entirely. While West Virginia was remarkably resolute in decidedly conflicted times, Martinsburg's likewise determined nature brought them nothing but trouble as the powerful railroad and slave interests wrestled for control of the area.

The original territory of Virginia, as claimed for the British Crown and stolen from the American Native Peoples, was enormous. It stretched from the Atlantic Ocean to parts of what is now Minnesota. But by the early 19th century, the Virginia territory had – for the most part – been carved into states.

Virginians in the western part of 18th century Virginia didn't identify with their eastern slave-owning aristocratic neighbors. Consequently, Western Virginians began toying with the idea of becoming an independent state pretty much from the time the United States was founded. Still, it wasn't until the state of Virginia voted to secede from the Union and join the Confederate States of America that the independent separatist movement gained the required momentum and leverage to bring about statehood.

Two months before the firing on Fort Sumter, Virginia held a convention where delegates could vote whether or not to secede from the U.S.. A Library of Congress website states, "Pioneering individuals, mountaineers, settled in the western portion, while a slave-holding aristocratic society developed in the eastern portion." Those easterners were heavily represented at the Virginia Convention and when the secession vote came, there was little doubt that Virginia would go. Still the nonbinding convention decision had to be backed up by a vote of the people. For the most part, the every day folk in western Virginia wanted nothing to do with slavery, and they didn't want to leave the U.S. along with the rest of the state. Especially because their mineral rich natural resources made them rely heavily on free and open trade routes with the northern states.

When the referenda vote was put before the people, the town of Martinsburg and surrounding Berkley County voted, "no." The secession vote carried through the rest of the state, but the Martinsburg region had proven itself disloyal to the secessionists and Virginia troops were sent to the area to "quiet" protesters.

Western Virginians wanted independence from Virginia and worked to create the United States' 35th state. When Virginian office holders vacated their constitutional offices, it gave separatists just the opportunity they needed. Union supporters and independent "West Virginians" met in Wheeling. Their intention was to request leave of Virginia, but they couldn't separate from a state that had no government. So the first thing they did was elect a new one.

Things got so much easier for the advocates of a new West Virginia when the people at the Wheeling Convention simply put their own supporters in place. They selected a new governor, lieutenant governor, attorney general and other necessary office holders. Not surprisingly, these new Virginia representatives happily agreed with West Virginia's desire to become an independent state and voted to let them go.

The West Virginians sent the Confederacy the strong message that the state was forged, in part, out of the anti-slavery movement by selecting the motto, "Mountaineers are Always Free." The motto not only mocked slavery but it emphasized the rugged individualism of the West Virginia lifestyle.

Even before the civil war, Martinsburg had strategic significance. In the 1840's it had become a significant railroad hub. Martinsburg was the gateway to Harper's Ferry and Pennsylvania just beyond the rivers. It boldly stood against slavery but also harbored dangerous spies and agitators. Because of its location – its proximity to the north – and key railroad infrastructure, the town was occupied by both rebel and union forces several times during the war.

Eventually southern troops – rather than have the railroad continue to feed supplies from the wilderness and ore rich mountainsides to the Union forces – sacked the railroad yard. The Virginia Foundation for the Humanities published in its Encyclopedia Virginia a narrative of the devastation wrought in 1861, "Confederate troops under Jackson's command entered Martinsburg on June 20 and set about dismantling the railroad, further outraging Unionist residents. In addition to the tracks, the Confederates destroyed the round house, various railroad buildings, fifty-six locomotives, and at least 305 cars. Thirteen locomotives were spared by Jackson and seized for use by the Confederacy."

The troops continually beat on the town. By the end of the war Martinsburg was – again according to the Encyclopedia Virginia – a "'peculiarly undesirable place of residence,' observed a Northern reporter in December 1864. 'Its streets have been trampled ... the ruins of the depot buildings, and of houses burned in former attacks upon the town give the usual air of desolation.'"

But Martinsburg's spirit of independence was strong. As gateway to the industrial north, after the war, the town was rebuilt. By 1877, just 12 short years after the surrender at Appomattox, the town had its train yard back and – despite a deep recession – railroad business was booming.

Virginia had lost its grip on her western territory while businesses and individuals had lost their ready supply of free labor. Without slave labor, wages for everyone else needed to go down if company profits were to remain high.

Slaveholders are guilty of many crimes. At best they are kidnappers who then press their captives into service and auction or sell their families to other kidnappers and thieves. At worst they rape and murder their captives to keep them producing and living in fear. Among the many atrocities that make up slavery, the theft of a person's labor is one that can be perpetrated on free men as well as slaves.

President Lincoln best summed up the contemptible nature of stolen labor in his second inaugural address. His words condemn the southern states for this just as Western Virginians condemned them when West Virginia became a state and re-joined the union.

In 1865, two years after West Virginia became a state, Lincoln said, "It may seem strange that any men should dare to ask a just God's assistance in wringing their bread from the sweat of other men's faces.'"

Even more remarkably, in this address Lincoln finally admits that the Civil War was over slavery, the value of humans as assets, and over this theft of another man's labor, "One-eighth of the whole population were colored slaves, not distributed generally over the Union, but localized in the southern part of it. These slaves constituted a peculiar and powerful interest. All knew that this interest was somehow the cause of the war."

Lincoln closed his speech by praying for a speedy end to the conflict. If prayer is answered, his was. The war ended a month later.

By 1877, even though the civil war was over and the 14th amendment ending slavery had been ratified nine years earlier, labor was still being stolen from the people. Frederick Douglass in his autobiography, *My Bondage, My Freedom*, explained that black slavery provided the added benefit of making poor whites see themselves as somehow better off than slaves, even though they surrendered their labor as well. In part, besides the free work, and the buying and selling of human chattel, controlling the poor white was an additional benefit of enslaving blacks.

The poor whites of the south were complicit in this manipulation. These American serfs were so steeped in racism that this differentiation between themselves and the slaves helped them feel superior. This racism trap helped them surrender the "bread from the sweat" of their own faces.

Douglass wrote about the exploitation of racism among poor whites, "The impression is cunningly made, that slavery is the only power that can prevent the laboring white man from falling to the level of the slave's poverty and degradation." But with slavery gone, and a powerful post war economic depression sweeping the land, a day's work – by either black and white laborer – had to be further exploited by greedy masters of industry and property.

None were more rapacious than the railroads.

When the railroad workers in Martinsburg learned of Baltimore and Ohio Railroad's intention to cut a brakeman's pay by 10 percent, the workers knew they and their families could not survive. Brakemen worked hard at a very dangerous task, and already couldn't get by on the $1.75 they earned for a 12-hour day. Additionally, the reduction of wages removed the last separation between the worker and the slave. Slaves take what is given them; only free man set their own wages.

Historian Howard Zinn, in his essay on the railroad strikes of 1877, described the sort of thoughts in a slave wage worker's mind, "Had he simply risen to a breakfast that did not fill him, seen his children go off shabby and half-fed, walked brooding through the damp morning and then yielded impulsively to stored-up rage?"

The Martinsburg workers – in a style not unlike the one that birthed the state in the first place – would not accept the pay cut. Zinn reports, "At the Baltimore & Ohio station in Martinsburg, West Virginia, workers determined to fight the wage cut went on strike, uncoupled the engines, ran them into the roundhouse, and announced no more trains would leave Martinsburg until the 10% cut was cancelled."

The people supported the workers. They crowded the depot area and the police couldn't control them. Newly minted WV Governor Henry Matthews asked President Rutherford Hayes for federal troops. Again, Zinn explains that Matthews didn't want to use local militia to quell the riot but made up a story to the president about them being "insufficient" instead. Zinn wrote, "In fact, the militia was not totally reliable, being composed of many railway workers."

In 1877 the federal government was just about broke, making the request even more difficult for President Hayes to grant. An expensive civil war and Indian Wars on the frontier zapped the treasury. Wealthy bankers, sympathetic to the plight of the railroad, offered to lend the government the money they needed to pay the military to respond to the strike. "J. P. Morgan, August Belmont, and other bankers now offered to lend money to pay army officers (but no enlisted men). Federal troops arrived in Martinsburg, and the freight cars began to move."

What started with a small action in Martinsburg ended up being the largest industrial dispute – up to that point – in U.S. history. Before the railroad strike of 1877 ended, 100 people were killed – mostly workers – with Martinsburg suffering the first fatality. Over the course of the strike, half the rail lines were shut down and the entire national guard of Pennsylvania was called out to quell riots in cities from Philadelphia to Pittsburgh and Altoona to Harrisburg. Other workers joined the strike. Steel workers and firefighters supported the railroad men. A 6000 person rally was held in Chicago and a general strike was called in St. Louis, where black and white workers struck together.

The U.S. in 1877 was a terrible place to be a poor worker. Sanitation and public health were virtually nonexistent in the poor neighborhoods and infant mortality was alarmingly high. In fact, death rates were so high that morbidity recording changed and 1877 was the first year infant mortality statistics were collected.

Inadequate or nonexistent public works infrastructure – not disease, per se – caused many more poor children to die. Sanitation, hygiene and nutrition were the villains. In the first week of July of 1877, the year of the railroad strike, "in Baltimore, where all liquid sewage ran through the streets, 139 babies died."

In one week, 139 babies! Looking back, it's no surprise that thousands of ordinary Baltimore citizens came out in support of the striking railroad workers.

Even though this key movement began in Martinsburg, the readily available side of the sign near the railroad depot reads: "The B&O Railroad reached Martinsburg in 1842, and by 1849, a roadhouse and shops were built. These first buildings were burned by Confederate Troops in 1862. The present west roadhouse and the two shops were built in 1866. The east roadhouse was built in 1872. These buildings represent one of the last remaining examples of American industrial railroad architecture still intact and in use. These structures serve as important reminders of the status of the railroad in the mid-19th century and the role it played in the economic development of Martinsburg, the county, and the state."

On the other side of the marker – the side one could risk life and limb to see – it reads, "On July 16, 1877, workers of the Baltimore and Ohio Railroad went on strike and closed the railroad yard to protest a cut in wages. Their action sparked the largest nationwide strike the country had ever seen. Extensive damage was done to company property at Pittsburgh, Baltimore, and Wheeling, and over 50 workers were killed before the strike was crushed. Federal troops were used for the first time in a labor dispute. As the country's first general strike, it focused national attention on labor's grievances and made workers aware of the power of collective action."

The fact that the story of America's largest strike is buried behind a narrative about architecture and the importance of the railroad – but not the railroad workers – is telling. We started our trip exactly where we should have: In an all but forgotten town where forgotten workers fought for themselves and their forgotten families.

Chapter 8 It's All About the Regress
λ λλ

It was early June and the days were still getting longer. Rick's kids had run around the parking lot at the Martinsburg railroad station turned quasi-museum. We went inside but didn't stay long. Some of the facts seemed pretty accurate and others, well, let's just say that a white man paddling a canoe wearing a tri-cornered hat and a leather suit covered in fringe left out a lot of the true story and required way too much gullibility on the part of any savvy visitor.

Well past dinner time – with the kids still bouncing off the walls – we made our way to Charleston, West Virginia's capitol. For our first night on the road we planned to stay like many truckers with sleeper cabs and the way snow-birding seniors in their RVs do. We thought we'd saddle up to a Wal*Mart parking lot and tuck in for the night.

Wal*Mart has a policy allowing transients in vehicles to stay the night – and from the look of some of the vehicles parked in their various lots across this country, even longer. There's no electrical hook up and the amenities just aren't there, but to a road weary driver that's of little concern. In the case of truckers and RV drivers, they generally have internal power back up and the ability to survive at least a few days self-contained.

On the ride down from Martinsburg, Rick asked me to find us a place to stay. There really weren't any camping spots available and because we were pulling into town so late and planned to leave again quite early, I'd come up with the idea that we just stay at Wally World.

Rick bristled at the notion at first. He said that he just couldn't stomach the thought of endorsing any part of a Wal*Mart operation. I explained to him the way I look at it. And it's a point of view that I think is very important to emphasize. Although I whole-heartedly agree that Wal*Mart itself is a big part of the reason that the U.S. middle class is vanishing.

I believe that it's to Wal*Mart's advantage to let folks sleep in their parking lot free of charge. Wal*Mart's corporate website seems to agree,

"While we do not offer electrical service or accommodations typically necessary for RV customers, Walmart values RV travelers and considers them among our best customers. Consequently, we do permit RV parking on our store parking lots as we are able. Permission to park is extended by individual store managers, based on availability of parking space and local laws. Please contact management in each store to ensure accommodations before parking your RV."

Firstly and as Wal*Mart noted above, lot lizards, as some call them, are good customers. Many undoubtedly shop when they get there or in the morning after they get up and prepare to hit the road. But the second reason they allow people to live in their lots – and I have nothing to substantiate this claim but my own gut – is to set precedence. As Wal*Mart's pay checks and benefits become more and more commensurate with the ever burgeoning poverty class, Wal*Mart's own employees will one day need to sleep in their vehicles in the lot as well. So think of this as a long-range employment plan for the world's largest private employer owned by the nation's richest family.

One of the best tools we brought along for the ride was a mobile WiFi unit. It allowed us to do research on the fly: both for the radio interviews and for the trip's logistics.

Because we'd never done this before, we didn't realize that with school just let out, the tourist season would tick up considerably. We really should have made our sleeping arrangements ahead of time. Many of the places we'd hoped to stay were full when we contacted them last minute. That's not ever the case for a Wal*Mart though, they've got parking lot to spare in the wee hours of the night.

We planned to meet up with perennial West Virginia candidate for governor, Jesse Johnson. When I went online to find the nearest Wal*Mart to his home just a little north of Charleston, there wasn't one. Jesse's yard is on a hill, and if you've ever slept in a mobile home, the one thing you learn quick is that level ground is pretty important. Not far from Johnson's house was a grocery store, and we thought we'd try parking the RV there overnight and see if we got thrown out.

It turns out that people sleeping in any parking lot since the great depression of 2008, doesn't surprise anyone. Nobody seemed to care that the RV was parked there over night.

While the family stayed at the Kroger's plaza, I went back to Jesse's house and interviewed him about West Virginia politics. I asked him what happened to the labor union strength that was West Virginia's legacy. He said that the West Virginia miner legacy for fighting back had given way to desperation when the coal companies got more and more powerful. Politicians, supported by big coal, began backing them over organized labor. That sounded familiar. The research I'd been doing on the Battle of Blair Mountain and the Mingo County Coal Wars was evidence of the power of elected officials and court judges over the outcome of labor struggles. And back in the early 20th century, if an elected official got in the way of the coal companies, they found themselves dead: Just as dead as Matewan Mayor, Cabell Testerman.

Wait, I'm getting ahead of myself. And besides, the politicians who didn't cross the coal companies and instead aided the corporate cause, found themselves very much living and living in style. Now choosing between dead and alive and comfortable seemed pretty easy for most of the lawmakers in West Virginia at the time. Most politicians chose the coal companies over the workers. Not Sidney Hatfield, he stood with the miners and well, yeah, he ended up dead too.

But like I said, that's ahead of where I want to be right now. Those killings are among the causes of the Battle of Blair Mountain and that's not until chapter nine. So for now, it's suffice to say that in addition to having favorable elected officials – favorable for the coal companies – there's a level of disinformation coming at the average consumer in West Virginia and Jesse feels that's one of the biggest problems facing the mine workers today.

Back at Jesse's house, I asked Jesse how West Virginia had regressed back to the way of thinking before the union victories of the early 20th century. I asked him if the media was anti-union and he said, "Everything here is anti-union. The corporate message is killing West Virginia. It doesn't let up, it 'de-brains' you everyday." And Jesse's solution? "We need progressive media in West Virginia. Every channel carries Rush Limbaugh two or three hours a day."

He didn't have to tell me that twice. Listening to Rush Limbaugh is bound to "de-brain" you. The Pulitzer Prize winning political fact checker, Politifact, says that 6% of the time Rush's statements are mostly true and another 12% of the time they are partly true. Their site goes on to say that in the statements fact checked by their staff, 82% of Limbaugh statements are either "mostly false, false," or boldfaced purposeful lies. A category the aptly name, "Pants on Fire."

Jesse has a point. There needs to be a media outlet that reminds people that the minimum wage, the 40 hour work week, the abolition of child labor, work place safety measures, and many other workplace improvements were brought about by the labor movement. There needs to be a concerted pushback against the lies told by Limbaugh and many of his ilk. Just a few examples of the Limbaugh bias against organized labor: He has gone on the record, on his show, on innumerable occasions comparing union activity to rape. He also compares union organizers to Ku Klux Klansmen and Nazis. And yet this is an unchallenged source for labor news on talk radio in West Virginia. No wonder things are going backward.

Chapter 9 Daddy, Why Does That Man Have a Gun?

We got up the next morning and began our trip to Blair Mountain. Our little caravan increased by a third that morning. In addition to the RV and Carol's minivan, Jesse led the way in a friend's borrowed sedan. I'd been through the mountains of Logan County before, writing stories about mountain top removal coal mining, and every time we'd gone through coal country we'd picked up a conspicuous tail or two on those rural back roads. It certainly could have been a coincidence, but rather than arouse suspicion, it seemed best for Jesse to travel in an unfamiliar car, and by unfamiliar, I mean unfamiliar to the group "Friends of Coal."

Indeed we weren't very far into Logan County when our first *Friends of Coal* escort joined us. We knew who they were because their vehicles had *Friends of Coal* markings. One vehicle's entire rear window had the logo emblazoned across it.

According to the *Friends of Coal* website, "The *Friends of Coal* is a volunteer organization that consists of both West Virginians and residents from beyond our borders. Membership is free and the level of involvement by members is at their own discretion."

And on the day we met them, their level of involvement included surrounding us at our host's house and putting up road signs for litter removal. At first the only folks from *Friends of Coal* to approach us were women. Judging from their website, these folks must've been members of the *Friends of Coal* Ladies' Auxiliary.

It was pretty creepy to be descended upon so soon after our arrival. It was hard to believe their litter patrol claims; the roadside was already clean and tidy. At least the road leading up to and away from Brandon Nida's house was immaculate. Perhaps this "clean up crew" comes fairly often to check on what Nida is doing. And really, in all fairness, we should have known that we'd pique someone's interest just by going to visit Nida.

Nida, a West Virginia native, an organizer with the Blair Mountain Heritage Alliance and a U.C. Berkley Doctoral Student, lives above what used to be an old gas station in the center of town. The service station office is now a make shift museum for some of the less valuable relics Nida has salvaged from Blair Mountain's battlefield. The more valuable ones are tucked away elsewhere. Nida says he often identifies, photographs and buries artifacts so that the coal company won't find them. He believes the coal companies would like the historical markers to disappear just like they're working to make the town disappear.

Directly behind Nida's house is a turf berm with a concrete side. That berm used to be the landing for a train station. The tracks are gone, the landing's gone, and there's nothing left of what used to be the station. It's remarkable really, because in late August 1921, thousands of men waited there – and at stations all through the area – for trains promised by then Governor Ephraim Morgan, trains that never came.

In an effort to stave off the violent show down that would become the Battle of Blair Mountain, President Warren Harding had dispatched one of his finest generals, Harry Hill Bandholtz, to negotiate a truce and get the miners to go home.

Brandholtz banked on the fact that the miners were loyal citizens. The miners had no beef with the federal government. They wanted to fight the coal companies and their hired guns, not their brothers-in-arms with whom many had served during the Great War.

The miners agreed to leave if they could just go home. Governor Morgan, working from a playbook drafted for him by the coal companies, promised to send trains for the miners. The trains never came, and days later the miners were still waiting and consequently available for battle when the fighting began. Morgan also used the fact that they hadn't moved on, to persuade the Harding administration that the miners weren't serious when they promised to go home.

Today, when one looks out behind Nida's house, the train station's been expunged from the landscape, removing all evidence of the double cross and giving a 2013 alibi to Gov. Morgan's 1921 betrayal of the agreement between the workers and Pres. Harding.

Thanks to our posse, our *Friends of Coal* Ladies' Auxiliary, we learned real quick that some of the folks in West Virginia think Nida's a bit of a troublemaker. So as we unpacked our gear and prepared to interview him as well as Jesse Johnson, and C B Bella – third generation miner whose granddaddy fought in the battle of Blair Mountain – more clean up crews began to arrive. One of the women who had been the first on the scene started talking about Nida being an environmental polluter. They didn't like him being there, she told us, because, "he put raw sewerage into the water." She said that's why people shouldn't live in Blair because Nida and others had done poisoned the water and it wasn't fit to drink.

When we went inside, we asked Nida about the water. Nida shook his head over her claim. He said that she was right about part of it. The water wasn't fit to drink but it was because, "there's selenium in the water." Selenium is a by-product of mountain top removal coal mining.

Up the road, one of the last holdout homeowners in Blair, 73-year-old Jimmy Wesley, leaned on his oxygen tank while he told me that his well had been contaminated too. And even after the coal company dug him a new well – 80 feet deeper than the old one – the water still smelled and tasted of methane. Now Wesley buys his water at Wal*Mart. He lugs it down into his holler where his is the only home. Wesley said that there used to be 37 homes in his holler and 470 homes in Blair when he was a boy. Wesley said now the whole town "is down to about 35."

Carol was shepherding the kids as they ran around the parking lot. Brett had unloaded the mixing board, mics, and video gear. About the time we headed into Nida's office/museum, some more *Friends of Coal* drove up. These fellas weren't the auxiliary. They were men with guns.

To be fair, the women may have had guns too, but we didn't see any. Like in the days harkening back to the Wild West – or even a century ago Blair Mountain – the fella who seemed to be leading the group had his gun strapped to his hip.

I've done a lot of radio and there was no reason to wear guns and show up uninvited at a radio show. It was obvious to us that the women had been talking on the phone with this second group who came to assist them in their "litter control."

We all believed that the guns were merely for show. While Rick, Brett and the folks we were there to interview weren't intimidated, we still didn't like the kids being in the middle of our conversation as long as there were people there who felt the need to make such a show of force. Carol packed the kids into the minivan and took them to a state park about 40 miles away so that we could work without worrying that our new *Friends of Coal* friends might like to make some sort of point.

After Carol disappeared up a hill and around a bend, we settled into our interviews. C B Bella, the retired mine worker who just recently lost his retirement in the Patriot Coal bankruptcy shell game, shared stories of how "scab" operations undid the good work labor unions had done over the decades in West Virginia. In his experience, the owners closed down a mine so they could reopen it later without the union, "After a job is dissolved for so many years, they can open it up any way they want, union or scab." And with deep mine jobs being steadily replaced by surface mining, there's a glut of miners. Bella also spoke of the trouble caused when workers are brought in from outside, "A lot of workers are brought in from out of state, from right to work states."

Bella explained that he wanted to do the interviews with us, even with the intimidation factors going on outside, "Because of the union, without the union, people wouldn't be making decent wages, wouldn't have no benefits, no hospitalization, anything like that."

It's also Bella's legacy that made him talk. Bella's Pappaw – as he called him – fought at Blair Mountain, "I believe in protecting what they fought for. The day he died he died with a bullet in his ankle from this Blair Mountain War."

Bella wanted to stand up for his Pappaw, just as Bella's great grandmother did at the time, "The wounded miners and things would come through the mountains, go to her house and she would feed them and help bandage them up and take care of them and everything."

It might have been easier for Bella's ancestors to stand up for the union, before the regression Johnson mentioned had started. We asked Bella if attitudes toward unions changed. Bella agreed with Jesse, "Most everybody around here wanted the union here."

During the interview Rick asked Bella about people fighting for coal companies. He pointed out the contrast between today, with the *Friends of Coal* showing up to keep an eye on us or scare us off. Rick asked Bella what had changed in 90 years to take folks from fighting for a share of the wealth in the area, to strong-arming for the coal companies. There never did seem to be an answer, other than the fact that the coal companies will give a dollar or two an hour to keep their workers from joining a union. Bella speculates that once all the unions are busted those higher wages will all be gone.

Bella had one last reason for speaking with us. A surface miner himself, he wanted to speak out against the practice, "I've learned over the years that this mountain top removal is a cowardly way of mining coal. It destroys the landscape, the trees, the land. It'll never be worth nothing in future years. Trees won't hardly grow on it. It's hard to get weeds to grow on it."

This big burly miner hadn't gone all tree hugger in his retirement. He disapproved of surface mining on a human level too, "This mountain top mining destroyed our communities too… it just got so nasty here and noisy and dusty, and the vibration from the blasting would shake your house to pieces. People just didn't want to stay in this pigpen, you might say, and people kept moving away. And before you know it we didn't have enough students, uh children here to keep our schools open. And that was the first thing they attacked, our schools."

Nida agreed, "The railroad landing was gone ten years ago. The High School was gone in the 1990's. Kids have to be bussed 1 ½ hours depending which direction you want your kid to go to school. In the winter we're left with no electricity for weeks at a time. We have bad water, who would stay?"

As we drove out of town, we climbed through the gap that separates the two peaks of Blair Mountain. Permits have already been issued – and if Arch Coal has their way – those peaks will be blown to smithereens sometime very soon. What appeared to be private roads intersected the road out of town. Jesse explained, "Those are the old state highway roads that cross straight through the battlefield. They never belonged to the coal companies, but West Virginia has allowed the coal companies to rope them off. After a while the ropes turn to boulders with big 'no trespass' signs on them. It seems everyone forgets that those are state highways. And we are denied access to the battlefield and to our history."

Gun toting *Friends of Coal*, disappeared train stations, 400 or more erased homes, and toxic drinking water, it sure would be hard to argue that someone wasn't trying to forget that 10,000 miners marched from Mingo County to Blair Mountain to battle the coal companies and their hired thugs. But for now we still know it happened and for now archeology grad students like Nida still have the proof.

λ λλ

Chapter 10 Largest Episode of Class War in U.S. History

"Largest episode of class war in U.S. History," that's what Brandon Nida called the Battle of Blair Mountain, and that's what it was. But it wasn't class warfare the way most think of it. It wasn't a battle of one class to eliminate another class. No, for the wealthy coal mine owners it was a war to keep the working class exactly where they wanted them. It was a war to keep the miners poor, subjugated, landless, filthy and in such absolutely desperate situations that they would never find the strength to rise up in rebellion again.

The miners fought a very different class war than what the prevailing propaganda about them claimed. The workers didn't crawl out of the mines and take up arms to eliminate the wealth class. Quite to the contrary, they fought to maintain capitalism and in turn get to a higher rung – or any rung – on the ladder of success. They wanted some wealth for themselves, they wanted to buy things, have things, and better enjoy their lives. At no time did the miners give up on the theory of the American dream, at no time did they embrace a Bolshevik ideology. If the coal companies hadn't hired the Baldwin Felts Agency and employed strikebreakers and thugs to maim, starve, and kill the miners, a peaceful resolution of their grievances could have occurred.

In the early 20th century, coal miners tunneled deep into the earth. They worked long hours for very little pay. The coal companies provided housing for miners and they got their provisions from the company store. When they got sick they went to the company doctor. If they were paid they were paid in printed notes – company script – that was only negotiable within the workings of the mine economy. And when the miners got too sick, or too injured, or died, their family was turned out of their housing – unless – there was a son who could take the miner's place or there was a service his wife could provide to the managers of the mine. Child labor and this sort of forced prostitution were last resorts for mine families, but they were options nonetheless.

The United Mine Workers, founded in 1890, enjoyed organizing success in the southern coal mines of West Virginia during and immediately after World War I. During the war, coal demand soared. In West Virginia new mines were sunk and thousands more men went to work. After the armistice was signed on November 11, 1918, demand for coal declined sharply. Suddenly there were more miners than needed and the coal companies took this opportunity to lower wages.

With tens of thousands of miners living in company housing, and using company currency that had no value anywhere else, it was easy for the mine companies to pressure the workers. Anyone who didn't want to work for less – and eventually anyone who had the audacity to join the union – was put out of their housing.

While the miners had little recourse against losing their jobs, their subsequent evictions came under the scrutiny of local law enforcement. Many ranking West Virginian politicians were beholden on one level or another to the coal companies. Here and there, there was a police chief or a mayor or a judge who sympathized more with the plight of the worker than they did the mine owner. In Matawan, in coal rich Mingo County, Police Chief Sid Hatfield and Mayor Cabell Testerman were two men who could be counted on to defend the rights of the miners.

Hatfield is and was a prominent name in southern West Virginia. In October of 2013 Bennett Hatfield, the chief executive of Patriot Coal, is still battling over miners' rights, but Bennett – unlike Sid back in 1920 – works against the miners.

Putting miners out of their homes is dirty work, especially when the miners don't want to go. Mine operators weren't ones to do dirty work. Southern West Virginia mine owners hired private security companies to do their dirty work for them. The Baldwin Felts Agency guns-for-hire showed up in Matawan – as they did in mining communities all across the region – and evicted miners that the companies deemed troublesome to have around. Mayor Testerman and Chief Hatfield demanded legal justification for the miners' evictions. The Baldwin Felts agents could not provide the necessary paperwork and they were ordered by the police chief to leave town. The next day – May 19, 1920 – the chief, the mayor and a few dozen newly deputized officers met the agents downtown so that they could escort the corporations' mercenary army to the train.

Their departure should have been peaceful. But the day before, a couple of telephone operators listened in on a conversation, heard Chief Hatfield planning with the others to escort the agents out of town and the women then called friends of theirs at the coal companies and told them what they'd heard. With the Baldwin Felts agents tipped off, and with a street filled with armed gunmen on both sides, there's little surprise that the Matawan Massacre occurred. When the shooting was over both sides had taken losses. Mayor Testerman and Albert and Lee Felts were among the seven detectives and three locals killed.

The last remaining Felts, Tom Felts, blamed Chief Hatfield for his brothers' deaths. Felts couldn't prove who killed his brothers but he blamed Hatfield all the same. Even at the murder trial, no one person's story corroborated another's about what happened during the massacre or who shot whom and when.

Exonerated of murder in connection with the Matawan Massacre, Chief Hatfield went home to a jubilant Matawan, leaving Tom Felts' blood lust anything but satisfied.

Government officials loyal to the coal companies were regularly bringing charges against Hatfield and others in hopes of curtailing their rebellious ways. Eventually Tom Felts got his revenge when his agents gunned down Chief Hatfield as he walked into a courthouse for arraignment on different charges.

The murder of Sid Hatfield enraged miners all across West Virginia. Thousands descended for a rally at the capitol in Charleston and vowed to march through Logan County to Mingo County and rid the state of the hired gunmen who had been turning miners out of their homes, raiding their tent villages and murdering their leaders like Hatfield and Testerman.

Indeed the class warfare and union busting had gotten so severe that the hillsides of West Virginia were littered with tent villages housing discarded miners and their families. Malnourished inhabitants littered the access roads to the mines earning this Appalachian region the nickname: The Valley Forge of Labor.

Logan County lay between Charleston and Mingo County. Logan County Sheriff Don Chaffin – an unrepentant corporate toady – vowed that no miners would cross through his county and began preparing for all out war if the miners tried.

With thousands of miners amassing in preparation of the march, the sheriff – whose paycheck came directly from the mining companies – his men, all the militia the governor could muster, and the remaining coal company's mercenary force set up a defensive line along the Blair Mountain Gap. From this lofty perch they could turn back any assault made by the miners.

Governor Ephraim Morgan, like Governor Jacob Cornwell before him, declared martial law. Ever since the civil war, court cases had disqualified declarations of martial law because it necessitated the elimination of the judicial branch of government. President Warren Harding – among others – held the opinion that the federal government could not activate the military while the courts system was still in force. Pres. Harding therefore bristled at Gov. Morgan's request. Instead, Pres. Harding sent one of his ablest generals to survey the situation. Harry Hill Brandholtz seized control of the situation, convened a meeting with labor leaders and negotiated a way out for all parties.

The agreement promised trains – sent by the governor – to pick up the miners and bring the miners home. Word spread quickly through the worker's lines that they would be searched when they approached the train yards and their weapons would be confiscated. While the miners were willing to cancel this particular march, they were unwilling to surrender their weapons and be unable to strike at another time. So before they left the hills for the train stations, they buried or otherwise hid their arms.

Whether the governor never intended to send the trains, whether it was just a ruse to commandeer the miners' weapons, or whether the trains were legitimately delayed, nobody came to get the men and they were still there – able to dig up and retrieve their hidden guns – when skirmishes began.

Gov. Morgan once again called on Washington for help. This time he claimed the miners had not gone home as they had promised they would, and Brandholtz activated three different U.S. army units and deployed them to surround all sides of the conflict.

Before the army could get there, the coal companies and the Baldwin Felts agents had employed three airplanes and bombed various miner strong holds. When the United States Army airplanes arrived these bombings stopped.

After the battle, Gen. Brandholtz filed his report, he made note that part of the reason the miners did not disperse was that the trains they had been promised never arrived.

The Battle of Blair Mountain cost fewer than a hundred lives and lasted less than a week. The conditions for the miners did not improve and union membership declined. But these losses resulted more from decreased demand for coal than a lack of determination on the part of the workers. Had the miners revolted during World War I when the demand for coal was at its zenith, they might have won many of their demands. But the miners were patriots; they would not strike when their country needed them, just as they would not fight against the soldiers who were sent to quell the uprising.

The company won, and as Johnson pointed out, they continue to win even today. The coal industry is highly subsidized. In fact, the U.S. coal industry is the most profitable it's ever been. Domestic demand for coal is at its lowest and most of the product is exported to Asia and Western Europe. The CEO's make millions, the companies take billions in subsidies, but still the workers are called greedy for wanting decent wages, healthcare and pensions. And in 2013 the gulf between the poor and the rich is greater than it was at the time of the battle of Blair Mountain. The class war rages on.

Chapter 11   Jesus and the Faithless Economy

Once we left West Virginia, Rick, the old Teamster that he is, drove straight through to Knoxville and got us to a small campground along a verdant levy just outside the city. Our little troop hails from Central Pennsylvania, a region that is steeped in a number of religious traditions. Known best for the Amish and Mennonite settlements, visitors who fully expect to see horses and buggies are often surprised by the frequent display of triple crosses along the roadsides there. Still, if we thought we'd hailed from the Bible belt, when we turned down from Kentucky into Tennessee we landed right in what must've been the buckle of the Bible belt.

As we pulled into the RV and camping park, we drove between the campground swimming pool and a Christian Outlet Center. The Christian Outlet Center marquis boasted a vast array of "Books, Bibles, and Gifts." Just past the fenced-in swimming pool was the bathhouse where the ladies' and gents' rooms both featured spacious, clean, hot showers. Above the bathhouse was a wire sculpture draped in lights. We pulled in just as the sky was getting dark and we hurried to our campsite.

While Rick and Carol set up the campsite, the kids ran off to the playground and I went to look around. I promised the kids I'd take them swimming, but when we went up to the pool, it had already closed. This scene would play out over and over again along out trip. We'd pull in too late to go swimming, and leave early in the morning, before the pool would open. Still the kids asked every day if we could go swimming and every day Carol would say "yes" as long as they'd behaved and the pool was open. The kids behaved far better than the pool hours of operation did all across the country.

Just past where Sammi, Alex, and Aly played on the swings a wooden structure like a chapel without walls flanked one side of the campground. There were rows of benches and a stage with a lectern for revival meetings and worship events. At first I stood at the lectern and looked out at the benches, then I took my seat on one of the benches and imagined the hubbub of a congregation packed in all around. After a few minutes, I looked up the hill to the bathhouse. Dark as it was by then, I could finally make out the message the light sculpture on the roof said. Half again the height of the building there were five giant lighted letters spelling out "JESUS."

The Jesus sign shone brightly enough to light my way up to the warehouse sized megastore, the Christian Outlet Center. I'd hoped to take advantage of the amazing 75% off sale that was advertised with huge banners strapped to the awnings of the retailer. It appeared that even situated right next to a revival campground with outdoor worship and eight or nine-foot tall Jesus sign bathing the bathhouse in light, a Christian megastore just couldn't stay in business in suburban Tennessee.

According to the United States Census Bureau, about 50% of the United States is religious while in Knoxville, Tennessee that number is closer to 70%. And Knoxville has four times the number of Baptists as there are in the rest of the country. Knowing these statistics made the failing Christian discount store even more remarkable to me, until I researched the Knoxville economy. See, Knoxville has staggering poverty statistics. Poverty is 40% higher in Knoxville than it is in the rest of Tennessee and 69.2% higher than the national average. It clearly wasn't a shortage of believers that shuttered the Christian Outlet Center. It was their ever-vanishing disposable income.

人

Chapter 12 Rosa Parks Boot Camp

Up and on the road before the pool opened, we wound our way through rural routes outside Knoxville to the Highlander Research and Education Center. Chief Financial Officer and Operations Coordinator, Stephanie McAninch, greeted us at the library located atop a rolling hill of farmland and pasture.

Founded in 1932, as the Highlander Folk School, in Monteagle, Tennessee, the mission of the organization had changed little even though over the years both its name and location had. Highlander's brochure explains that founders Myles Horton and Don West, "believed that society should be fundamentally restructured to promote democracy and address systemic problems of poverty and injustice, and that poor and powerless people should play the leading role in addressing the problems facing their communities."

Keeping on track to broadcast nightly from the road, we interviewed McAninch at one of the library's round discussion tables. Upton Sinclair started each library – the original one in Monteagle and the one where we sat in New Market – with a donation of his work. Once we understood the work done at Highlander, the poetic nature of these contributions by the 20th century's most famous muckraker became clear.

During our radio interview, McAninch explained the theory behind the Highlander Center, "In the folk school model people learn from each other. Everyone has the solutions inside them. Everybody has the information and the ideas to solve problems in a community together."

McAninch went on to describe Myles Horton's vision when he started the folk school, "His goal was to get people to work for themselves, to know that they can make a change in their community and to give people the tools to do it." Over the years many famous activists would come to Highlander to get those tools. From great U.S. civil rights leaders like Dr. Martin Luther King, Jr., and Rosa Parks to international leaders like Nobel Peace Laureate Wangari Maathai, creator of Kenya's Green Movement.

Horton started organizing for the labor movement in the 1930's. Horton came from a poor Appalachian family and went off to Seminary School. McAninch told us, "Myles Horton saw the poverty, saw what was happening to his own family, to his friends, to other people in the community." She said that he knew, "If you didn't have that push for labor organizing, people would just be taken advantage of." He decided to start his folk school, teach communities to advocate for themselves and to do so regardless of perceived differences. McAninch went on, "When Myles accepted contracts he did it for everybody – black, white, everybody – and often times they would find out at the end of the process that they had negotiated a contract for white and black workers."

Organizing workers, championing the labor movement in the Deep South, in Tennessee, and – as McAninch pointed out – "having integrated meetings when it was illegal to have integrated meetings," put Horton at a certain level of risk.

McAninch told us a story about the chances Horton took by insisting on social color blindness. "Myles was threatened a lot and he was actually given a pistol at one time to keep in his hotel room. Someone in the community that didn't like the work that Myles was doing at the time actually sent some thugs after him."

McAninch smiled, "So Myles saw them coming and they were yelling at him that the community didn't need an organizer and Myles says and well, you know, he shows them his gun and says, 'One of you is going to have to come up those stairs first. You're going to have to organize among yourselves and figure out which one that is.'"

Sitting and talking to McAninch, with her gentle demeanor and fond regard for Highlander's founder, it was hard to imagine the really tough and frightening work that had gone on there. Until we climbed up the hill to that library and sat down to record the show, I had no idea that Rosa Parks had been taught community organizing. I thought her courageous stand was a spontaneous act of defiance. But by chatting with McAninch, I understood what I should have known all along: All the great accomplishments of each and every community movement – the labor movement, the civil rights movement, the suffrage movement – were often attributed to one or another great individual, even though they often worked with many others who got no credit for the outcome.

Even after individual acts of intimidation like the thugs at Horton's door, or the more public displays of disdain like when Horton's enemies rented billboards, "all over the south saying that Highlander was a communist training center," McAninch said Horton maintained perspective and a sense of humor. She added, "Myles said he wished he'd known [about the billboards]. He'd have put the phone number to the Highlander Center on the Billboards."

Eventually, those who hoped to destroy Highlander got their chance to shut them down. One night following a function at the center, Highlander was raided and the authorities found a tub with soft drinks and beer as well as a jar filled with coins. Highlander was accused of illegally selling alcohol, their charter was revoked, and the property was seized and sold.

The very next day, Myles Horton applied for a new charter under the name, Highlander Research and Education Center. More land was donated, Upton Sinclair gifted new books, and their mission continued. I guess when you've spent your life training people to refuse to get to the back of the bus, you draw on your own similar reserve when that prejudice and ignorance is leveled at you.

McAninch concluded, "The Highlander Folk School made a difference through the decades. And for that it was targeted by powerful groups and individuals. So, we always have to have that push to make people do the right thing, to make companies to the right thing."

And Highlander is still pushing. McAninch says the process is the same but the battles have changed. They're still fighting for the rights of labor, to put an end to poverty, and they probably always will be. But now the struggle for equality includes teaching individuals and agencies to advocate for immigration reform as well as lesbian, gay, bisexual, and trans gender (LGBT) rights.

When we were leaving we asked McAninch what happened to the old land; The land the state of Tennessee took from them and sold off. She said – when we met with her in June 2013 – that it was for sale again. On August 14, 2013, USA Today featured a story headlined, "Preservationist work to save Highlander Folk School." The story goes on,

> "More than 50 years after the state of Tennessee seized Highlander Folk School's property, not much remains of a place that gave so much inspiration to people who fought for social justice while posing such a visceral threat to the status quo that its founder was accused of being a Communist agitator.
>
> "But a Nashville-based historic preservation group has started working to buy what it can of the Grundy County property, restore its historical look and protect it from development."

Seems wrong they have to buy it back after it was taken from them. But that's an oft-repeated tale that we haven't even touched upon: a legacy many a Native American could share. The history of the United States isn't just a story of stolen labor, it's also a story of stolen land.

Chapter 13 Walking in Memphis
♪

It took us all the rest of that day to cross Tennessee. Rick and Brett were up front in the cockpit and the kids and I stayed down back playing cards and coloring. Carol followed in the car behind us. Because the RV was rented, we didn't have the equipment necessary to tow the Smith family car. Traveling was far more comfortable for the kids in the RV, so – at the outset – on the long legs of our journey Carol was often left alone.

Jim Hoffa, Teamster's General President and son of the late Jimmy Hoffa, endorsed the People's Tour. We issued a press release when we were in New York and pulling out of Highlander we realized that the story hadn't been picked up by any mainstream press outlets. None of us was terribly surprised by that, it was nothing harrowing and news worthy like when conservative neocon Glen Beck set up a worship tent in D.C. for a few days. No, we were just a couple of radio hosts and their producer with a family full of little kids traveling the country and reliving America's powerful and often violent labor past. And now the head of a 1.3 million-member labor union had endorsed it, and son of a gun, but I'd been a journalist for decades and I thought that was more than a little bit news worthy too. So I decided to post something at my page on the Huffington Post.

I've written from the road for so many years, I figured that I'd just bang something out and get it done before we got to Memphis. Of course, I'd never traveled on the road with an 11, 7 and 4 year old that I'd only just met. I turned to the kids whose ribald exuberance was shattering decibel levels in the little RV and asked them if they could be silent for me for about 2 hours. Wanting to know why, I told them that I needed to write and that I couldn't concentrate with so much as a radio playing in the background. Satisfied by my answer, they went up back to the double bed with their books and games and played quietly by themselves.

It turned out that this was the last time I'd have the opportunity to write. Our trip became far too involved to section off two hours to myself, but the sheer willingness of those kids to accommodate my need for quiet stunned me. Nobody's kids are perfect, but those Smith kids – traveling 9600 miles in 28 days – were darned close.

When we got to Memphis we stayed at one of a number of RV parks on Elvis Presley Boulevard. Right behind our park was a low-income housing project. All asphalt and a smattering of broken glass, this camping area might have been an extension of that project. Graceland and all the Elves Presley Entertainment (EPE) properties were about a mile up the road from us and with the exception of that sideshow theme park atmosphere, the whole region looked depressed and stereotypically urban.

Memphis had something for every one of the grown-ups on this trip. Rick couldn't get to Beale Street fast enough. Brett and Rick had worked for months and gotten a host of great interviews lined up for our visit there. Carol – a professional photographer who would snap thousands of pictures along our way – wanted to take the kids to St. Jude's Hospital. She and Aly had raised money for the sick kids there, and she wanted a picture of her children out in front of the hospital. As for me, I wanted to go to the Lorraine Motel.

Oh, and there was barbecue.

We didn't have much time so we prioritized. First things first, we all piled in the minivan and headed to Beale Street. Downtown Memphis was surprisingly deserted. We parked across from a park around the corner from Danny Thomas Boulevard. Beale Street had been closed to motor vehicle traffic so we walked over with the kids in tow. Hungry, we just needed a place with some good southern barbecue.

Live music filled the street. Music spilled out of every open bar room, bands played on the street corners and in the infamous Church park. Robert Church, renowned as America's first black millionaire, founded Church Park. Born a slave, he escaped during the civil war. When he returned to Memphis he opened a saloon and bought up land and property all along the Beale Street section. He worked tirelessly for everything from black enfranchisement to anti-lynching legislation. Church's devotion to community went further than civil and human rights. Church brought music to Beale Street, built Church Park and Auditorium – all of were open to black and whites alike – and music plays there in his honor to this day.

The one thing everyplace on Beale Street had in common – other than the music and the pulled pork – was that they didn't allow children in the bar. Well, everyplace but one: The Jerry Lee Lewis Honky Tonk and Café. And yeah, you can't make this stuff up.

The food was more than decent and the service was excellent. I admit, it took us 10 or 15 minutes to stop cracking jokes to each other about how The Jerry Lee Lewis Honky Tonk and Café had to allow children, so Jerry Lee's wife could dine with him. But after a while we settled down and had dinner. We didn't start clowning around again until after everyone ate.

Rick can and does talk to strangers with impeccable ease. Rick's an everyday man. He doesn't have a snotty bone in his body and people identify with him easily. He befriended a bouncer by chatting up football and before we knew it, the bouncer, his buddies and the bartender staged a scene – while we photographed it – of them throwing Rick out of their saloon.

After a good laugh we loaded sleepy children into the car and headed home to bed.

Scheduling show production was a work in progress for the first week or so. We knew that somewhere along the trip, we'd have to tape the filler pieces in each night's show that introduced segments, discussed where we were and what we were doing, and recapped the important things we'd learned along our journey. We hadn't yet perfected the process of taping while we drove, so that night we had an hour or so of taping left to do.

When we got back from Beale Street, while the kids got settled into the back of the RV, Rick, Brett and I finished taping the Shows from West Virginia and eastern Tennessee.

The next morning, the Smiths and I walked up to Graceland and left Brett behind to edit and uplink the programming for that night. Because we started making shows over the weekend, our shows actually aired a few days after we'd left the town in which they were taped. We planned to keep that sort of lead-time so that we'd never find ourselves without enough programming. Because we worked seven days a week on show content, we managed to keep our lead going right through to the end of the trip.

It was hot and oppressively humid as we walked up Elvis Presley Blvd. to Graceland. A stone wall circles the property and literally every inch of that wall is covered with graffiti, messages and signatures of folks who had happened by the "King's" house.

When Elvis daughter, Lisa Marie, turned 25 she inherited the entire estate. Less than a decade ago, Lisa Marie sold 85% of Elvis Presley Enterprises (EPE) to Core Media. Core Media is better known as the owners of the rights to the television shows "American Idol" and "So You Think You Can Dance." Just about the time we started our trip, with the exception of the family home, Graceland itself – which Lisa Marie owns outright – EPE put the rest of the facility up for sale. According to insiders close to the deal, EPE is hoping to get around $200 million and intends to expand their television holdings.

If a buyer can be found, everything from the "Heartbreak Hotel" to the tour service and gift shops would change hands. We wandered through the EPE facility that is directly across the street from the Graceland Mansion. Winding our way past young men in Elvis garb, along photographic mosaics of the King, Rick started asking employees of EPE what they thought of their jobs. He asked them if they thought they were paid well considering how expensive everything was in the gift shops and along the tour route. This was the first time, but far from the last, that Rick would be shown the door by employees and/or management made uncomfortable by his probing questions.

A couple of women who were sideshow barking at passers-by and inviting them to tour one of Elvis' two private jets that were on display. I asked how much it was for a ticket. They told me, "$12 but the little ones are free." I said, "$12, I have to work almost two hours to make that." One of the women replied, "Tell me about it." And went back to work.

We walked back to our RV park and packed everything up. Brett was done editing, and because of the mobile wireless uplink, he could send the show on the fly. We decided to give one more barbecue place a try. This time we decided on a place legendary as one of the King's favorites, Marlowe's, the home of the giant pink parking lot pig.

I mention this for one reason and one reason only. Marlowe's allowed patrons the option of ordering one of their various barbecued meats stuffed into a baked potato. This culinary innovation inspired awe from conception to execution and deserves note in any book written about Memphis.

I stopped at the gift shop to get a few post cards. An older fellow stood behind the cash register. He told me stories about Elvis. He never introduced himself but he regaled me with anecdotes about when Elvis Presley Boulevard was nothing but a dirt road and the night Elvis dropped by on his motorcycle with friends. He said that he'd locked the place up and Elvis and his buds ate there all alone.

And later – years later – Elvis came back in his limousine, having made it to the big time. I didn't ask this guy for proof or to tell me who he was, because it really didn't matter. Elvis in Memphis now is like Santa to the rest of the world. The legend's the important thing, and the stories are better the more often they're told.

Because the men who volunteered for interviews on Rick's show were all workingmen, they wouldn't be available until after 4 p.m. Consequently, we had time for a few more stops before heading over to the Teamster's Local 667 where we'd scheduled talks with several representatives of various unions, including the Memphis sanitation workers.

45 years and two months earlier, Dr. Martin Luther King, Jr. had visited Memphis is support of the same sanitation workers' union we had come to interview on our People's Tour. MLK, Jr.'s support of the sanitation workers was an integral part of his Poor People's Campaign. He had been there several times, but that visit ended in violence and without a contract for the workers. When he returned on April 3, 1968, MLK, Jr. hoped for a better outcome.

We left Marlowe's and headed over to the Lorraine Motel. 1968 Memphis offered little option for where a black man would stay. Back on the night MLK, Jr. was assassinated, his hotel was in a far less gentrified neighborhood then it was the day we visited. The National Civil Rights Museum consists of the motel and several of the properties around it, including the boarding house where James Earl Ray stood when he allegedly shot and killed Dr. King. Unfortunately, the museum was closed for renovations. The best we could do was stand in the parking lot and look up at the balcony in front of Room 306.

A few other visitors wandered by while I stood staring at the now famous setting, solemnly imagining that fateful evening. Across the street, standing at her permanent station, a former resident of the Lorraine Motel continued her decades long protest of the National Civil Rights Museum.

On the night MLK, Jr. died, Jacqueline Smith lived at the Lorraine Motel. Many hotels in poorer neighborhoods rent by the week or month – often for years – to low-income people who don't have the up front money for an apartment. Even after King's assassination, Smith didn't have the money or the inclination to leave her home. It wasn't until the Martin Luther King Memorial Foundation purchased the motel in 1982 that Smith left. She was forced to leave.

The eviction from her home, so that low-income housing could be made into a gentrified museum, galled Smith. She felt that the emphasis was all wrong and the repurposed motel glorified the death of a great civil rights leader instead of honoring his life. And 31 years later, Rick, Brett, Carol, the kids and I all stood face to face with this passionate woman who would not back down.

Smith has a card table with just an umbrella to shield her from the brutal Memphis sun. She displays protest signs that say, "Stop Worshipping the Past, Start Living the Dream" and "Welcome to the $27 Million James Earl Ray Memorial." She's guarded and mistrustful. I wanted to interview her. I gave her my card. She said she'd think about it.

I did a few web searches but couldn't find any formal interviews with her. There were a few blog entries from people who claim to have spoken with her. They report that she feels affordable housing or a civil rights training school would be better tributes to Dr. King's legacy than a fancy museum that costs $12 per person to visit. She notes that a poor family can't afford entry to the "James Earl Ray Memorial" as she calls it. She thinks that would bother Dr. King. And she thinks that goes against everything the late civil rights leader defended in his lifetime.

Unconfirmed stories about Smith claim that she became homeless after her eviction from the Lorraine Motel. And while I couldn't get her to answer that question directly, one of the banners on her table may have answered it for her.

The sign read, "Just because you can't see the homeless, it doesn't mean they don't exist." The sign goes on to state, "Gentrification is an abuse of civil liberties."

Smith has a website www.fulfillthedream.net, where she devotes most of the pages to quotes from the object of her devotion, Dr. King. There are about as many clues to her day-to-day existence on the webpage as we found on her table across from the hotel. And there's very little about her eviction from the motel. But there is a picture of white men throwing her bodily from the parking lot after it had been fenced in with 6-foot chain link. The old black and white photo looks remarkably like the gag photos we'd staged of Rick being thrown from Jerry Lee Lewis Honky Tonk and Café. But it was no gag.

And after 29 years standing vigil, Smith continues to protest outside the home she lost because someone gunned down Martin Luther King Jr., a man Smith believes would be fighting right beside her to get her home back.

Chapter 14 A Tale of Two Johnsons
♪ ♪

On February 1, 1968, two Memphis sanitation workers died on the job. Their deaths prompted a strike by their coworkers for better, safer working conditions and recognition of their labor union. Even though the city council voted to negotiate with the workers, Mayor Henry Loeb refused.

One month later civil rights leader, Martin Luther King, Jr. marched with the sanitation workers in a demonstration that unfortunately got out of hand. A young man was shot by a police officer and died.

As time wore on, the workers were getting nowhere with their grievances. King, upset over the violence that broke out at the last rally, initiated negotiations with all sides in the dispute. He returned to Memphis to support the workers and assure a nonviolent protest. A new march was planned for April 5th but the city secured an injunction against the protest. Following a meeting with King's supporters on April 4, Judge Bailey Brown revoked the injunction and the march was rescheduled for April 8th.

Shortly after King received word that the sanitation workers' demonstration would go forward, Dr. King walked out of his room at the Lorraine Motel and was shot to death.

Keith Johnson, Chairperson of AFSCME (American Federation of State, County & Municipal Employees) local 1733 sat patiently at the conference table while Brett performed his sound check. Johnson, a giant of a man – at least four inches taller than Rick and Rick's 6'4" – clad in the neon t-shirt he wore to promote visibility while he worked hauling trash, came to the Teamsters office to share what it's like to be one of the sanitation workers King died fighting to protect.

Our first question was a throwaway. A throwaway's a question you ask to warm the guest up because you figure you already know the answer and it ought to be a fairly straightforward way to start the interview.

We asked if the sanitation workers' shop was full of pictures of King.

His answer was anything but predictable. We were shocked. The Memphis sanitation workers are NOT allowed to hang a picture of King, not on the walls, not anywhere for that matter.

Johnson replied, "We work at different sites, at barns, there are a lot of things at work that they don't want us to wear. We come into there with something, with a shirt with Dr. King on there, we can't wear that."

Stunned, Rick asked, "Really?" Johnson answered, "Really."

We needed to back up. Because we naïvely underestimated management's fear of worker unity, we'd wrongly assumed that the legacy of Dr. King and his sacrifice for their cause, inspired sanitation workers every day at work. Now we redirected our interview to ascertain just exactly how much the new youngest generation – Johnson had been a sanitation worker for 28 years, starting a full 17 years after King's assassination – learned from the men who marched with King in 1968.

Rick asked what those striking workers passed on to him.

"They passed on that you have to fight for what you believe in and don't give up. And you have to stand and fight during conditions that were so bad. I mean just terrible conditions." Johnson told us what he knew about why the sanitation strikers went against the city and Mayor Loeb, "The filth was ridiculous. There were maggots. You had to put cotton in your ears… you put cotton in your nose. When you got home your wife wouldn't let you in the front door. You had to stop on the porch and by the time you shake your clothes, take the cotton balls, there were maggots all over."

Johnson said that it wasn't like collecting trash is now, "because you had to tote the tubs to someone who was actually standing in the garbage. You had to tote the can. You had guys up in the trucks standing in the garbage when they poured the garbage in the truck. You had guys up there pouring the garbage in around their feet."

Johnson continued telling their tale, bringing us forward to the strike, explaining that theirs was an intensely dangerous job when it rained. He explained that the garbage got slippery and men would stand further inside the truck to shield themselves from the downpour, "In the rain, we had a couple of guys that actually got killed. They was up in the back of the truck and they said the truck malfunctioned, but you know, to keep them out of the rain, it was raining so hard and you know, the blade came down and killed them."

As a result of these deaths and the 1968 Memphis Sanitation Strike, for decades after, the city suspended trash collection when it rained. Until recently, "So now in the last year and a half they're forcing us to work in the rain again."

Johnson's keenly aware of why King and others fought, but that fight has not ended, "It's almost a deeper fight now, the conditions were worse then, the pay was lousy... they were actually fighting then for better working conditions and better wages. Now it's to the point that they're taking money from us... we're fighting to keep our jobs. We constantly hear about privatization. Every year."

Johnson feels that because King died during their fight, that they are bigger targets to some labor busters, but also better protected from others, "Once they called us sacred cows, to the point where we felt like we were sacred because of Dr. Martin Luther King, that we cannot be touched."

Johnson says that shield produced by King's legacy could easily disappear, "Every time privatization comes up they say we're always talking about Dr. King and what he stood for and they say we're not sacred anymore. There's a lot of people across the United States that think that we got it good. They don't understand the fight we had."

Johnson – feeling the need to bring up a new generation of labor organizers – explains the challenge before him with his younger colleagues, "We try to instill inside them the knowledge of how to fight. A lot of people get it wrong. They think that because I'm a representative of the union that they're going to pay their dues and I'm going to do all the fighting. I say to them that they are the union. It's the numbers, the more people we bring together, it makes it easier."

Johnson knows the guys he works with aren't lazy. He thinks they just don't understand how hard they all have to work to keep the benefits they have, to keep the jobs they have. Johnson wants them to work at their union membership after their long day hauling the community's trash, "Getting out on a truck, right now it's a hundred degrees and we pick up whatever people throw away... the smell... and all this." He wants the young workers to value what they do for the community, and value themselves for insuring public health and safely, "People try to take this away from you. We do this with pride. We are serving the citizens. We do this with pride." His younger co-workers have to turn that self-respect into self-defense, "You're in a union for a reason. We represent you when management does you wrong, but you're in there to make it grow. We want it better for them than we have it now."

Johnson feels that there's a lot to learn from the historic march of 1968 that remains unlearned. The lack of commemorative signs, the absent mention of Dr. King and the protest marchers, the unlearned lessons of organizing, these things keep his co-workers from knowing that there's real safety, real power, in numbers. Johnson explains, "We have family, we have to have protests, we have to bring our families and go to the streets. Get our families involved like in 1968, there were a number of sanitation workers out there but they had their sons, their daughters, they had their mothers, their sisters, their brothers, they had all of them out there. They were actually standing out there as well and that meant the citizens of Memphis were behind them. And we all have to come together, not just for sanitation workers, and we all need to bring out families."

Johnson pointed out that sanitation is an important part of the public trust. Johnson knows that as soon as corporations take over vital services the functional bottom line will shift from serving the people to making a profit, "It will affect citizens and the workers. It would affect everybody in this city. All this privatize, when it comes out, it's not going to get better. We have to get the knowledge to the citizens, let them know, it's not going to get better. Right now, you have a voice. Simply cause of a city council, you elect them in. Ok you have a voice. But if you set up there and privatize this out, let them do this, the bottom line is a private company is going to come in and the first year they'll treat you nice. But then you've taken it out of the citizens' hands because it's privatized now. And then it's going to blow up and you can't go back."

The current political leadership in Memphis – with its modern day Mayor Loebs – has told Johnson and the other AFSCME leaders that they'd like the union to bid on the contract for sanitation against private industry. The city is effectively inviting the union to work against it's own membership to cut corners, cut wages, and eliminate benefits. Johnson can't even explain how an idea like that came about, "Management competition where we can come in and bid against a company like BFI. We are the workers, how are we going to bid against ourselves?"

And it isn't even like they have a retirement to sell off. Yeah, that's another little shock we got in Memphis talking with Chairperson Keith Johnson. Even after Martin Luther King, Jr. paid the ultimate price, the sanitation workers of Memphis never did get a pension.

None of this made any sense to any of us. Not to Rick, not to Brett, not to me, and it sure as heck didn't make sense to Keith Johnson. Luckily, this is a tale of two Johnsons though, and Chad Johnson was waiting to speak with us next.

Chad Johnson, executive director of AFSCME Local 1733, explained that in 1967 the sanitation workers agreed that the newly invented social security insurance would serve as their retirement program. And because of this, they have no other pension plan, "By some provisions of Social Security statute it is impossible for you to become a part of a defined pension benefit and receive social security at the same time. That is unless your employer makes the social security payments and most employers take one tract or the other."

Johnson blames many of the problems that face public employees on the Taft Hartley Act. In 1947 this act was passed over the veto of then Pres. Truman and is summed up by Johnson, "fundamentally there's no protection for public employees to deny their labor if they feel like they're being mistreated on the job."

For every minute Keith Johnson spent walking us through the vital facts swirling about one of the American working class's most important single events, Chad Johnson spent a moment summing up the nation's current events big picture. He feels the rules of unions are pretty straightforward, "The point is you're supposed to have an agency that advocates for working people, just like every other group has someone who advocates for them."

Rick played possum a little and challenged him, saying that we might have needed unions a hundred years ago, but we don't need them anymore. And of course, Johnson disagreed, "We're in a country right now, where the wealth divide between the top 2% and the rest of the country is greater than between the Pharaohs of Egypt and their servants."

Johnson continued, "You need unions at a time when retirement security is going out the window, you need it at a time when they're now cutting back on healthcare benefits, on healthcare at all. You need it at a time where a college education or any sort of education is slipping from the grasp of the majority of people."

Johnson, with all his big picture wisdom knows that the problem is a lot bigger than just union busting, it's who is doing the union busting and where these players get the nerve to think they should have any say in municipal decision making at all. Johnson explained to us how things work in his state, "Tennessee is one of the few states that doesn't have a payroll tax, does not have an income tax. All we have to support our public services are property taxes and a gigantic sales tax. Interestingly enough... Tennessee is on the list with the 5th lowest tax burden in the country. I'm not an economist but if low taxes meant wealth than Tennessee should be paved in gold. But it's not. When you look at all the indicators it's still on the bottom when it comes to poverty and women's health and children's health and education."

And yet, Johnson points out, amidst all this suffering, businesses like Fed Ex pay absolutely no property taxes, "People may not know this but, many municipalities and states in their attempt to lure in big companies will say, 'hey guess what, big company, you don't have to pay the property tax or you don't have to pay the income tax even.' And then they [the big companies] have the bold nerve [to say] 'by the way we're going to form a group to tell you what to do with your public tax dollars that we're not paying.'"

As the executive director of a labor union representing the government workers who are regularly caught in the ideological crossfire between big business gunning for their jobs and big businesses unwilling to pay their fair share, Chad

Johnson has coined a new slogan that he really hopes will catch on. Chad Johnson says, "If you don't pay, you don't get a say."

And what about the huge corporations that do more than just free ride off the infrastructure necessities paid for by the little guys in their communities? What does Johnson think about the corporate welfare recipients who get incentivized to relocate to a region? Well, Johnson thinks they should, "reclassify them as public employees. Cause if you're getting public dollars, and when you look at the amount of money that is moving, these companies are getting more public dollars than people who actually work for municipalities."

That's when we asked Chad Johnson to run for president.

Chad Johnson pointed out in an off handed and simple gesture that the huge multi-national corporations that leverage their way out of paying taxes and take mega subsidies for locating in a region collect as much if not more money from municipal, county and state tax payers than the public servants who actually perform a service and live in these communities. And in a state like Tennessee with no personal income tax, all those executives with seven figure incomes pay no income taxes. And yet it is the sanitation worker like Keith Johnson who – if it weren't for King and 1100 striking sanitation workers would still need cotton balls to keep the maggots out of his nose and ears – is maligned and portrayed as greedy.

I want bumper stickers that say, "Johnson/Johnson 2016."

𝄞

Chapter 15   Guns in the Workplace but No Living Wage
ʎ ʎʎ

We drove around and around – turning this way and that – and even though all three of us had our iPhones out, nobody could find the St. Jude Hospital.

We all pulled over next to the overgrown vacant lot that our GPS's said was St. Jude's and Carol said, "How could it have vanished?" Of course it couldn't have, but we all laughed anyway. For the life of us we couldn't find it and we'd hoped to be well on our way to Little Rock later that evening.

Carol called for Aly to get out of the car and said, "Well go stand in that field, we're not coming all the way to Memphis and leaving without a picture."

But really, we'd been batting a thousand in Memphis. In town for only 27 hours, we'd seen the historic and cultural sites that most of us wanted to see. We stuffed ourselves silly with smoked meats and with the exception of a missing children's hospital, we'd done pretty well. In addition to the two AFSCME Johnsons, we'd interviewed three Teamsters, a trolley driver with the Amalgamated Transit Union and the president of the Memphis AFL CIO.

When Carol saw our radio line-up earlier that evening she took one look at us, hopped in the minivan and said, "I'm taking the kids and going to Mississippi for an ice cream."

The kids had reading projects, coloring books and crafts, electronic games for extremely special occasions and blank maps of the United States that were theirs to decorate as soon as they entered a new state. Knowing they had hours to kill waiting for us to conduct our radio interviews, Carol took advantage of the opportunity to add an unanticipated state to their maps.

Traveling with a Teamster, it seemed as though we'd have an inside track on life on the road. But some of these Local 667 Teamsters were driving long before Rick was born.

Robert Seay started driving truck at 17. He remembered earning $1.14 an hour in 1950. And that was a darn good wage. The minimum wage at that time in Alabama – where he started driving – was a whopping 75 cents an hour. Seay spoke of their many hard earned gains. He walked picket lines in all kinds of weather. He feels like a pioneer, one of the early truckers who laid the groundwork. In 1955 they got their pension.

Bill Edwards agreed. Another retired trucker, Edwards remembered when the union got them air-conditioned trucks.

Edwards worked hard to get a union job. He knew that the union guys got paid by the mile. In the 1960's his pay went from less than $100 per week to more than $500. Both Edwards and Seay educated their kids and have retired in comfort. They know they wouldn't have been able to do that without collective bargaining and good employers. Edwards and Seay gave a good days work for a good days wages. Seay said that because employers and unions worked well together, by the 1970's, they felt like they were all in the drivers seat together – figuratively as well as literally.

Richard Creekmore spoke of that winning cooperation and remembered it working for Jones Trucking. Creekmore said, "I've been in management, I've drove a truck. I know both sides of this question and at Jones trucking we had some of the best people there ever was to work for. When Jones started he had a section of the country that he hauled freight in. When deregulation was approved by Congress that cut our little section of the country out. Now we're in competition with every truck line in the country." And Creekmore feels that deregulation hurt truckers and shipping line owners equally.

All three of these retired Teamsters spoke fondly of their benefits and their retirement. Creekmore summed it up most poignantly, "See, I had insurance on my wife. And when she died, she went into the hospital and died." Creekmore is perhaps most grateful for that small kindness and the dignity and comfort his wife experienced at the end of her life. It's a dignity that should be available to everyone.

Seay, Edwards, and Creekmore are all worried that the younger kids are up against too much negative public opinion when it comes to their union membership. He knows they are hard pressed to organize and push back against the anti-union sentiment that seems to be sweeping the country. Seay still works as a Chaplin for the Teamsters. He brings Bibles to people whenever they lose someone. He hopes that people get a different idea when they see him. Seay said, "We fell short on educating the pubic on what a union does and what a union is. They probably think we're a bunch of bad guys, but we're not."

And they all hope the younger Teamsters start getting more involved in union activities. They hope so for the sake of other Teamsters and for unions in general.

Seay remembered MLK, Jr.'s assassination. He remembered that he was where he should have been when it happened. Seay was volunteering under a tent helping the sanitation workers with their strike. Seay's worried that not enough people stick by the other unions the way he thinks they should.

Larry Miller drives the trolley that runs through downtown Memphis. His dad drove trolleys before him. Miller doesn't know how anyone can expect the downtown to stay alive without "good solid public transportation for business." A business needs customers and a business needs workers. Miller remembered the first big federal cuts to public transportation during the Reagan Administration. They lost hundreds of drivers then, and they're poised to lose more now. Miller says he just, "feels sorry for people waiting on the bus."

Irwin Calliste, President of the Memphis AFL CIO, can't understand what's going on politically. Nationally and locally, laws have stopped making sense. The unions worked on a living wage ordinance for subcontractors and then the state took it away. Calliste pointed out that this is the first time in Tennessee since reconstruction that the democrats are completely out of power. The republicans control both houses of the legislature as well as the governor's mansion.

Calliste is frustrated. He feels that selfishness is encouraged in American culture to the detriment of all else. Why should someone pay dues if they can get the same thing for free? People are supposed to want something for nothing. People care about the wrong things. Workers have become self-absorbed and self-destructive.

Calliste said, "Things that are important take a back seat and what's important isn't important." Calliste pointed out that workers in Tennessee can carry a gun to work but they don't get a living wage.

Calliste said it's an education problem as well as a cultural problem. Pulpits have to preach respect for the workers. Worker's rights need to be as important as profit. And schools have to teach labor history.

Mr. Calliste, you said it. And when we met back up with the kids after these interviews and their Mississippi ice cream break, we loaded up and moved 'em out. We headed west for our next labor history lesson.

λ

Chapter 16 Little Rock Nine

We knew we wanted to go west because we knew Brett had only about a week left before his planned immersion in all the progressive sunshine that Netroots Nation could deliver. But while we had a dictated time frame, we dictated our route. Rick made most of the calls based on the history he wanted his kids to learn. Once we identified must-see-history, Rick and Brett contacted authorities in the area. Sometimes they were historians and other times they were labor leaders, but they set up interviews with the folks who could clue us in on the specifics of a region.

Rick really wanted his kids to see Central High School in Little Rock, Arkansas. Shame on me for having been to Little Rock before and not giving Central High School a second thought.

The U.S. Department of the Interior has a museum diagonally across the street from Central High School. The museum – like the events that took place there in 1957 – should be overkill. Really, nine black kids went to an all white school, should that really be national park worthy? How could the task of desegregating one measly southern high school have been so noteworthy? But once you learn how powerful the anti-black sentiment was in Little Rock at that time, it all starts to make sense. Perspective is pretty important when it comes to understanding the "Little Rock Nine."

The civil war may have freed enslaved blacks but it did nothing to make them equal to their white captors. In 1892 Homer Plessy broke Louisiana law by not surrendering his seat on a train to a white man. Plessy claimed that the 14th Amendment guaranteeing equal protection under the law nullified the Louisiana law requiring him to move. In 1896, the United States Supreme Court voted 8 to 1 against Plessy.

Justice Henry Billings Brown wrote in *Plessy v. Ferguson*, "The object of the [Fourteenth] amendment was undoubtedly to enforce the equality of two races before the law." However, Brown wrote that the court also determined, "If one race be inferior to the other socially, the Constitution of the United States cannot put them upon the same plane."

So they ruled that all races were entitled to the same things legally, but socially they could still be separated. And from that came the concept of separate but equal. Separate lunch counters, separate bathrooms, separate movie houses, and of course, separate schools.

In the early 1950's five cases challenging educational segregation were brought before the Supreme Court. The Justices consolidated them under one name: *Brown v. The Board of Education of Topeka*. May 14, 1954 the court unanimously changed their opinion, "We believe that in the field of public education the doctrine of 'separate but equal' has no place. Separate educational facilities are inherently unequal."

With appalling deference to racist state governments, the Supreme Court waited a year before demanding desegregation. During that year, the Attorney's General from segregationist states were asked to suggest methods of desegregation that would be less jarring to the general public. Finally, on May 31, 1955 the Justices decreed that public school departments use "all deliberate speed" to desegregate.

Regardless of that mandate, complete desegregation did not occur until the Civil Rights Act of 1964.

In Little Rock, Arkansas, in 1957, a federal court ordered the schools to integrate immediately. The school department had 4 high schools. The showpiece of these schools was the all white Central High School. When school began in September, nine black children were enrolled and expected to attend.

I often wondered why only nine teens got the chance to move over from their blacks-only school to the infamous Central High. When we got to the museum, I asked one of the park rangers. It turned out that 200 students had initially volunteered to go to Central High but only nine made the cut.

Once kids elected to go to Central, they had to agree to certain conditions. The school department had been ordered to give black youth the same education as white youth, and that's where the school department intended to leave it. No black student in Central High would be allowed to play sports or participate in extra curricular activities. And no matter how they might be taunted, bullied, pushed, pulled, spat upon, or ridiculed, the black kids had to promise they would not defend themselves. The Little Rock Nine promised they wouldn't talk back or act out in any way toward an abuser.

Only nine young black students were willing to sacrifice every other aspect of their high school careers to get what they believed would be a better education. They went to counseling over the summer leading up to their transfer, but it is doubtful that they fully understood how much courage they'd need before they were through.

Resistance to the Little Rock Nine was pervasive. From the Governor on down, these kids were resented far worse than even they imagined they would be. Melba Pattillo explained, "After three full days inside Central, I know that integration is a much bigger word than I thought."

September 2nd, Governor Orval Faubus got on TV and explained to the state that he would be dispatching the Arkansas National Guard to Central High School. The National Guard would stand sentry and bar the black kids from the school. He said that he wanted to "prevent violence."

When the Little Rock Nine tried to go to class on September 4th, the guardsmen obediently turned them away. When you watch the video of them trying to get into school, it's alarming how many angry, yelling, white women you see in each frame. The face of racism is often assumed to be male, but the newsreels over at the museum tell a very ugly tale of racist women in America.

Turned away by the National Guard, condemned by the governor, and bullied by the crowd, the Little Rock Nine all but gave up on attending Central High.

The federal courts were committed to desegregation and on September 20th, Judge Ronald Davies ordered the Governor to stop using the National Guard to abrogate the kids' constitutional rights. The Governor complied and withdrew the National Guard. But once the kids got back to school, riots broke out and the Little Rock Nine were chased from the building. It wasn't until Pres. Dwight Eisenhower intervened that the kids actually got a chance to learn in Central High School classrooms.

Appalled by the rioting, Pres. Eisenhower deployed the 101st Airborne Division and – adding insult to Gov. Faubus' injury – he federalized the National Guard sending them back to Central High, but this time to make sure the kids went to school.

The military stayed in Little Rock for the entire school year. After one of the kids was attacked in class, they each received an individual military escort every day, all day. It wasn't easy to put up with the consistently overt racism and disdain, but Minnijean Brown was the only one who lost her temper and finally fought back. The administration expelled Minnijean Brown from Central High. Brown moved to New York and finished her schooling there.

I don't know how indicative my personal education is of the rest of the country, but from what I learned about Central High, I thought that was the end of the story. I thought the racist governor learned his lesson and integrated life went on as it should have all along. But that's not what happened. If I hadn't been along on Rick Smith's journey to teach his kids U.S. history, I never would have known that racist Gov. Faubus refused to give up.

See, Gov. Faubus was furious that black children had sullied the once pristine Central High, and rather than have more black children at the school the next year, Gov. Faubus shut down all the Little Rock High Schools. Rather than integrate, Faubus denied 3600 students – black and white – an education. The race struggle became a labor dispute as the teachers and staff of all four high schools were idled by Gov. Faubus' decision.

I mentioned the videos of racist women, yelling taunting and tormenting the Little Rock Nine. One of the black girls, Elizabeth Eckford described her surprise at the intolerance back when it the riots broke out, "I tried to see a friendly face somewhere in the mob – someone who maybe would help. I looked into the face of an old woman and it seemed a kind face, but when I looked at her again, she spat on me."

In reality, racism has no gender but the source of resolution to this conflict did.

After the governor closed the schools – in a move eerily similar to how malicious governors all across the nation rejected federal 2013 Medicaid money for the poor in their states – the schools remained closed for an entire academic year.

In 1958 the Women's Emergency Committee to Open Our Schools – which became better known as WEC – decided to get the schools back in business. According to the Department of the Interior, "Infuriated by the lack of response from business and community leaders, they [WEC] formed the first organization to publicly condemn the school-closing action and to support reopening the schools under the Little Rock School District's desegregation plan."

The women published flyers reminding their fellow citizens, "Wake up Little Rock, your public school system is being destroyed." The women forced a city wide recall of all anti-integration school board members and the schools reopened in August of 1959.

I'd always known that racism, hatred and fear allowed for the abuse of black children all across the country. It still does. But I had no idea until the People's Tour for America visited Little Rock High School that racism, hatred and fear actually closed off educational opportunities to every high school student in the city. Was Little Rock indicative of social problems plaguing all of America? It must have been. It became the flash point because, with a racist and arrogant governor leading the way – 92 years after the civil war ended – prejudice had a home in the Arkansas state house.

Smaller fights were waged all across the nation, for which the Little Rock Nine would become the poster children. As Daisy Bates, director of the Arkansas NAACP, put it, "Any time it takes eleven thousand five hundred soldiers to assure nine Negro children their constitutional rights in a democratic society, I can't be happy."

The kicker is, a year later, it took an entire recall election to grant 3600 children their right to an education because Pres. Eisenhower had the intestinal fortitude to commit those troops to defend the Little Rock Nine.

λ λλ

Chapter 17 Yes Virginia, There is a Middle Class

We really underestimated how we'd interview folks when we pulled into various towns. While many folks were happy to talk to us, not many got back to us ahead of time with very many specifics. And unlike some big network operation, we didn't travel with a production truck. Although along about Utah and every stop after that – when Rick and I would take the time to talk about something other than our next immediate broadcast need – Rick started saying, "Next time we're pulling a broadcast trailer behind us."

And even though we'd communicated with regions in advance, we really didn't have any idea what kind of set up might be available for us to use when we got there. We felt a little needy every time we'd say, "Do you have WiFi, do you have an office or a conference room we could use for our interviews, and how long can we hang out here?" Heck, in Memphis we'd moved in and stayed put for about four hours straight. Regardless of our feeling that we'd imposed on folks, not a single soul made us feel anything but welcome.

Melanie Orman greeted us at the Teamsters Local 878. Orman, a young bright beautiful woman, appeared to fulfill every requirement for a Miss Arkansas candidate and matched not a single stereotype of a Teamster. Although when Rick jokingly said, "You're a Teamster? Where's your baseball bat? Do you have a baseball bat?" Orman didn't miss a beat and replied ever so sweetly, "Of course."

Orman welcomed us and set us up at the desk in her office. The suffocating temperatures in Little Rock, Arkansas made it way too hot to work outside. And, without a traveling studio, we wilted at the idea of inviting guests out to our overcrowded RV to do the show.

Orman made us feel right at home. As political coordinator she brought us up to speed on the state of Arkansas labor laws. The picture wasn't pretty. Arkansas's a "Right to Work State."

According to the Free Online Dictionary, *Right to Work States* have "State laws permitted by section 14(b) of the Taft-Hartley act that provide in general that employees are not required to join a union as a condition of getting or retaining a job." That means that if a union secures certain gains in a workplace, folks can be hired who don't need to become a part of that union to take advantage of the gains. Therefore, "Right-to-work laws forbid unions and employers to enter into agreements requiring employees to join a union and pay dues and fees to it in order to get or keep a job."

On average, union dues amount to two hours pay each month. The Arkansas AFL-CIO website says that as a result of their membership, the average union worker is 52% more likely to have health insurance, about three times more likely to have a pension, 50% more likely to have paid personal leave, has an average of 28% more vacation time, and makes about 30% more per week than a nonunion employee. Unions are even more important for Latino workers. In Arkansas the average Latino union employee makes nearly double what a nonunion Latino makes! Double! That's because unions don't discriminate based on race. All union members get paid equally for equal jobs.

When employers look at saving 30% on wages and reducing all those benefits, it's no surprise that so many set up shop in *Right to Work* states.

When we drove though Tennessee, we made a detour so Rick and Brett could hop out of the RV and tape some video out in front of Carlisle Tire and Wheel's new plant. Carlisle Tire and Wheel shuttered their namesake in our hometown of Carlisle, Pennsylvania –putting thousands of our neighbors out of work – simply to bask in the warm glow of worker exploitation in *Right to Work* Tennessee.

Right now you might be wondering just what they did in that video. I, like you, felt my pulse quicken at the possibilities. I can only say that the video and all the interviews we taped along the way are available at our People's Tour website.

During her interview Orman had some good news to share though, too. The workers and their advocates in Arkansas had just succeeded in pushing back against the legislature when they attempted to reduce unemployment compensation. Orman explained that the average post-reduction benefit would have been about $50 per week per family. That wasn't the amount of the cut; that would have been the amount of the benefit.

Orman said that dozens of workers went in to testify. They really activated their base and they managed to win that one.

Another legislative representative, Glen Stell, joined us for an interview after Orman. Stell's a member of Teamsters Brotherhood of Locomotive Engineers and Trainsmen (BLET) and he warned us of a threat to public safety that he and others around the nation were fighting. Freight trains had long ago lost their caboose, and prevailing political wisdom was that technology had rendered a second trainman unnecessary – regardless of the size of the train. Stell believed that nothing could be further from the truth.

I'd heard for years that unions weren't just about wages and benefits. I'd been told that because union members do the job, they are keenly aware of the hazards and are often the advocates for safety. Stell's cautionary words made sense. I understood his concerns, especially the fear that – with only one person on the train – no one would be available to operate the train should the conductor become incapacitated, fall ill, or die on the job.

A few weeks later, when a deadly train accident in Lac-Megantic, Quebec revealed that there had been only one crew member on board the train, I was shocked into understanding how important workers' feedback about safety is. But without organized labor, who listens to workers? Certainly history has shown – as we'd continue to see along our trip – that without unions, management did not listen.

A few weeks after the tragedy, Dennis R. Pierce, National President of the BLET, issued a statement offering condolences to the victims of the train wreck and admonishing the U.S. federal authorities to heed this tragic lesson. Time will tell if anyone in power actually paid attention.

When we left the union hall, we drove to an adorable home in suburban Little Rock. The neighborhood was lovely. The flowers and gardens were colorful and lush. We left the oppressive heat and humidity outside and walked into a spacious, cool and comfortable house with a number of luxuries. The owners had plush furnishings, a flat screen TV, loaded bookcases, a well-stocked sewing room, a patio with a grill, and a kitchen full of groceries featuring all the necessary appliances one might use to prepare them.

Melanie Orman had called her grandparents and asked if we could stop by for a visit and a few interviews. Melba Collins and Gordon Brown couldn't have been more hospitable. Both well past retirement age, these two labor leaders had struggled their whole careers to organize and in turn lead various aspects of the labor movement.

Collins told us that as a single mom, she'd likely not have survived and certainly wouldn't have thrived without her union job. Brown explained hard battles – some won and others lost – that shaped his career and brought Melba into his life. But through it all, the best representation of how they'd lived their working lives was how they were living in their retirement. They were comfortable. Brown reclined in a chair, recovering from surgery to repair an injury from a fall.

According to the Arkansas Department of Human Services, Division of Aging and Adult Services, 23% of retirement-age folks there live in poverty; but not Orman's grandparents. And that's because – Collins and Brown will both attest – they had union jobs, with union wages, and retirement compensation when their careers ended. And retiring in comfort helps define the middle class.

Chapter 18   Dealey Plaza
ג ג

Texas ended up being largely about me and what I wanted to do. We knew we had to get to Roswell, New Mexico and Rick had already put Little Rock, Arkansas on the map, so that meant we were crossing – one way or another – through Texas.

Originally, it didn't much matter to any of us how we crossed that giant state. Rick came up with the idea for the People's Tour about eight months before we actually took to the road. West hadn't blown up yet and all anyone really came up with for an easy Texas tie-in was the fact that Texas had the jump on eliminating the middle class when compared with the rest of the nation.

If Texas specializes in anything, it's poverty. One third of Texas children are impoverished. One third of the working adults have no access to health care. Incredibly, one tenth of all the nation's homeless children live in Texas. The saddest part of all this: poverty that pervasive was a good thing for our schedule. We could have talked about those statistics from pretty much anywhere in the state. That meant we could take the shortest route and cut across the top.

But then April rolled around and a fertilizer plant explosion rocked the sleepy little town of West, Texas. Workers died. Firefighters died. And a school, nursing home and several neighborhoods were blown to smithereens. Getting to West, Texas became our prime objective. And it's the anchor around which we scheduled our other stops as we traveled through the Lone Star state.

The events of November 22, 1963 have mattered to me most of my life. Since I was a little girl my mom would tell and retell the story of where she was when she heard the 35th President of the United States had been shot. My mom and I were alone in the front seat of her car listening to the radio. It was 4 days before my 3rd birthday and my mom said she put her arms around me and just cried and cried.

My mom's parents immigrated to Boston from Ireland. This much-loved Irish Catholic president meant more to my mom than he might have mattered to others – even though he mattered an awful lot to others as well. Perhaps 21st century African Americans identify with my mom as they know how it feels for one of their own to have made it to the White House.

While we mapped our route from Arkansas to West, I asked Rick if we could go to Dallas. Ever the accommodating host, he said, "Sure."

We found a campsite that was more like a parking lot. We had left the verdant campsites back east and exchanged them for rocky, sandy, desert-like settings. We got in too late to do much but shower and sleep. Private shower rooms flanked the office.

It appeared our suburban Dallas campsite had many long-term or permanent campers. That's another phenomena we would encounter as we moved to regions of year-round warm temperatures. Lots of people live in campgrounds. Once we paid closer attention, we noticed school busses stop in campgrounds, too.

Most RV parks have large public rest rooms with a row of toilets, a row of showers, a row of sinks, and a small area for keeping one's things and changing one's clothes. The ability to use a bathroom like you have back home afforded a luxury – and privacy – we'd almost forgotten existed. We even got a little spoiled because we stayed at that particular spot for two nights. Unfortunately for Sammi who didn't have one of us in the next shower over, these private baths meant she was alone when she figured out how things worked.

A few days later when we left to go to West, I remarked on how hot it was. I said that I – already – could use another shower. Sammi, said she could use one too, that she hadn't had one in days.

"Why?" I asked.

The adorable 11-year old replied, "There was a sign in the bathroom that said, 'bathing 25 cents' and I didn't have any money."

Oh man, did I feel bad. I had seen that same goofy sign painted on a piece of worn wood with a graphic of an old wash house and it never dawned on me that sweet Sammi would take it seriously and demure from asking for a quarter. Luckily that place had a pool, and – of course – we went swimming. But poor Sammi had to wait about 36 more hours more from the time she told me – until we got settled outside Roswell – to wash three days of sweating and chlorine from her skin.

Kids who don't complain or ask for things are a bit of a shock to the system.

The day after we settled into camp near Dallas, Rick, Brett, and I taped the rest of the commentary for the Arkansas show and then Brett got editing while the Smith family swam and I went for a walk. Morning walks would become my routine for the rest of the trip. Every day I got up a little early and stretched my legs. The distance we traveled got longer each day, as did the hours we spent interviewing guests. Within a few days of adding a daily walk to our routine, I added a destination for those walks. The only coffee drinker in the RV, I began jonesing for coffee about two days after my French Press broke. Just like the airlines say, people should, "Use caution when opening the overhead bins as objects shift while traveling."

Texas had bugs like you read about, at least you will here. I walked on the pavement out to the street but then I decided to walk back through a field. The deeper I got into the field the more evident it was that in the 4 inch high grass there were thousands – if not millions – of grasshoppers or locusts or something. I looked up infestations and in the appendix at the end of the book there is a link to a site with pictures of a number of probable varieties that were the jumping, hopping, noisy "problem invertebrates" all around me. By the time I got halfway across the field the bugs were thick in the air and jumping high enough to hit my out stretched hands.

One of the great limitations of this trip – and perhaps a great limitation built into American History in general – is that when we study workers we never focus on slavery. Oppressive temperatures, bug infestations: the working conditions for folks enslaved in the south must've been ferociously cruel. Their masters stole their labor, their liberty and their families. The sort of greed that motivates one person to hold others captive didn't end with the civil war, it just shifted to other methods. And that's where our American labor history begins.

When I got back to our RV, it was time to go. We all piled into the minivan and headed for Dealey Plaza. I wish I'd never seen Abraham Zabruder's film of Pres. Kennedy's assassination. That said, I've seen it so many times I practically have it memorized. We stood at the corner of Elm Street where Pres. Kennedy's motorcade had to turn in front of the Texas School Book Depository and Carol, Rick, Brett and I all noticed the exact same thing: everything looked so small.

The streets were surprisingly narrow and marked with two white X's painted on the pavement. These X's indicate where the president was when the bullets were fired that killed him and wounded Texas Governor John Connally.

The schoolbook depository faced North Houston Street. The motorcade came down North Houston Street headed toward the window from which Lee Harvey Oswald is alleged to have killed the president. Then, right in front of the window, the vehicles turn a very sharp left hand turn onto Elm Street. It was not until the car carrying the Pres. and Mrs. Kennedy and Gov. and Mrs. Connally had traveled down Elm Street several dozen feet that Oswald is alleged to have fired at all.

We had a couple of questions. Why wouldn't Oswald have fired as the motorcade traveled straight at him on North Houston Street? Why wait until the motorcade turned down and around the corner, heading down Elm Street? In fact, the first shot fired was much closer to the infamous grassy knoll than it was to the schoolbook depository.

While we walked around the museum and surveyed the murder scene, folks who had various opinions of what "really" happened to the 35th president approached us. One guy escorted us to the fence on the grassy knoll and showed us how easy it would have been to hide there and do the shooting. The argument over what happened to the president will likely go on forever. But one thing is certain; the middle class took a hit when the president took those bullets.

Pres. Kennedy supported federal assistance for nutrition programs, healthcare, worker pensions, and education. Pres. Kennedy promised federal funds for teacher salaries, and he supported assistance to the poor even if it raised the deficit. In his short time as president both social security benefits and the minimum wage were raised. And lastly, Pres. Kennedy believed in both technology and humanitarianism. His two legacy programs – the Peace Corps and the Race to the Moon – created jobs and secured super power status for the U.S. without resorting to war.

Pres. Lyndon Johnson continued much of the work begun by Pres. Kennedy, with one possible exception. Pres. Johnson accelerated a war that many believe Pres. Kennedy would have ended. Military conscription pulled many middle and lower class boys from the homes and returned about 5% of them in coffins. Pres. Eisenhower had warned future generations about war for the sake of profit as he handed the keys to the White House to Pres. Kennedy, "Every gun that is made, every warship launched, every rocket fired, signifies in the final sense a theft from those who hunger and are not fed, those who are cold and are not clothed. This world in arms is not spending money alone. It is spending the sweat of its laborers, the genius of its scientists, the hopes of its children."

When we left Dealey Plaza, I halfheartedly looked over my shoulder expecting to see Jacqueline Smith from the Lorraine Motel. Indeed, the Texas School Book Depository – like the Lorraine Motel for MLK, Jr. – is more a tribute to Pres. Kennedy's death than to his life. Dealey Plaza needs a big sign that reads, "Welcome to the Lee Harvey Oswald Museum." And in both cases someone should add, "We made a memorial to the 'official' story, we insist you believe it."

𐂃 𐂃

Chapter 19 Governor Bush's Presidential Library
λ λλ

"If I had more time, I would have cried a bunch of times." So said 11-year-old Sammi Smith, as we exited the George W. Bush Library in Dallas.

If the curators of the Bush 43 Library were going for "uplifting." They missed their mark by a country mile. Granted, they didn't have much with which to work. And though their captions and narratives attempted to make every tragedy sound like some sort of victory, their point was lost on Sammi. I'm not surprised that it didn't dent Rick's, my, or even Brett's younger twenty-something year old cynicism, but when a grade schooler sees nothing but tragedy, you've lost the spin war, for sure.

Carol and the A's (the family nickname for Alex and Aly) launched off for New Mexico without us. Carol's mom was born in Roswell and she wanted to visit family.

Sammi is a voracious reader and a pretty darned good writer. She wanted to – and did – stay with us all along our portion of the trip, making radio and interviewing guests. She was consistently polite and helpful. After a week or so on the road, she was helping us set up and tear down. She ran errands back and forth to the RV and when we got back on the road, her *kidness* kicked in and she'd remind us to do the important things, like stop for ice cream.

John Orrell, Public Relations Director for the George Bush Museum and Library, greeted us in front of the Freedom Registry. The first image that assails your eyes as you walk into the library is a marble wall engraved with the names of donors to 43's library. I've never referred to President Geo. W. Bush as "43," but I guess I missed the inside track. 43's how he's known. Even the stickers that proved you'd paid for admission to the building just said "43."

Over the last few months, I've placed a number of calls to the Bush Foundation. Even after Orrell gave me a contact name to ask for directly, my calls were not returned. I had a number of questions I'd have liked a foundation spokesperson to answer. I especially wanted to know how much a donor had to give in order to get their name carved in stone.

According to the foundation website, a donor's name will appear in the electronic Freedom Registry for four of five levels of giving. There is a mega cheap membership for $25 that doesn't include mention in the Freedom Registry. It appears that – at least according to the friends of 43 – Freedom costs at least $50.

The four giving levels at which a person may have their name added to the program on the electronic tablet inside the door to the facility are $50, $65, $85, and $100. All five levels earn you a 10% discount when shopping at 43's gift shop. And when you're willing to pay a little more for Freedom, you get free admission for two adults. At the $100 level, you can bring your kids for free, too. But, disappointingly, nothing is listed on the site for how much the *chiseled in stone* donors paid.

Freedom Registry members who come in at these $50, $65, $85 or $100 levels are only listed for one year. Don't renew your Freedom purchase? Some tech guy somewhere in 43's foundation hits the delete button.

There's no deleting marble, so I'm thinking that former Texas Governor William Clements and all his buddies on that wall parted with a pretty penny to be there.

Orrell couldn't help me with any questions about the donor lists because Orrell works for the National Archives and Records Administration (NARA) and they only use half the building. They don't have anything to do with sucking up to fat cats or perverting the word "freedom" until it means financier.

Orrell explained that in 1939, Pres. Franklin Roosevelt decided to donate the personal property he acquired as president – and even part of his family's Hyde Park estate – to the United States. It was Roosevelt's belief that while president everything given to him was actually given to America. President Harry Truman followed suit. It wasn't until 1955 that the Presidential Libraries Act was passed and this formality became law. President Hoover's library was the first one officially founded under this new system.

In 1978 the Presidential Records Act went into effect. As a result, a president cannot keep any of the records generated during his tenure. This, no doubt, raised the ire of folks would've liked to keep items like the Nixon Tapes – Pres. Nixon's unlawful recordings from the oval office – away from public scrutiny. Sure enough, if you go to Yorba Linda, California, you will see things at the Nixon Library that undoubtedly would have embarrassed the 37th president.

But 43's library is so young that it's unlikely any potentially incriminating information is on display in the museum. Unless – like Sammi – you feel that the "positive" items stressed in the displays are – in actuality – depressingly horrifying.

It will be another 46 years (2059) before the federal government reveals the classified documents from 43's term. And Freedom of Information Act (FOIA) requests will not be entertained until January 20th of 2014.

So what's in the archives?

Orrell says that more than half of their 200,000 plus documents concern "No Child Left Behind." In 2011, Colorado became the first state to request a waiver from the federal government to dump 43's signature education policy. In 2013, 43's home state of Texas was the 42nd state to withdraw. And according to the Associated Press, one month after we left 43's library, the United States House of Representatives – with its Republican majority – voted to "dismantle the troubled No Child Left Behind law for evaluating America's students and schools." Considering the failure No Child Left Behind became, odds are good that Orrell's office won't be flooded with requests for those documents.

Considering the national archives don't have much to archive yet, the museum looked amazingly full. Orrell explained that the presidents generally keep someone nearby whose job it is to collect historically significant items. Orrell said that's how they got the bullhorn from 43's speech in New York City following 9/11: "So right after 9/11 Pres. Bush is there down at ground zero and he's talking on the bullhorn. You know that's a very, it's a very famous scene. There's somebody there that's always on the staff that has the foresight to say, 'we need to hold onto this.'"

Orrell continues, "So he comes down off the rubble and there's usually a staffer there that goes, 'Sir,' you know, 'May I please have this.' And then they'll hold onto it. It becomes part of the national archives."

It wasn't until Orrell said, "comes down off the rubble," that I got really revolted by that scene which had lived in my head – as it does in the heads of the rest of my countrymen – for more than a decade. I suddenly realized that "Down off the rubble" meant that 43 was likely standing on top of hundreds of unrecovered bodies.

43's museum was filled to overflowing with these artifacts from his presidency and before. In fact, the entire room in which we sat to interview Orrell came from the White House. While president, 43 had the Situation and War Rooms renovated. He saved the original two chambers and rebuilt them in presidential libraries. The War Room is now part of the Reagan Library and Museum and the Situation Room is just down the hall from 43's museum gallery. Even the table and chairs are the real McCoy. Orrell expected that one day the two rooms would be linked up and school children in California and Texas would be invited to play *president and his cabinet at war* real soon.

Playing president should be the name of the displays in the main museum. Orrell encouraged us to check out the Decision Points Theater. In the theater four scenarios play out and participants get to put themselves in the shoes of the "decider in chief." Visitors can choose between The Surge, The Rise of Saddam Hussein, The Financial Crisis, and Hurricane Katrina.

Orrell explained that once a person has selected a scenario the person is given guidance from both sides of the aisle. Advice also comes from the CIA, FBI, and White House Advisors. He did caution us that the advice isn't the real advice 43 was given in those circumstances. Rick piped up politely but emphatically, "The argument can be made that you're getting false choices."

Orrell agreed, but assured us that this exercise wasn't supposed to help people understand the decisions made by the president, just how fast he had to make them and how difficult making them must have been.

When we left the Situation Room, we thanked Orrell – who had done a bang-up job considering we were anything but an adoring crowd – and then we mixed in with the folks who had paid as much as $16 to visit the library. That of course was the price for adults. Prices went as low as $10 for kids under 12 years of age and children under four were free. As members of the media we got in for free too. I'd have had to do an awful lot of soul searching to pay full price as an adult. But a word to the wise about bringing your kids: leave them with Grandma. I'm certain a five-year-old will be hard pressed to get their $10 worth.

43's museum and library perfectly fit the tragedy theme our People's Tour had taken over the last week or so. From the Lorraine Motel to Dealey Plaza, and then the Geo. W. Bush Presidential Library and Museum. Walking into the main hall, smack dab in the center of a person's line of sight stood 20 or more feet of twisted steel from the World Trade Center.

If a satirist had planned the George W. Bush Museum and Library they couldn't have done a better job. I wouldn't be the first to point out that during 43's tenure the economy collapsed, but not because of terrorist attacks. The United States encountered the worst economic collapse in a hundred years because of failed economic policies. 43 inherited a nation out of debt and plunged it into debt with war and taxation policies that didn't match up. And yet, remarkably, walking into the first chamber of his museum, there is a sign that touts 43 as a business man, the "first president with an MBA." The sign – leaving nothing to chance – reminds the reader that MBA stands for "Masters in Business Administration." It also notes that 43 owned an oil company but mentions nothing about the investors that bailed him out when he teetered on the verge of bankruptcy.

Harken Oil and Gas – at a time when 43 referred to himself by saying, "I'm all name and no money" – bailed out 43's oil company. It turned out that his name was just what Harken was after. According to a Washington Post series written by George Lardner, Jr., and Lois Romano, "Harken's executives saw a bonus in their target's CEO, despite his spotty track record."

None of the nepotistic or influence-peddling financial wheelings and dealings were mentioned in the museum's discussion of "George W. Bush the businessman." The posters just damned him with a faint praise reference to this first ever presidential Masters Degree. And that's the general theme of the entire museum.

There are countless self-congratulations for 43's initiative to combat AIDS in Africa – President's Emergency Plan for AIDS Relief, PEPFAR – but no mention of cutting funding to the UN Population Fund and Marie Stopes' clinics, both of whom supply condoms in Africa.

43 also brags about the Proliferation Security Agreement which states that starting May 31st of 2003, the United States would work with other countries "to stop the spread of WMD." It makes no mention that the Bush Administration launched this initiative 72 days after the U.S. bombed Iraq with their "shock and awe" campaign: waging war – employing depleted uranium and cluster bombs – against a nation that 43's administration mistakenly thought had weapons of mass destruction.

All references to the Iraq War have to do with spreading democracy. There is no reference to failed intelligence, and again, the gains in Iraq were never set against a backdrop of military and/or civilian deaths. The center also fails to mention the Justice Department scandals that rocked the career of Attorney General Alberto Gonzales, resulting in a formal reprimand.

And ironically, photos of purple-fingered Iraqi voters waving their hands in the air to show that they'd voted were across the hall from the details of 43's 2000 presidential election. Sandra Day O'Connor stepped in during the recount of Florida's election and stopped the counting. People's votes just didn't matter that much. This Supreme Court intervention is how Governor Bush became President Bush even though he lost the popular vote and apparently the electoral vote as well.

With all the spreading democracy back patting, there was certainly no mention of Justice O'Connor's interview with the Chicago Tribune Editorial Board on April 26, 2013 – 4 days before 43's museum opened. Not only did she voice disappointment with Geo. W. Bush's presidency, but she said it likely would've been better had the Supreme Court not taken the *Bush v. Gore* case in the first place.

Now remember Orrell told us – and yeah, after seeing all this "love is hate, war is peace" inversion, I wanted to replace one of the "r"s in his name with a "w" – the museum and library are owned by the NARA. So why the trickery and spin in the museum? Well, Orrell explained that they received ownership of their half of the building from 43's foundation the day before it opened. All those exhibits were already in place.

After spending a decade of my life as a political columnist and commentator, I'm not offering even a pretense of impartiality. Adding to my career in the media the fact that I ran for U.S. Vice President in 2004 and was defeated by 43's running mate who went on to shoot one of his best friends in the face, you may take my description of 43's Museum and Library with a grain of salt. And if you've got $16 that you'd rather set fire to than use toward a good cause, I recommend you verify my claims. But I stand by Sammi's assessment. "If I had more time, I would have cried a bunch of times." Still, I was relieved that we didn't have time to linger.

In order to leave the library we had to pass through a revolving door that plunked us into the gift shop and bookstore. There was a surprising dearth of merchandise. If you didn't play golf or wear a ball cap, you likely wouldn't find much to purchase: Unless, of course, you wanted to scare children.

A children's book about the plane crashes into the World Trade Center, The Pentagon, and a field in Somerset County, Pennsylvania was prominently featured and available for sale. The design on the cover of the powder blue dust jacket looks like a newspaper masthead. The phony newspaper is the "Actual Times" with a story, "The Day the Towers Fell" touting that "America is Under Attack."

Like most children's books, *America is Under Attack*, has full-page pictures with text wrap. Only this text wraps around the ghastly drawings of death and destruction. Heck, it's no *The Pet Goat* but this is no ordinary children's book. It's fear-mongering propaganda meant to bring the people into line at a very early age. After all, you can't bring up a bunch of sheep by reading to them about goats.

☖ ☖ ☖

Chapter 20   I'm Busted
λ

Trish Griffin, a realtor with a website at Kelly Realtors that's also labeled "Waco Real Estate," had fifteen listings the last week of October 2013. Extrapolating from these listings– and assuming her listings are indicative of the region – the average home price in McLellan County, Texas is about $280,000.

April 18, 2013 – the day after Adair Grain, Inc.'s West Fertilizer Co. exploded – a Washington Post story claimed, "more than 50" homes were destroyed. Fifty homes at 280 grand would be $140 million worth of damage, just for the homes. That doesn't count the nursing home, middle school, roadways, trees, vehicles, and everything else that got wrecked by the blast.

When a company violates regulations, penalties often have little to do with the actual damage done, and yet it still seems pretty amazing that the fine levied on Adair Grain, Inc. in October of 2013, came to less than half the likely selling price of one of the houses they blew to kingdom come. The total fine that the Occupational Safety and Health Administration (OSHA) proposed for all 24 safety violations was $118,300. Company owner, Donald Adair, responded to this little slap on the wrist with, "I'm busted." It appears that the massive explosion blew Adair right out of business.

According to the Los Angeles Times, Daniel Keeney, a spokesperson for the West Fertilizer Co., is pretty sure the fines don't have anything to do with the explosion anyway. He thinks it's just OSHA taking exception to other environmental infractions that put the health of workers at risk. While there may have been bad air at the plant – they exposed the workers to dangerous levels of anhydrous ammonia – the company certainly couldn't imagine that their lax safety practices would reduce their corner of town to smoking piles of mangled metal, glass shards, charred rubble, and dead firefighters. Unless someone working there knew that stock piles of ammonia nitrate might detonate under certain circumstances. And one would think someone owning the fertilizer might have known it as well.

Much like the Triangle Shirt Waist Factory Fire more than a hundred years and a thousand miles before, it seems nobody knows what caused this disaster.

Still, the fines issued October 2013 are precedence setting. The last time OSHA inspected the plant was 28 years earlier. While the violations were much the same, last time no fines were metered out at all. Perhaps OSHA stopped inspecting West Fertilizer Co., because inspections can be costly to the agency. And when OSHA demurred of fining them in 1985, the agency may have reasoned that it'd be cost saving to discontinue inspections of companies that aren't going to be held accountable even when they flout the law.

We pulled into West not really knowing which way to go. No one walked the street so we were fortunate that our fairly random route took us past the fire station. The entire town looked deserted, and while the firehouse looked like folks had been there recently, it was hard imagining that anyone was ever coming back.

USA Today reported, "Nationally, the West blast was the highest single-incident firefighter fatality count since 9/11, when 340 firefighters were killed responding to the terrorist attacks in New York, according to the National Fire Protection Association." It was also the second worst in Texas history. Ten of the 14 people killed were firefighters.

West's first responders are largely volunteers and that might have accounted for the deserted firehouse. Loved ones, towns people, visitors, or all three decorated the building by hanging yellow ribbons, leaving patches from other fire houses, memorial messages and photographs of the victims. A big white sign with black letters on the door of the office entrance implied that the town had grown weary of all the attention their disaster had garnered. The sign read, "NO PRESS."

Shortly after the explosion, Texas Governor Rick Perry issued a statement that more regulation would not have saved the town of West from the calamity that decimated neighborhoods, a school and a nursing home. Last inspected in 2006 by the Texas Commission on Environmental Safety, they wouldn't have mentioned fertilizer storage anyway. The agency does regulate the anhydrous ammonia but it appears the West Fertilizer Plant's ammonium nitrate stockpile caused the blast. Expanding the agency's regulatory purview might have mandated that the firefighters be notified in advance where the fertilizer was stored.

Still other regulatory agencies have found West Fertilizer Co., in violation. In 2012, "the U.S. Pipeline and Hazardous Materials Safety Administration assessed a $10,000 fine against West Fertilizer for improperly labeling storage tanks and preparing to transfer chemicals without a security plan. The company paid $5,250 after reporting that it had corrected the problems."

Perhaps extremely strict regulation accompanied by plant closure for violations would help owners like Adair manage their hazardous chemicals more effectively and in turn help them avoid getting "busted."

We drove away from the firehouse and toward the blast site. Adair's finances aren't the only things that got busted. Having never seen West before the disaster we couldn't guess what had been vaporized out of existence by the blast. Later, looking at pictures, we saw buildings and other structures that used to be there and had completely disappeared. What we could see was scorched earth all around a couple of gnarled metal structures.

The blast sheared trees off mid-trunk, blew the windows out of every building for city blocks, lobbed debris that caved in the roofs of a school and the neighborhoods around it, and shook a nursing home until it looked more like an earthquake had rattled the individual rooms apart. The fissures created by this shaking allowed the walls to collapse in on themselves.

If I hadn't seen it with my own eyes, I wouldn't understand the concept of an explosion destroying outdoor basketball courts. The concussive force twisted the metal poles that held hoops and streetlights like a toffee maker twists candy canes. Once twisted and broken, the blast flung them across upheaved asphalt.

And again – just like at the firehouse – nobody was there.

We knew people had been there. Some folks had placed brightly colored signs on sticks into the ground. Among other things, the signs said, "Hope" or "Pray for West." It seemed everything said "Pray for West." It was painted on the side of at least one destroyed home and it was printed on beer cozies for sale at a business on the edge of town.

A stop sign across from the destroyed school had an older message printed by Kiwanis International that read, "Drive Carefully Protect Our Children."

We wandered wherever we wanted. Nothing and nobody stood in our way. It appeared a few contractors might have started work on some individual homes, but nearly two months after devastation rocked West, no large-scale disaster relief had begun.

When we pulled out of West, we discussed the Federal Emergency Management Agency (FEMA) and their recent decision to deny assistance to the region. According to USA Today, "In its original letter to the state, FEMA said the explosion was 'not of the severity and magnitude that warrants a major disaster declaration.' That ruling affected both public assistance aid — which provides funding to the city to rebuild — and further individual aid, which provides crisis counseling and other services."

But on August 1st of 2013, FEMA reversed their decision. By October 7th more than $16 million in FEMA funds had found their way to West. Few were happier than Gov. Perry that the feds reversed their decision and pumped money into the town. Seems Gov. Perry's dislike for big government – when it comes to regulation – evaporates when that same big government redirects tax dollars into his district.

Chapter 21   The Ups and Downs of Gender in the Workplace
⅄⅄

On our way out of West, we stopped quickly at a Czech Bakery to try some Kolaches. Brett's unofficial job – which he embraced completely – was to check out regional foods and make sure we didn't miss anything important and/or tasty.

Brett read us a Yelp website rating for Kolaches. It went something like this, "The little donut put West, Texas on the map before it got blown off the map."

The Czechoslovakian pastry made of dough filled with sweet or savory filling didn't disappoint. We got a few to eat in the sad little café. Frankly, I didn't see anything in West – even far from the blast site – that wasn't really sad. Before we left the sweet smelling shop, we bought some more Kolaches for the road, and then headed toward New Mexico. The long day threatened to get a lot longer.

We had hundreds of miles before us and a whole radio show to record. Driving through western Texas we put taping-while-driving to the test. Despite a few additional challenges like road noise, Brett sitting on a cooler hunched over the gear – holding it so it wouldn't slide – and some occasionally broken concentration, it worked pretty well. For the rest of the trip that was the only way that Rick and I taped our narrative portions of the show.

We'd been on the road a couple of hours when a big storm blew up. Because the terrain is so expansive and flat, we could see lightening off in the distance and watched intently as we got closer. Rick and I were each holding our microphones with one hand. With his other had Rick was steering the RV and with my other hand I got weather updates on my phone.

We finished recording a 19-minute segment and Brett needed two or three minutes to edit the ends and attach them to an earlier interview. I whispered to Rick, "Would you want to know if there's a tornado warning in this area? I would have asked you back when it was just a tornado watch, but it changed while we were recording and I didn't want to have to recut our audio."

Rick said he didn't mind me waiting. He said he'd have waited too. Then he whispered, "What do we do? Keep going or stop somewhere?" There's no weather event more exhilarating than a tornado. And by exhilarating, I mean frightening. I answered him with a shrug, "If we set still it could get us and if we move it could get us. There's no way to predict where cyclones touch down." We decided to just keep traveling. By the time we came to that decision the wind was blowing so loudly and so strongly against the side of the RV that we decided to take a break from taping and Rick put both hands on the wheel. The only thing that made the late night trip really scary was having Sammi with us. It's a menacing thought, wondering what would have happened to that traveling tin hotel room, if a cyclone had knocked into it.

We pulled into the downtown Roswell RV Park pretty late at night. More a parking lot than a park, we pulled the camper into the only available space and silently and automatically we moved all the gear, made our beds and fell asleep. Carol and the A's had gotten a hotel room and that meant we'd have a nice place to shower the next morning.

The following day – and after those showers – we headed to the Cowboy Café for breakfast. Roswell, NM is home to one of America's most uniquely employed individuals. We had an appointment to meet LJ Dolin, a female elevator mechanic, and she told us to join her at Cowboy's because they had the very best breakfasts. Dolin clearly wasn't the only person who thought the food at the Cowboy Café was great. We pretty quickly realized that we wouldn't be interviewing Dolin in there. The only place we really had available to talk to her was inside the RV. After our hearty southwestern breakfast, Carol took off with the kids in search of aliens, while Rick, Brett, and I showed Dolin to our cramped little camper.

We opened the windows and propped the door. The weather was seasonably warm but if we ran the air-conditioning unit, it really wreaked havoc with our audio.

Everywhere we'd gone to interview workers, folks greeted us with kindness and helped anyway they could. Dolin went beyond all that. Dolin's career – and decades spent fighting for a fair shake – conditioned her to bring volumes of paperwork and photographs to document her story.

Dolin said that she wouldn't have chosen to live in New Mexico if her grandmother wasn't there. Dolin moved back to be near her seven years ago. She knew that with a union card and a willingness to travel she'd find work. Eventually Dolin landed a job repairing elevators in and around Roswell.

Dolin says that the wages are lower in New Mexico than anywhere else in the country. I couldn't find statistics for elevator mechanics but I did find wage and gender statistics in general at the American Association of University Women website. In 2011 the average wage for men in the U.S. was $49,398, but guys only make $41,211 in New Mexico. In 2011, women in the U.S. earned an average of $37,791 while gals in New Mexico made only $33,074.

Men in New Mexico make a little better than 80% of what men in the U.S. make. And women in New Mexico make 80% of what the men in New Mexico make. That means that a woman working in New Mexico – on average – makes 1/3 less than the average guy in the U.S. makes. But that's a sacrifice Dolin makes to be near her grandmother, and she knows it. Low wages are among the sacrifices Dolin willingly made to become an elevator mechanic and live near family. Many of the other sacrifices she ended up making were completely involuntary.

When Dolin first started out, sexist exclusionary men in the industry forced her into uncomfortable and often unlawful situations, just to try and get a job as an elevator mechanic. She's hit a few rough spots along her journey after landing that job, as well.

Dolin's interview – like all the interviews from the road – is available at the People's Tour website. But rather than just encourage you to go there and hear her tell her own story, a portion of it bears rewriting.

LJ Dolin became a light wheel vehicle mechanic while on active duty in the U.S. Army. After her enlistment ended she moved to San Francisco, California and became a mechanic contracted to work for the United States Postal Service.

One day she heard that a construction company had been advertising for female elevator mechanics. Dolin loved heights and already had all the tools necessary to work on elevators. She immediately applied for the job.

When she inquired, Dolin says her would-be employer told her to call back, "Next Tuesday. And I called every Tuesday for the next five years." Dolin reminisced about the run around she had been given. Finally after calling week after week, year after year, the foreman told her, "Why don't you just go get in another trade? You have no high-rise experience." This infuriated Dolin. The men didn't have high-rise experience when they started either. But, Dolin says, what they did have was family in the trade and male anatomy. Oh and it didn't hurt that they were white.

Dolin refused to give up, so she did as he demanded and apprenticed with a carpenters union working on high-rises. For three years Dolin, "Picked up scraps off the floor. Me and the Chinese guys and the black guys, we were all picking up garbage. There was a lot of discrimination."

It wasn't until eight or so years later that Dolin broke down and filed a lawsuit and won her place on equal footing way up high, building elevators in sky scrapers. Once she became an elevator mechanic the shenanigans didn't stop, but she had a union card and it became more difficult for men to harass her. Whether they were union men or management men, Dolin finally had an advocate to go to bat for her.

She's had battles over her pension, and a few years ago when Dolin came out and asked her girlfriend to marry her, Dolin again lost her job. It hasn't been easy to push for gender and sexual orientation equality. And while Dolin didn't pick those fights, she didn't walk away from them either.

Dolin knows that some folks feel it's been a big waste of her energy to spend decades fighting for opportunity when there are so many other battles that could have used her talents. But Dolin said her union needs folks who know how to fight. For example, New Mexico has no elevator codes. The legislature recently passed a set of codes but Gov. Susana Martinez pocket vetoed the legislation. Dolin's a hard working part of the movement to make her job – and everyone riding elevators – safer.

Dolin speaks now of a time when she'll no longer have a reason to stay in New Mexico. Her Grandmom is 97 and Dolin knows that one day she'll be gone. Dolin would like to move back east or to Canada where her fiancée lives. And because she has a union card in the International Union of Elevator Contractors, she can work anywhere – anywhere that will hire her.

One other victory Dolin claims – as she acknowledges the 34% pay differential between women working in New Mexico and men working across the United States – because of her union, no job can pay her less than it pays a man. And after 30 years of struggling, that's one sweet advantage Dolin feels she finally has on her side.

Chapter 22 Bruce Scabbit
⅄ ⅄⅄

Traveling 9600 miles in 28 days has to be one of the most stressful ways to learn U.S. history, but at least it's an eye opener. We pulled into Tempe, Arizona looking for a woman we'd met back at the LAWCHA conference in New York. During one of the LAWCHA general assemblies we had the chance to announce our then upcoming People's Tour to the conference attendees and ask if anyone out there in the American hinterland had interesting projects brewing. Archivist and historian, Xaviera Flores, invited us to drop by Arizona State University (ASU) and check out the work they've been doing, recording and preserving labor history.

Flores, a young archivist, is the first fluent Spanish speaker to translate and maintain the Spanish language labor records of Arizona workers. Yep, we, too, were amazed that she's the first Spanish speaker to translate the insurance and employment records of native Spanish speakers in – of all places – Arizona!

Not all of the labor records Flores went to ASU to restore and recapture are in Spanish. The AFL-CIO locals – for example – documented everything in English. But without the Spanish language records from many of the other labor organizations, no true historical perspective can exist. The contributions of Mexicans and Mexican Americans who labored, lived and died making the desert southwest what it is today – until Flores work began – had pretty much been lost.

For some better-known modern day Arizonans like Maricopa County's controversial sheriff, Joe Arpiao, forgetting Mexican labor history makes perfect sense. Arguably the sheriff would have a harder time racially profiling suspects and populating his 110-degree tent prisons if Arizonans started valuing the contributions made by immigrant populations in the area. Writing a people's history is the first step to respecting the folks from that culture.

We didn't have time to stop and interview the 80-year-old Massachusetts native turned hardball Arizona lawman, but I have in the past. Should I get the opportunity again, I must remember to ask Arpaio what he thinks of the repository ASU has built to preserve the contributions of a population he so vociferously targets.

When we sat in one of the ASU conference rooms interviewing Flores, she did point out that Arizona history cannot be studied without studying Mexican history, "Because at one time Arizona was Mexico."

By the time our People's Tour arrived in Tempe, the United States' penchant – and Britain's, France's and Spain's before this nation's founding – for stealing land, property, labor and resources was fast becoming the dominant theme of our trip.

First the Native Americans were robbed of their land and their lives, then the Africans were robbed of their origins and liberty, and now the 21st century's newest wave of impoverished immigrants are being robbed of their history. Consequently much of the US has lost sight of Chicano social and economic contributions.

In every case of theft – whether it is land, liberty, labor or legacy – the disabused masses suffered for the benefit of a few. All attempts at reparations for abuses have fallen dismally far short of adequate. Only contributions like Flores' – and others like her – preservation of the history of the working class, will make any real difference. No native will ever get the land his or her ancestors lost. No descendent of enslaved blacks will ever be financially compensated for the wages his or her ancestors lost. Heck, even sanitation workers – made famous fifty years ago for their unequal treatment – still don't have a pension!

Flores arranged for us to meet and interview an ASU historian. She's not just an historian though, she's also part of Arizona's living history. Christina Marin, Ph.D., archivist and curator emeritus of ASU's Chicano/Chicana research collection, didn't just work with the library on this project; she's one of its founders.

Daughter of a copper miner, Marin shared tales of living in a copper town and how the union made her life better. Marin explained Arizona and the five C's that make Arizona famous: copper, cattle, climate, citrus, and cotton. Marin explained that every school kid in the Grand Canyon State learned about these five resources. Accurate as that list may be, Marin had another list that really told the story of Arizona history but all her words began with M: "Missionaries, Military, Mormons, and Mexicans."

Marin was an undergraduate when ASU – once called the Arizona Territorial Normal School – decided to collect research and build a library devoted to Chicano history. It was Marin who convinced them to include labor history.

The whole experience of visiting ASU and talking about preserving historical truths without racist or cultural bias seem paradoxical. After all, the beautiful campus was situated on stolen land. Not far from Apache Boulevard, classrooms, rec halls and dorm rooms sat on land that once belonged to tribal peoples. Apaches and other tribes first owned the land where ASU built their campus.

The legacy of stolen land is bad enough when it's stolen once, but in ASU's case their property was arguably stolen twice. After the natives were run off from their homes and before the coeds swarmed the sprawling campus property, the area where we stood was a Chicano community known as San Paulo.

The state of Arizona used eminent domain to remove the San Paulo residents from their homes. Once they negotiated Chicano homeowners' land away from them, school officials expanded the Normal School as a college. That college later became a University. The San Paulo residents could not refuse eviction even if they found the compensation that accompanied their eminent domain eviction inadequate. The law said that they had to go.

Marin explained that the Chicanos accepted their fate even thought they tried to compromise. The prices would not come up, but the school did make them promises, "University officials told these families, 'Don't worry, we'll take care of you. You will always have a job at ASU.' So what do those children do? What do the women do? What do the men do? These Mexican families then become our cafeteria workers, our landscape workers, our kitchen help, our housing workers who clean up the dorm rooms."

Marin believes this destroys much of the social fabric and in part explains the "Sheriff Joe" level of disrespect for Hispanics over all. Marin continued, "Those kind of workers do get a job, but they lost everything. The point is this. There was a viable community of Mexican American families." A community that is now disparate and all but gone. They lost their neighborhoods, their community structure, and their cohesive collectives. And now Marin says that those jobs they were all promised are pretty much gone as well.

ASU – in an effort to lower cost and increase revenue – has outsourced many of the services university employees used to provide. The food service around campus consists of many fast food chain kiosks. The buildings and facilities are named for corporate sponsors. And on our way to the interview we drove by an on-campus ASU Wal*Mart. The sight of this ruthless power retailer snuggled in among the campus buildings left Rick and me slack-jawed and speechless.

Thanks to folks like Marin and Flores, students at ASU can still access information about Arizona's rich labor history. There are historians on staff who can speak of the big labor issues through Arizona's history. Historians at ASU discuss the 1917 Bisbee deportations. And college freshman studying nearly 100 years later can learn how Phelps Dodge mining company thugs kidnapped more than a thousand foreign mine workers and sent them hundreds of miles away from their jobs and their homes. These workers' lives were threatened if they ever came back.

Students can learn about Arizona's rich agricultural history. They can study Cesar Chavez and his struggle to organize farm workers in Arizona. Students have an opportunity to learn about political struggles and the growth of the middle class through labor organizing. They can learn personal stories from scholars like Marin whose dad provided adequately for their family of seven because he was a member of the Mine Mill Smelter Workers local 586.

And once they've learned the origins of Arizona's middle class, they can find out how everyday economic security all started to unravel. Marin speaks candidly of the union busting that was such a big part of the Reagan Revolution. President Ronald Reagan – the only U.S. president that also served as the President of a labor union – fired the nation's air traffic controllers in one of his better-known and early on union-busting stunts. But Pres. Reagan's infamous battle to destroy Patco (Professional Air Traffic Controllers Organization) was only the start.

In 1983 workers went on strike at mines in Clifton Morenci. This time, American mining workers found themselves with no allies. The Republicans under Reagan supported the dissolution of all collective bargaining while Democrats in leadership barely raised a whimper. Bruce Babbit – then governor of Arizona – sent in the Arizona National Guard to put down the strike at Clifton Morenci. If the Arizona unions had ever fooled themselves about the Democrats being on the side of the workingman, Gov. Babbit's strong-arm show quelled that misconception entirely. That was when Bruce Babbit became Bruce Scabbit.

Marin's a plain-talking woman who speaks with ease about the truth as she knows it. With her Ph.D. and her life's education as a Chicana – in a state that often scapegoats Mexicans – Marin is an excellent teacher.

As we wrapped up our radio show at ASU, Marin added, "Bruce Scabbit was in the pocket of Phelps Dodge all along. You know how we know? After he helped break the strike, Phelps Dodge funded his exploratory committee when he thought he'd run for president." And when the Phoenix Indian School property went up for sale, the governor bought some prime real estate. Marin said, "Phelps Dodge lent him the money he needed. There's Bruce Babbit buying a lot of that property."

What kind of a governor purchases land stolen from the Natives with money stolen from the workers? Well, Bruce Scabbit is one. But there've been many politicians who have profited – if not from collusion like his – at least from looking the other way. We learned even before we got to Arizona, the ubiquitous tale of power mixed with greed, as it runs through U.S. history.

We finished the interviews and packed our gear to head out of town. Carol and the A's had gone ahead of us. They were bound for the Grand Canyon, and we were hot on their trail. But not so hot that we couldn't take another food detour: this time Brett Yelped directions to an "In and Out Burger."

"They'll wrap your burger in lettuce if you don't want carbohydrates," Brett told us. Interesting fast food option, but none of us took them up on it. When you're eating all those French Fries, really, what are a few more carbohydrates?

Chapter 23 The Grand Canyon Between the Rich and the Poor
λ

Rick scheduled a few extra stops into our People's Tour agenda so that the kids could see some great American wonders. We headed north out of Arizona State University and straight for the Grand Canyon.

Folks who control history books and tourist literature say that it was 1869 before anyone climbed to the bottom of the canyon. John Wesley Powell explored the Colorado River and that's where man's interaction with majesty began. In the available literature, few speculate about the untold numbers of Native American peoples who undoubtedly scaled the canyon in both directions. It appears without seeing – and recording – there is no believing. And yet despite a marked dearth of Anglo eyewitness observation, geologists can tell that Precambrian basement rocks lie at the bottom of the canyon. They also know that they got there, "1.8 billion years ago when the North American continent collided with an ancient chain of volcanic islands, much like today's Hawaiian Islands."

It's astounding that scientists and historians could have such apparently divergent skill sets. Clearly scientists don't view their knowledge of continents colliding as speculative, but without proof that the Havasupai – who have lived at the Grand Canyon for thousands of years – climbed up and down its interior, historic documents and tourist guides don't mention them doing so. It needn't take too large a leap of faith to speculate that people have been climbing in the canyon since people came in contact with the canyon.

Even in the 21st century, historic accounts that concern themselves with events predating western Europeans and their descendants – contributions by Native populations – are left out of the conversation and consequently any meaningful discussion. It's easier to forget that the U.S. was stolen and that various peoples and their cultures were destroyed if all discussions of the majesty, beauty and bounty of the land begin after the thieving and genocides were through.

Perhaps that's because there's no way to mention –casually – millions of dead Native Americans or the millions more displaced and re-deposited far from their original lands. Recounting the slaughters of indigenous tribes would serve the same purpose as tallying the contribution made over time by enslaved Africans and their descendants; it would remind modern U.S. citizens that nothing is free. And I'm not talking about that sop fed to generations of discarded military veterans about their sacrifice.

No, I mean the cost paid by the original occupants and subsequent laborers.

The U.S. as it exists today wasn't free. The U.S. as it exists today was built on stolen property by stolen labor. In all these circumstances, the myth that the military made us free needs to be replaced with the truth that the military was used by industry, corporate bosses, ruthless oligarchs and their politicians to pillage resources and enforce oppression.

If 21st century Americans understood this heritage of greed, then modern labor history would matter too. And by modern, I mean everything that's happened since the end of the civil war. All the additional labor stolen from poor whites, post-slavery poor blacks, and immigrant classes – who came here as cultural outcasts – make up the history of the labor movement since 1865.

Instead of Rick's three kids learning the truth of American History in an overstuffed camper traveling the country, they would have been taught in their schools sitting next to their peers.

Sammi, Alex and Aly would have learned about the beauty of their country, the wars fought to expand it, and the casualties of those wars. They'd have been taught that the Native American genocide and the horrors of slave holding were just the first steps in building a nation of ruling classes, opportunism, and oppression. And that nothing would stop greedy land grabbers and slave holders, but an organized populace united to demand social justice, fairness, and freedom. Without that united populace, humanity faces everything from segregation to mining disasters, as was evidenced along our trip.

🚲

It might be the understatement of the millennia to call the Grand Canyon merely grand. It's 277 miles long and anywhere from one to 18 miles wide. Surprisingly, it is not undeveloped. There are an awful lot of places to camp, rent a hotel room, dine, or shop along the canyon rim. As we drove up from Tempe, I called RV parks looking for a place for us to stay. Because we booked our sleeping arrangements last minute, and because school vacations in most of the country had already begun, one facility after another told us that everything was full.

The stress level in the camper increased as I unsuccessfully searched for an available campsite. Finally we found one at the Railway RV Park. Relieved to have a place to stay, it didn't dawn on us how cool – or expensive – this place was going to be until we got there. Rick took Sammi inside to pay for Railway RV's second-to-the-last available campsite. When they came back out, not only did we have a spot – and yes, it had a pool – but Rick also had seven tickets to ride the Grand Canyon Railway straight to the south rim. We were so excited.

Not knowing quite where we would stay along the hundreds of miles of available rim space, Carol and the A's had traveled further east than we had. So once we secured our stay, we waited for them to join us. The kids wanted to swim and I walked into downtown Williams, leaving the Smith family to play in the pool and Brett back at the campsite to work on his computer.

Historic Route 66 bisected the town across from the railroad. It was a lovely summer night and street bands played. I sat to listen to one and some guest workers from Ireland chatted with me about what they should see while on vacation. These two engineers had been brought to the U.S. by a California power plant and they hoped to see as much of the "wild west" as they could.

We spoke for a while about natural wonders, then the conversation turned to politics. It seems every conversation I have ends up with politics. But President Obama had a trip to Ireland scheduled and this prompted our discussion.

The engineers marveled at the excesses they encountered in the U.S., especially the excessive beauty and size. They were a little dismayed by the other excesses. They understood how the U.S. winner-take-all system worked. Unlike parliamentary rule and proportional representation, the U.S. model provides that a totality of the power goes to the "winner" even if they get only a plurality of the vote.

The engineers viewed the disproportional concentration of power as the cause of a lousy healthcare system, expansive ghettos, and an over-arching emphasis on the military. They were engineers after all, and none of this lopsidedness made sense to them. They explained to me that lopsided structures don't hold up well under adverse conditions.

When I walked back across the tracks to the Railway Campground, I made better note of the signs around the property. I realized Xanterra Parks and Resorts owned it along with the hotel nearby and the Railway itself.

If you read the "Territorial Times" – the newspaper put out by Grand Canyon Railway – you learn that Xanterra Parks and Resorts "has operated lodging and restaurant facilities at some of the most beautiful places on earth" for 106 years. You don't learn a thing, however, about Xanterra's controversial owner, Philip Anschutz.

Anschutz purchased Xanterra in 2008. And while I could tell you a lot of nasty things about his reputation, I might be considered biased. So I'll quote an article written about him and published by the United Church of Christ.

"Philip F. Anschutz is a conservative patron and former oil and gas baron with an estimated net worth of $6 billion. He operates one of the largest nonprofits in the United States, and has a variety of media holdings including Anschutz Entertainment Group, Walden Media and the daily The Examiner. Given Anschutz's ties to the extreme right—including the funding of homophobic groups, anti-union organizations, and climate and evolutionary science deniers—his recent foray into education reform is very troubling."

And given our purpose for taking this trip, learning that touristy side trips all across the national park system were owned by an anti-union, homophobic, climate science denier had us in complete agreement with the United Church of Christ. This lopsided ownership of so many of the U.S. national park properties proved troubling to us as well.

𓀀 𓀀 𓀀

Chapter 24 The Chinese and the Irish Built America's Railroads.
 λλ

On April 29, 1999, Republican Congressman John T. Doolittle stood on the floor of Congress and praised the contributions made by Chinese immigrants in building the transcontinental railroad. Harvard University Library Open Collections Program documented that in 1868, 12,000 Chinese were working for the Central Pacific Railroad on any given day. This immigrant labor force coupled with the Irish immigrants and ethnically Irish Americans, who worked west from their eastern homes, built the rail system for the wealthy robber barons. Men like Leland Stanford, who owned the profits and the tracks.

At the time the Central Pacific Railroad Company was founded, Stanford was the governor of California. Federal subsidies helped make Stanford wealthier and even more powerful, even as his acceptance of them while in office flouted ethics and social justice. Of the many railroad men taking advantage of their positions, Stanford's abuse of power was the most flagrant. And yeah, Leland Stanford Junior University – better known as Stanford University – is named for that Leland Stanford.

Cong. Doolittle's comments to Congress highlighted how vital the Chinese laborers were to the growing nation and her capitalist economy. Merchants who wanted the railroad to connect population centers with western mines and other natural resources did not intend to build the infrastructure themselves. Building a railroad through dangerous unforgiving terrain amongst jilted – consequently angry – Native Peoples required skilled builders who would rather take their chances fighting these obstacles than suffer with certain hunger and depravation. Here again proof that when upper classes pit the lower classes against each other – regardless of who loses at the bottom – the upper class wins.

In 1863 – prior to importing the Chinese and at the height of the American Civil War – only 600 laborers hired on to lay rail. Because of Central Pacific Railroad's meager workforce, it took two years to build 50 miles of track. After the war ended, thousands of Irishman left the battlefields and went to work for the Union Pacific Railroad headed toward the west. On the last day of construction – when the Central Pacific met Union Pacific and drove home the golden spike – the Chinese and Irish immigrants together built 10 miles of track in just 12 hours.

More than any other force – except possibly the merged interests of governmental and corporate corruption – racism built the railroads. The treaties that negotiated the land away from the Native Americans weren't honored, the Irish immigrants were paid poorly and the ethnic Chinese paid even less. Both Cong. Doolittle and the Harvard report cite Chinese courage and industry when describing how the railroad conquered difficult terrain. The Chinese risked their lives as they blasted tunnels and hung in baskets off the sides of cliffs, moving the project forward.

Fighting the Native Americans was left – for the most part – to the U.S. Army and the Irishmen.

The Grand Canyon Railway, begun in the late 19th century, originated in Williams, Arizona and didn't make it the whole way to the south rim until 1901. It was one of hundreds of small rail spurs built across the country, as rail travel became a preferred method of moving people, products, and raw materials. In the 40 odd years after 1869 when the Transcontinental Railroad was completed, the railroad industry boomed.

Unfortunately for the worker, the increased construction of railroad track was not accompanied by increased regulation of the railroads or increases in workers pay. The owners' immense wealth made them politically powerful. More than a million people were employed by the railroads, strikes were everyday occurrences on the east coast – as was strike breaking – and because racism built these western railroads there was little concern when workers got hurt or died. In just one year – 1889 – 22,000 railroad workers were killed or injured on the job.

The Grand Canyon – at one time accessible only by the most intrepid travelers – was full of valuable ore. Gold, copper, iron, lead, and zinc had all been discovered and entrepreneurs wanted to mine the canyon.

The invention of the electric light bulb increased demand for copper 1500 percent between 1880 and 1910, but hauling copper away from the Grand Canyon was not feasible by stage coach, the railroad had to be finished.

None of the tourist literature we received while riding on the Grand Canyon Railroad told us anything about the original owners or who laid the track. Our tour guide, an elderly gentleman so old that he had an emergency pack of nitro glycerin clearly marked on his belt, told us that the railroad was built by the Chinese. He said that there was a memorial down in Flagstaff, Arizona praising the contribution made by these Chinese workers.

The tour guide – his name tag said Bill – explained to us that prior to 1901 passengers and packages would have to travel the last thirty miles to the canyon rim by stagecoach. As our train chugged along the track, we passed old concrete buildings. The roofs were gone, as were the doors and window glass. Bill said locals used those old bunkhouses for target practice lately, but that railroad workers lived there from 1916 or 17 until the 1930's.

While quarrying and pillaging natural resources may have been the reason the railroad got its start from Williams to the Grand Canyon, hauling tourists became its real purpose. Once the awe inspiring vistas became better known, the railroad brought resort building materials and the people who would stay in them. Road weary travelers preferred a more direct route than the original one that wound around limestone hills and cliffs. These concrete bunkers then housed later workers that blasted the limestone away and straightened the tracks.

At least that's what Bill told us. Our guide said that the bunkhouses were used then. He thought it likely that the earliest workers lived in tents.

The first time I saw the Grand Canyon the prevalence of resorts shocked me. I'd expected a pristine and unaltered landscape around the rim. Learning on this trip that speculators hoped to mine the canyon angered me. Not because unbridled greed of that magnitude is new, but because I'd naïvely believed anything could remain outside greed's grasp. Even though people petitioned Congress as early as 1882 to protect the canyon, not until 1893 did the Grand Canyon receive any federal protections. And 3 years after the establishment of the National Park Service, in 1919, the Grand Canyon became a National Park.

In 2012 about four and half million folks visited Grand Canyon National Park. The number is expected to be lower for 2013 – the year Rick Smith took his radio show and his family on a detour from their "People's Tour" to check it out. But that's because a few months after their trip, the canyon was shut down along with all the other National Parks while the U.S. Congress fought over the Affordable Care Act and whether or not the middle class had a right to healthcare. Yeah, that's the same body that took 37 years to decide that the Grand Canyon would make a nice National Park.

𝝺 𝝺𝝺

Chapter 25 Women Laborers and the Servant Class

Before we set off on our People's Tour, Carol and the kids prepared all kinds of food to take along. Carol had cooked family favorites and frozen them while Sammi chopped fresh vegetables for us to munch along the way. By the time we got to the Grand Canyon those provisions were gone.

We stopped at grocery stores and restocked yogurt and purchased staples like milk and cereal, but we relied on restaurants and burger joints for the rest of our meals. Truck stops provided fast food options that came in handy on those days when we traveled many hundreds of miles and made few stops. But for the most part, Rick and Carol tried to make sure we got to a decent restaurant and ate fresh local food at least once a day.

When I first went to the Grand Canyon, I wasn't sure what it'd be like but I sure didn't expect a south rim lined with resort hotels. The luxury accommodations sat so close to the edge that I feared for the safety of visitors who sleepwalk. The train let us off just below the Bright Angel Lodge. Built in 1935, it's on the National Registry of Historic Places and has a museum inside. I brought Sammi inside with me to see check out the museum and to learn about the Harvey Girls.

Fred Harvey, an able entrepreneur with experience in both train travel and restaurants, noticed that the post-civil war American frontier offered little hospitality to the average traveler. Fred Harvey convinced the executives at the Santa Fe railroad to let him open a chain of restaurants and rest stops along their rail service so that he could cater to weary and hungry travelers. Eventually, Harvey and his cadre of women restaurant workers – the famed Harvey Girls – delighted customers at resort destinations as well as travel lodges.

It takes quite a bit of imagination to compare the underpaid and overworked truck stop fast food venders along U.S. Route 40 making $300 in 2013 with the provincially dressed waitresses and hostesses Harvey paid $17.50 a week in 1890;

especially because according to the Morgan Inflation Calculator, that $17.50 is worth more than $440 in 2012 dollars.

Harvey was very particular about who he hired. Prospective Harvey Girls should be "young women, 18 to 30 years of age, of good character, attractive and intelligent." They couldn't get married while in his employ and they had to promise to stay at least six months from the time they hired onto his workforce. Many of these young women eventually met their husbands while at work. A website for the city of Florence, Kansas boasts that 20,000 Harvey Girls married their regular customers.

What might seem no more than a shrewd approach by a savvy businessman who learned from his own travel experiences while crossing the desert southwest ended up changing – at least in part – the American workforce. The innovation known as the Harvey Girls actually heralded radical change for young women, especially young white women.

A 1977 study published in the Journal of Economic History explains that in 1890, 39.1 percent of non-white women worked outside the home, but only 16.3 percent of white women did. When Harvey added tens of thousands of white girls to the work force, he didn't give them fancy jobs of high station requiring specialized education. Harvey put white women to work as servants. This servant class had – since slavery ended – been largely reserved for women of color.

Harvey got a lot of these new employees out of their inner city homes and off of their farms. He paid them well and they were expected to serve their customers with poise and efficiency. Today's servers – regardless of color – are certainly not treated the way Harvey treated his new class of white worker. Somewhere along the way – especially as that percentage of white women in the work place soared to upwards of 40 percent by the end of the 20th century – the servant class in the U.S. began to rely on the benevolence of the customer and not on wages from their employers.

Just as other occupations dominated by women, minorities and ethnics enjoy fewer labor protections, so, too, do food service workers, barbers, and others. Agricultural workers and waitresses don't have to be paid a regular hourly minimum wage – even as meager as the current minimum wage.

A *Bloomberg News* story from April of 2013 points out that the federal minimum wage for servers is $2.13 per hour and has been since 1991. While some states have legislated a higher wage for servers, thirteen states still pay this low wage, even though the minimum wage for other hourly workers was increased to $7.25.

The Harvey Girls made Harvey rich even though he paid them today's equivalent of $11 an hour. Ignoring this fact, current day restaurateurs claim that increasing a server's minimum would kill their businesses. Lawmakers and entrepreneurs who resist increasing server minimums argue that increasing the wage would force establishments to close and wait staff to lose their jobs.

The Bloomberg story cites statistics that counter that argument. "A 1994 analysis by Alan Krueger, now [Pres.] Obama's chairman of the Council of Economic Advisers, and David Card, director of the Labor Studies Program at the National Bureau of Economic Research, compared fast food restaurants in New Jersey and Pennsylvania after New Jersey raised its hourly minimum to $5.05 in 1992 from $4.25. 'The increase in the minimum wage increased employment,' they found. For low-wage workers, they found job prospects improved in New Jersey."

Time after time it seems decision makers who work to keep wages and benefits low forget to calculate the positive effect on the economy that naturally results when low wage earners make more money.

As the 2013 holidays approached, a news story bubbled to the surface stating that power retailer and grocery giant, Wal*Mart, had placed collection bins for donated food so that their own employees, "can enjoy Thanksgiving Dinner." If Wal*Mart associates are that destitute, it's only logical to assume that any increase in wages would be spent right at Wal*Mart, where they work.

Somehow that logic hasn't made it to the corporate decision makers. After all, if it had, then some decision makers must've considered the possibility of adequately compensating folks and in turn benefiting from that extra buying power. If they entertained this notion, they clearly ruled out the idea and opted instead for placing bins begging for folks to help them. Perhaps number-crunchers in the Bentonville home offices have calculated that they will sell more goods to the kind-hearted customers who donate food to help Wal*Mart's impoverished workers.

Or perhaps, greed blinds the greedy to common sense.

If power retailers don't trust that their own retail sales would reclaim the increased wages, and if customers aren't capable of filling the gap for low wages – even as management posts signs admitting their associates don't have enough food – then there may be some psychological pay-off to keeping a servant class that is also part of a begging class. Regardless of Wal*Mart management's agenda, with a 2013 year end effective unemployment rate well into the double digits, it's unlikely many Wal*Mart associates will quit their jobs before Christmas to protest their inadequate compensation. Impoverished people seldom fight for their own rights, or complain about the abuse of others if it would cost them what little they have.

𐤋𐤋

Chapter 26 $240 Million Tribute to Military Incompetence
λ λ

By the time we got back from our three-hour visit to the Grand Canyon, it was getting pretty late. The kids went to bed in the back of the camper, Carol took off in the car, and once Rick, Brett and I got on the road, we started taping another radio show.

We hoped to get from the Grand Canyon over to the Las Vegas area before stopping. Carol has family there and after a quick planned trip to Hoover Dam, she was going to take the kids for a visit. We had Las Vegas labor leaders to interview.

We had so many hours of radio to produce we didn't have time to call around for a campsite. Instead we decided to just sleep in a parking lot somewhere along the Arizona/Nevada line. I suggested to Rick that since he and Carol had spent the past couple of weeks sleeping in the same 200 or so square feet with five other people, that they might like to sleep alone together in a hotel room. It seemed to me that stopping in a roadside hotel, while Brett and I stayed outside in the camper with the kids, might make the most sense. Especially because the next day, we could all use the hotel room's shower.

Late that night we pulled in next to a little motel. The desert night air was relatively cool and Brett, the kids and I slept with the windows open. The next day, once the sun rose and as the RV heated up, the others headed into the hotel room with Rick and Carol while I went off on foot in search of coffee. I crested the slope along which the RV was parked and couldn't believe my eyes. It wasn't a coffee shop; it was the shimmering silvery blue expanse of Lake Mead. None of us knew it when we parked the night before, but we were just up the highway from the Hoover Dam and the massive body of water that damming the Colorado River had formed. The sight of that 247 square mile lake in the middle of the desert was breathtaking.

All clean, we drove over to the Hoover Dam. In the early days, the dam didn't just provide water and power for a handful of southwestern states; it also connected Arizona to Nevada. Since the September 11th events in New York, Washington D.C., and Pennsylvania, the roadway that ran along the top of the dam made the Department of Homeland Security a bit nervous. The idea of protecting the dam wasn't new. While standing on the structure, off in the distance one can see the World War II defense post built to protect the dam and the nation's largest manmade drinking water reservoir – Lake Mead.

The Hoover Dam is a colossal spectacle. And the new overpass – the Mike O'Callaghan-Pat Tillman Bridge – makes the dam look small. 1900 feet long, 4 lanes wide, and 890 feet above the Colorado River, the $240 million bridge was named in memory of a former Nevada Governor and an Arizona Cardinals football player turned soldier. Because the bridge is part of U.S. Route 93 connecting Arizona and Nevada, it is named for favorite sons from both states.

Mike O'Callaghan was a decorated veteran who served in Korea and later went on to the Silver State's highest office. Post 9/11, Pat Tillman quit his job as a professional football player to enlist in the army and defend his country. Killed in Afghanistan, Tillman's family, friends and fans were lied to about his cause of death. In a CNN interview, his mom, Mary Tillman, chided the false reports, "That is not an error; that is not a misstep; that is deliberate deception."

Tillman was killed by his own platoon and the information was suppressed for undisclosed reasons. Still, if one cared to speculate, protecting the war machine from undesired public scrutiny is the only plausible explanation for keeping the friendly-fire casualty a secret.

Construction of the O'Callaghan-Tillman bypass began in 2003 and was completed in October of 2010. The bridge may actually be a fitting tribute to Tillman's desire to protect his nation in the wake of the September 11th attacks. At least Tillman's namesake structure was built to protect the irreplaceable Hoover Dam. Untold lives would be lost if anyone or anything breached that remarkable structure or contaminated the water supply.

The facts that surround both the Hoover Dam and the bypass are similar in their statistical extremes. The dam is 726 feet tall and 45 feet wide at the top. It is filled with 3.25 million cubic yards of concrete with a base width of 660 feet. Four one-mile long tunnels were blasted through the walls of the riverbed and used to divert the Colorado in order to construct the dam. Boulder City rose out of the desert and housed the dam construction workers and their families. Boulder City is now one of the terminus cities for the O'Callaghan-Tillman Bridge.

The Hoover Dam cost $163 million to build, 2/3 the price of the bridge. Of course in 2012 dollars, the Hoover Dam would have cost a cool $2.7 billion. The

890-foot bridge is the nation's second highest and has the longest concrete arch in North America. According to the website, "Highest Bridges" dot com, "The best design trait of all might well have been the simple decision to include a walkway on the north side of the bridge. From here the majesty of the Hoover Dam can finally be seen straight on from a vantage point normally reserved for planes or helicopters."

The Hoover Dam was a vast investment in the nation's infrastructure. It harnessed the power of the Colorado River and pooled the water for irrigation projects as well as providing drinking water all the way to the Pacific coast. The skilled laborers employed on the project earned roughly twice the nation's average income and relocated their families to the desert southwest. The cost of building the dam was repaid by 1987, a little more than 50 years after the project began.

The debt to soldiers like Tillman who died fighting in the post 9/11 wars will never be repaid.

λ λλ

Chapter 27 Las Vegas' Biggest Gamble: Working for the State

Denice Martin opened the door and let us into the comfortable offices of AFSCME Local 4041. AFSCME stands for American Federation of State County and Municipal Employees. Denise and the folks she works with in Nevada set us up with a bumper crop of employees to interview. The cast of characters reminded me of every job I'd never want to do for myself, except for maybe the woman who worked helping the homeless.

We spoke to prison guards, welfare officers, social workers, paper-pushing public servants, and guys who worked outside caring for state property. One fella worked on roofs. When we spoke with Tom Young, a maintenance repair specialist for the state, the thermometer outside hovered around 100 degrees.

Young came by while we taped the show but he didn't want to speak on tape. He just wanted to show support for his friends who had agreed to help us put the broadcast together. He wanted to hear what his buddy Harry Schiffman, Secretary/Treasurer of Local 4041, had to say but didn't want to be interviewed himself. Young did talk to us off air, however.

Young told us that when he worked roofing, in order to keep his tools cool enough to handle, he kept them in a bucket of water. He might have to walk a few feet to get to the bucket, "By the time I took the tool out of the water and used it, it was dry." The weather was so hot and dry when we were there; it made perfect sense that the moisture would evaporate immediately from his tools.

Schiffman works as an electrician for the University of Nevada, Las Vegas. He's a native New Yorker and when the economy crashed decades ago, he took a letter of introduction from his International Brotherhood of Electrical Workers (IBEW) back home and brought his valuable skills to then rapidly-developing Las Vegas.

Schiffman said that Las Vegas had a long labor history, from the mines to the casinos. Nothing stood in the way of Las Vegas' expansion. All Las Vegas had to do about its rapid growth was move further out into the desert. Schiffman reminisced about when San Francisco Street was just "more sand." And as an electrician, it was pretty easy to find work in that building boom. When the boom fell off, he began working as a maintenance electrician. And college campuses require quite a bit of electrical maintenance.

In October of 2013, Corrections Director Greg Cox issued a report that Nevada's available prison space is insufficient to the demand. In June of 2013, when we interviewed Gordon Milden, he told us the same thing. Milden, who admitted that corrections work is safer and comes with far fewer hassles if you volunteer for the graveyard shift – especially because management's not there and you get a shift differential – told us that if inmates don't have anywhere to go when they leave jail, the jail won't let them go. People who have done their time are sitting in prison – often private for-profit prisons – because neighborhoods don't want them. These left over inmates are overburdening our incarceration-happy society.

All of the folks who spoke to us complained about the elimination of state jobs and cuts to state workers' benefits. Lou Lombarto Jr., President of his local, found it frustrating that union and non-union workers often couldn't see that they had more to gain from working together than being driven apart. Lombarto explained, "We all share one thing, we all share a paycheck. If you see your benefits disappear, we should all band together."

It hurts Lombarto's feelings as a U.S. citizen and as a veteran to hear how maligned unions are in general and state workers are in particular. Lombarto told us, "I served my country and I'm still serving my country, as a state employee." After fighting to secure the future of his countrymen when he served in the military, Lombarto reminds others, "Now, I'd like to secure my future."

As the day wound down, and after we'd heard countless stories about cut pensions, reduced healthcare plans, and dangerous working conditions – similar to stories that were playing out all across the U.S. in states where state employees had become fiscal scapegoats – in walked Jennifer Knight.

Knight had the same sort of experiences. She'd explained that while state workers got furloughed to balance state budgets, no "food fairy" arrived to feed her or her co-workers who still had mortgages and other bills to pay with their smaller paychecks.

And while everyone who came to see us in the Nevada AFSCME Local 4041 was smart and articulate, Knight was on fire. As workers got more and more mistreated, Knight – who admits she's better off than most because she has a great boyfriend who helps her make ends meet – has found her voice.

Knight is funny, sharp, bright, well-spoken, and unafraid. She's standing up to government officials who she says are getting, "on the job training for screwing America." In fact, one month before we arrived in Nevada, Knight had an op-ed published in the "Elko Daily Free Press." With her permission, we have reproduced it here. Knight says if anyone wants to read it and be inspired to tweak it to match their particular situation and push back against the "screwing of America" to do so with her blessing.

Nevada Must Be Made Whole
By Jennifer Knight

As the 77th session of the Nevada Legislature nears its close, I invite my fellow Nevadans to learn about their state employees before the final votes are cast to determine the economic fate of state employees, their families, and their neighborhood businesses.

We, the employees of the State of Nevada, are neighbors and fellow citizens of the State of Nevada. We are the patrons at local Mom and Pop stores; we dine at family-owned restaurants. We are friends, brothers, sisters, aunts and uncles, fellow parishioners. We are employees of the State of Nevada; we are not the government.

We provide vital services to our state. We apply law to administer the proper payment and distribution of benefits. We protect our fellow Nevadans by providing a structured environment for inmates to learn proper conduct before being released back into society. We protect the elderly and provide rehabilitation services to the disabled.

When the economy bottomed out, we rose to Nevada's call. We spent less time with our families so that fellow Nevadans could clothe and feed their children and maintain their dignity and independence. We sacrificed so that Nevada may recover because we believe in her recovery, and she is recovering! The average weekly wage just hit a record high! It is now time for Nevada to make its state employees whole, for our sacrifices have become untenable.

We are the first-year corrections officers who are paid straight time to work on Christmas keeping Nevadans safe. After we face the shock of our take-home pay, we have to then choose between welfare or leaving state service for a public safety employer who pays a living wage. We are the unemployment call center workers who qualify for Medicaid because our own pay and healthcare are that poor.

We are the first-year welfare workers who qualify for food stamps if we are the sole support for a household of two. Not five, two. We are the single mothers of disabled children who work full-time to aid our fellow Nevadans through hard times only to receive take-home pay that forces us to choose which child can see the doctor, and still we must sleep in our car.

We are the people who stayed in our positions through these cuts because we love our state, we care about helping our neighbors and businesses, and we believe in Nevada's recovery.

My fellow Nevadans, the State of Nevada does not spoil its employees; the State of Nevada has thrown its employees into the safety net that we safeguard and administer. If this is appalling to you, then I invite you to support us. Support Nevada's neighbors, Nevada's families, and Nevada's businesses. Let the legislature and the governor know that the State of Nevada must pay its employees a living wage. Make us whole so that we can once again say that we take care of those who take care of Nevada. You can find your representatives at http://www.leg.state.nv.us/ and Governor Sandoval can be reached at http://gov.nv.gov.

Chapter 28 Somebody's Getting Jumped

Carol and I hopped in the car to head out of Las Vegas. The kids were in the RV with Rick and Brett. When Carol got tired of driving I would take over for her. She wasn't that tired yet, but figured she would be before long, so I rode along with her. I loved riding up front in the minivan; the scenic views were a lot easier to see than they were from the back of the RV.

As we drove down one of the city streets headed out of Las Vegas, an older couple with an old jalopy waved us over to help them. Carol rolled down her window and the old woman asked if we had jumper cables. Carol said that she did and pulled over to help. Carol's a nicer person than I am. I generally offer to call a wrecker but Carol had the cables and anyway, they didn't look like they could afford to have their vehicle towed or to pay a roadside assistance bill.

While Carol pulled her car over, the old woman got back in the jalopy and got on her cell phone. Carol got out of the car to get the jumper cables from the back of the van about the same time that two other cars pulled up. These cars were considerably younger and sportier than the battered pick up in which the old couple sat waiting. One car pulled very close in behind Carol's van and the other tucked itself in behind the pick-up truck.

Carol and I looked at each other and said – I kid you not – "Uh oh."

What none of us had noticed during this big exchange was the RV parked around the corner. About a nanosecond after the other two cars pulled up, Rick jumped out of the RV and headed over to "help."

Now Rick's a big boy. He stands about 6'4" and probably tips the scale at 240 lbs. He's got the exact arms and shoulders you'd expect a teamster truck driver to have and at this particular moment – as he strode across the lawn beside where we parked – his chest was up and his shoulders were back.

"Can I help you with those, Carol?" Rick asked, taking the jumper cables from his wife's hands. For all of Rick's adrenaline rush, the four newcomers in the extra cars had a corresponding crestfallen look. You could read on all their faces, "Where the heck did that big guy come from?"

Suddenly, the older couple reconsidered their situation and decided their car would start after all. They told us that they no longer needed a jump and thanked us for stopping. Rick pressed them in a gentle manner. Were they absolutely sure? He assured them that he would be more than happy to help.

But no, they responded that they'd be just fine and thanked us anyway. They looked on as Carol started her car. Rick walked back to the RV and we all pulled around the corner to meet on the adjacent street and talk about our encounter. The incident shocked all of us and we needed a few minutes to decompress.

Rick looked over at Brett and goodnaturedly asked, "Where were you?"

Brett responded that someone had to stay with the children and besides, Rick had the situation well under control. And anyway, if he didn't, Brett thought it wise to hang back and call the police should things go wrong.

We all laughed.

Rick joked, "I could see it in your eyes, you were getting ready to peel out of here in the RV."

Brett replied, "You got me. I was all set to go to Plan B. I figured I'd take the RV and head for home. I still have $500 on my credit card. If things had gone wrong, I'd have been home raising a pig by now."

We laughed at that crazy image and hopped in our respective vehicles to get back on the road. If those old folks had tried setting us up, it didn't work. Their vehicle didn't get jumped, and neither did we.

But considering the purpose of our trip, we shouldn't have been so naïve, either. We'd embarked on this People's Tour of middle class America at a time when the middle class is shrinking faster than ever before.

Statistically speaking, increases in poverty cause crime rates to increase correspondingly. Nevada seems to prove this point with the second-highest violent crime rate as well as the second-highest foreclosure rate in the nation. That loss of economic security was one of the biggest reasons we chose Las Vegas as a destination on our trip.

Poverty creates desperation, and if the occupants of those three cars meant to rob us, they must've been pretty desperate to chance jumping a couple of broads in broad daylight. According to the *Las Vegas Review Journal*, a *Nevada Kids Count* report issued in 2011 states, "One out of every five Nevada children lives in poverty, marking the highest youth poverty rate in the state's recent history." So yeah, things are pretty desperate.

In fact, so many people are so poor now that record amounts of laundry detergent are being stolen. When crooks are stealing laundry soap, from well-lit stores with surveillance cameras and watchful employees, you could say the crooks have gotten bold. Perhaps robbing a couple of women on a side street in the middle of the day isn't that daring after all.

λ λλ

Chapter 29 Well, do ya, Punk?
ʎ

We pulled into the KOA Fairplex at Los Angeles County Fairgrounds some time after midnight. We had called ahead and the staff there left all of our registration information attached to the outside wall of the office.

Over the last couple of weeks, we'd spent a fair amount of time at big flat parking lot campgrounds, but this one didn't look like most of the others. Even in the dark it looked like a tropical jungle: full of blossoms, flowering bushes and a wide variety of palm trees. After we pulled into our camping spot, we did our usual graceless ballet of moving equipment and making our beds, and the whole tired crew fell asleep pretty quickly.

The next day the weather was gorgeous, and everything around us was blooming. We had no appointments until afternoon, and considering we'd spent three hours at the Grand Canyon and 45 minutes at the Hoover Dam, six wide-awake hours in one place had become quite a luxury.

The KOA, which is cutsie and short for Kampgrounds of America – just the kind of play on words that makes literacy volunteers cringe – had every amenity we'd been hoping to have. We made immediate use of their spacious laundry room, and the pool was delightful.

I got up early and went for my walk. Too early for the office to be open, I peeped in the windows and saw a well-stocked coffee station. I knew instantly that I could have set down roots and lived at the Los Angeles County Fairplex forever. That's when I noticed a school bus pulling into the campground. I wasn't the first person to think of living at the fairgrounds.

There aren't available statistics for the number of homeless children living in U.S. campsites. But a simple web search for "homeless kids in campgrounds" will bring up more anecdotal tales than a feeling person can bear to read. We had already stayed at a number of campsites with residences that looked pretty permanent, but that morning, waiting for the office coffee nook to open, was the first time I'd seen such conclusive evidence as a school bus picking up kids.

Twenty-two weeks after we left California, on November 15, 2013, the *Los Angeles Times* ran the story, "California Campground for the homeless is forced to shutdown." Seems the neighbors in Placerville, California didn't like "the state's only self-governing camp for homeless people" existing in their community. Might I add, "Way to go Placerville, and just thirteen days before Thanksgiving! Let the homeless celebrate everything they've got to be grateful for, just not in your back yard."

According to the U.S. Department of Education, 1.16 million homeless kids attended school in the United States last year. The number of homeless kids is up more than 75% since the recession began in 2008. Campgrounds may not seem like a good place for children and their families to live, but really, you should see the alternatives.

"Every generation wears their hypocrite coat." That's what Don Thornsburg told us a few hours later during our radio interview with him. And it pretty much sums up the dichotomy, as it exists in the U.S. today. Communities pour out support for the poor on the holidays and then too often resort to blaming them for their situation the rest of the year. Maybe that will be heartless Placerville's legacy. At least they abandoned the poor during the holidays, no hypocrisy there.

Thornsburg, a 69 year old labor historian and former Teamster, had been a paratrooper in Vietnam. Thornsburg's tall, slender, square jawed and fit. His curt manner and emphatic speech commanded us to conduct the interview they way he wanted it.

Thornsburg met us in an abandoned office building along with the other community and labor leaders who had taken time out of their busy schedules to talk about decent wages, hard-won working conditions, and the fair business practices that had – in Thornburg's words – allowed the "middle class to invent itself."

The difference between Thornsburg and the other guys was that he had a mission and he was going to achieve it. He'd agreed to share what he knew of California labor history, and Rick and I had one option: to shut up and listen. Thornburg told us that as a paratrooper in Vietnam he shipped out with 746 other graduates of paratrooper school. His 173rd infantry airborne sustained horrific losses and Thornburg was one of only 36 to make it home again.

After 20 minutes holding a microphone in front of Thornsburg's face, I jotted in my notes that he was the Clint Eastwood of labor historians: of all historians, for that matter. I bit the inside of my cheeks as I heard Eastwood's voice in my head, "You want to learn labor history? Well, do ya, Punk?"

Thornsburg explained that Los Angeles grew because ethnic groups – and lots of them – built the infrastructure that Los Angeles had to have in order to exist. Thorsburg said that various immigrant and ethnic populations "sacrificed so much in their lives and benefitted so little for it."

Thornsburg believes most people already know that Los Angeles, the state of California, and the nation as a whole, became great because so many suffered to make it so. But knowing that isn't enough. Thornsburg warned, "Anybody can point out the dirty laundry but you need someone to tell you how to clean it."

Thorsburg said that the water that came to Los Angeles was robbed from farmers further east, devastating their farms. The aqueduct, constructed at the turn of the 20th century, brought water to Los Angeles and eventually caused what came to be called the "water wars" as farmers struggled to keep their crops alive.

More innovation, more planned infrastructure, and more labor constructed Lake Meade and the Hoover Dam, which eventually brought some relief to the farmers in Owens Valley.

Thorsburg spoke of the Chinese who built the railroads, the Japanese fish packers immortalized in Steinbeck's classic, *Cannery Row*, the Mexicans and other Latinos who harvested crops and continue the back-breaking work of collecting the nation's food supply from the fields where it grows. Thornsburg told us, "America exploited everyone they could in every way they possibly could." And while, "understanding a fault never excuses it," there can be solutions discovered when the oppressed organize and push back.

Thornsburg credits the Jewish immigrants of East L.A. for the rise of organized labor in California. From Jewish baker's strikes in the early 1900's to current day protests by the Jewish Labor Committee in support of living wages for Wal*Mart workers, these organizations have been out-spoken in support of equality and shared reward commensurate with shared effort.

I don't know if Thornsburg intends to write his own labor history narrative, but one is sorely needed. There is a dearth of information available. I have read books with the words "labor" and "encyclopedia" in the title and not found 20% of the issues I've been looking for or describing things we've seen along the way.

As we finished up our interview with Thornsburg – or Clint, as I prefer to call him – he made passing reference to problems with "the modern working era." He cited the differences between shipping behemoths UPS and Fed Ex. UPS hires Teamsters and Fed Ex has independent contractors for drivers. Consequently the average pay for a UPS driver – according to a 2011 AOL Jobs report – is more than $20,000 better than that of a Fed Ex driver: $58,653 versus $38,465.

As for how these two companies fair profit wise, all the indicators support Thornsburg's assertions that sharing reward with the workers increases the overall economic health of a company. UPS appears at number 52 of the Forbes 100 with more than $3 billion in profits, nearly three times the corporate income of number 70, Fed Ex.

Thornsburg hopes workers will study the numbers and come to understand that good wages in the U.S. make better sense than union-busting or exporting jobs overseas.

Thornsburg concluded, "There's always been corporate greed. They took the American jobs and gave them to others who get a maggot lunch. And then send it [manufactured items] back; sell it at full price as though it were made here. They said it would be cheaper and it wasn't cheaper. They said it would be safer and it wasn't safer."

Yep, Thornburg needs to write a book.

Chapter 30   The Banditelli Brothers
λ λ

Eastwood, er Thornsburg, and the others made our trip to California worthwhile, despite the fact that we actually ran into our most difficult physical challenges recording those Los Angeles interviews. When we got to LA, none of the buildings that we'd been told could host us actually could. And when we finally found a building that some of the labor honchos said was vacant and available, they neglected to mention that these places were empty because they had no ceilings, few walls, and that pretty much every entry door was locked.

It turned out that none of us cared. After more than two weeks on the road, I wasn't so surprised that we – The Rick Smith Show – didn't care, but none of the fellas we interviewed cared either. Everyone just wanted to build awareness. Not a single person complained about any inconveniences. And for the first time since we'd left Carlisle we got to use the six foot folding table that spent its days on Rick and Carol's bed and its nights blocking the already too-limited access to the camper rest room.

We didn't have chairs for the interviews but we already knew Brett could pretty much edit the Super Bowl while sitting on a beverage cooler, so we grabbed those out of the RV. We hauled in one of the radio show banners and covered a wall-less wall as a backdrop for the YouTube videos we made along the way.

Carol and the A's had taken off for San Francisco shortly after lunch and when we finished up around dinner time, Rick, Sammi, Brett and I stuffed everything back into the camper and headed to a local Italian place to meet Chris, Brett's brother.

Chris works with teachers' unions. We spoke a little about his work and while a topic brought up even marginally along this trip could earn its own chapter here in *Daddy, What's a Middle Class?*, the corporate agenda sweeping the United States to destroy public education will not be discussed here. It needs and deserves its own book. Some of what has happened to destroy the middle class and the American Dream can be dismissed as bad timing or changing human needs.

But not what's happened to education. No, education has taken a full frontal assault by special interests with a plethora of agendas, none of which are good.

People like Chris are hired to work alongside educators and help them push back. Education is needed more than ever if the U.S. and her people are to stay competitive. Unless we only want to compete with the third world, then all that education will just get in the way.

Right wing neocon governors like Wisconsin's Scott Walker, Maine's Paul LePage, Pennsylvania's Tom Corbett, Florida's Rick Scott and others have been put in place by certain special interests to destroy public education and privatize it along with public transportation, housing and jails.

So, after we chatted shop, the Banditelli Brothers just reminisced a bit and we all felt bad when their too-brief visit came to an end.

We hadn't just split off from Carol and the A's – we'd planned for them to get as far as they could and stay in a hotel without us – but we still needed to get going. San Francisco was a five-hour drive from LA and we still had to find a Wal*Mart parking lot near wherever they ended up so that we could meet early in the morning and head in the minivan for the Golden Gate Bridge.

The Banditellis said their farewells while the rest of us moved toward the camper. I sucked up the free WiFi at the restaurant and found a Wal*Mart along the monorail line by one of the airports. Hours later when we pulled into America's largest retailer's parking lot, a very sleepy Sammi told me that I could make her sleep in their parking lot, but that I couldn't make her go inside.

Sammi never complained about all the interviews we'd dragged her to and she'd never been inside a Wal*Mart. Rick and Carol had done a fine job on that kid.

The next day, before Brett could finally touch down at Netroots Nation, we joined the California Nurses Association and marched across the Golden Gate Bridge. Thousands of nurses and their allies converged in Golden Gate Park to protest what they saw as an environmental disaster in the making: the Keystone XL Pipeline.

The Keystone XL Pipeline with its promise of good paying jobs and guarantee of environmental disaster emphasizes the history of the middle class. When the people in the middle are expected to compromise, the wealthy corporate interests never ask would the worker prefer higher wages or more vacation time.

No, the question is always, "Would you like to eat today or drink water tomorrow? Would your kids like to have clothes today or clean air tomorrow? Would you like a paycheck today or would you like the boss to find someone more desperate than you to take that check tomorrow?"

And without solidarity, without a plan, the worker trades his or her tomorrow for the necessities of today. And then those tomorrows bring more concessions and conditions get even worse.

Chapter 31 A Day Off
🐾 🐾🐾

Rick and Brett set up their booth at Netroots Nation. Some of the people there knew us already. Many folks knew the guys because of their work broadcasting working class concerns and labor issues. Other folks knew me because I'd run for Vice President. We don't get that sort of recognition on Main Street, USA. Suffice it to say that Netroots Nation was one of the few places on the planet where left-wing activism wasn't just revered; it dominated.

Rick and Brett hunkered in for the long haul. West coast fans of the show waited to meet them and they had a laundry list of cool folks to interview for the broadcasts back home. With the People's Tour past the halfway mark, Carol and I plotted a day to do something fun. The next day – while the guys went back for Netroots Day Two – we took the A's and headed for Crater Lake.

Crater Lake National Park, a 7 ½ hour ride from San Jose, only added about three hours overall to our trip. Our ride took us through some of the most beautiful farmland I'd ever seen. Hundreds, perhaps thousands, of acres of ripe produce and blooming sunflowers lined the roads we traveled. I'd never seen such abundance. At least that's how it seemed. Perhaps my mind had been starved after a week or more of driving through deserts. At any rate, it all proved irresistible. We detoured from our path a number of times to stop at farm stands, buy fresh produce, and stretch our legs walking in charming little northern California towns.

California, far better known for wines than for asparagus, feeds the US. According to a 2011 Mother Jones article, California produces, "99 percent of the artichokes grown in the US, 44 percent of asparagus, a fifth of cabbage, two-thirds of carrots, half of bell peppers, 89 percent of cauliflower, 94 percent of broccoli, and 95 percent of celery… 90 percent of the leaf lettuce… 83 percent of Romaine lettuce… 83 percent of fresh spinach, a third of total fresh tomatoes consumed in the U.S. and 95 percent of ones destined for cans and other processing purposes." Add to that fruit tally: "86 percent of lemons and a quarter of oranges come from there… Ninety percent of avocados… 84 percent of peaches, 88 percent of fresh strawberries, and 97 percent of fresh plums."

When you consider that most – and in some cases all – of various types of produce come from California and are shipped everywhere else in the nation, the value of two types of workers becomes evident. Without the agricultural worker and the transportation worker, Americans would starve.

And after all this intrastate shipping is done, there's still a lot left over. Wheat fields and cornfields in the mid-west produce surpluses, too. What isn't consumed domestically gets loaded onto ships. Our first official stop post Netroots Nation would take us to the northwestern most contiguous state in the United States. We had a gig the following day in Vancouver, Washington interviewing stevedores – longshoremen – who'd been locked out by their multinational corporate employers. This lockout wasn't just hurting dockworkers, it was hurting the farmers who needed to move their produce to foreign markets.

All these thoughts spun around in my head as we made our way past amazing views of Mt. Shasta and veered away from Highway 5, heading toward Crater Lake. In all we'd go about 800 miles from San Jose to Vancouver, but we'd left early and it was June, so we had the maximum daylight per day possible at any time of year. Besides, we had a 4-year old and a 7-year old to keep us company!

Okay, I said that for effect. But it's true and those kids were great. They helped us eat berries and reminded us how yummy homemade donuts could be. They told us stories and let us read to them. And when we drove up the caldera and first saw snow lining the National Park roadway, they were even more excited than we were.

Crater Lake became a National Park seventeen years before the Grand Canyon did. The country's deepest lake is perched 6178 feet above sea level. First noticed by ethnic western European explorers, John Wesley Hillman, Henry Klippel, and Isaac Skeeters, in 1853, these gold prospectors took notice of its beauty and kept moving.

Crater lake gets one tenth as many visitors as the Grand Canyon and while nowhere near as enormous, its beauty rivals any National Park vista. Speculation – or perhaps cynicism – dictates that the reason Crater Lake was so quickly preserved as a National Park was because it had no value to mine owners or any other prospectors.

As we drove the steep road leading up the side of Mt. Mazama, I couldn't help but wonder who might have built it. According to the National Park Service Crater Lake website, nothing but a dirt wagon trail wound its way to the top before it received National Park designation. Secretary of the Interior, James Garfield, listened to businessmen who had interests making the natural wonder more accessible. William Steele had built a concession stand for travelers by the lake, and railroad magnate Edward Harriman expected rail service to the region would be lucrative if visitors had better access to the site.

In 1910 Congress appropriated $10,000 for a feasibility study. The estimates came back in 1911. A road up the volcano and around the lake would cost $13,000 per mile. Paving it would cost another $5000. No one figured the cost of a guardrail. Not to sound like a wimp, but having ridden on that road a hundred years later, I can't imagine dismissing the idea of a guardrail.

In total the earliest road took six years to build and cost $416,000 dollars. As elevations increased, the available work seasons shortened.

Using beasts of burden and hand tools, creating mountain side drainage and road surfaces that wound around the outside of a volcano and across passes with names like "Devil's Backbone" is almost impossible to imagine. Especially in 2013 where even the smallest building project requires the use of heavy machinery.

All the work was done by day laborers who lived in camps. No contracts were signed. And though an Army Corps of Engineers project, there were no worker protections. The project went forward, picking up and losing workers as the bosses saw fit. Without access to pay records I can't tell you what these day laborers were paid, but it might have gone up when the US entered World War I and worker availability decreased, as hard working men were needed elsewhere.

Before we left Crater Lake, Carol and I took the kids into the gift shop and cafeteria located across the rim road. Another Xanterra property, along with cabins and campsites, known as Mazama Village, the gift shop is open year round.

Without businesses to push the federal government for infrastructure, one can't help but wonder if these necessary access roads would have even been built. And though city, county, state and federal expenditures provide infrastructure for developers, that infrastructure investment is seldom considered welfare or part of any welfare state.

I took over driving from Carol and wound my way down Mt. Mazama and north to Washington state along a road that was part mountain trail and part motocross competition.

We opened a paper map to see which way to go. This was our first and only use of a map. There's no cell phone reception at Crater Lake, so our telephone GPS devices didn't work.

Driving down that volcano and back to Interstate Route 5 – through the forests of Oregon – was more fun than any drive I've ever driven. And it was the first drive I've ever spent wondering about the folks who built the road I traveled, how they were paid, and how many of them were injured or perished while constructing it. Rick Smith was right. If we spent a little time thinking about the history of labor and the middle class, we'd change the way America views her surroundings and our concepts of who this country's founders really were.

I hadn't gone 20 miles before all my passengers were sound asleep. We had 350 miles more to go and pulled into Vancouver sometime after midnight. It was a grueling day. I crossed the bridge from Portland, Oregon to Vancouver, Washington, thinking about the agricultural workers and transportation workers who feed the people of the US. They couldn't do it without the construction workers who build the infrastructure, the roads. I hadn't thought of them before, but my drive to Crater Lake changed all that.

Chapter 32   Our Little Detour
λ

When Rick first mapped out the People's Tour, the route went straight from San Jose to Salt Lake City. There was no jaunt up to the Pacific Northwest. Sadly, we'd have missed Crater Lake, although we'd have shaved a whole slug of miles off our trip. But that original route was mapped out before foreign companies locked out U.S. workers at the docks in Vancouver, Washington and Portland, Oregon.

As reported in *Longshore and Shipping News*, Japanese-owned companies, Mitsui and Marubeni, locked out the workers after protracted negotiations produced a contract so lousy that it was rejected by more than 90% of the workers. And it's not like these big and burly stevedores shy away from a decent deal when they're offered one, "U.S.-based TEMCO, a joint venture of Cargill and CHS, reached an agreement with ILWU workers in February."

In light of the fact that a twelve-nation agreement is being negotiated as I type – albeit behind closed doors – with Japan as one of the players, it's frightening that the Trans Pacific Partnership (TPP) appears to increase vulnerability of workers in the U.S.

And lots of the would-be member nations' negotiators – the U.S. included – are in on the secrecy. Wikileaks documents show that Australian officials refuse to share details of their proposed concessions with the U.S. Senate. The Senate is, of course, the governing body in the U.S., which ratifies treaties, but clearly not the agency that negotiates them.

Most TPP critics fear – in addition to unfair labor practices in some of the member nations – the compulsory relaxation of environmental laws and protections of intellectual property. Again, according to documents released in December of 2013, "The TPP proposes to freeze into a binding trade agreement many of the worst features of the worst laws in the TPP countries, making needed reforms extremely difficult if not impossible."

Labor officials in both Oregon and Washington question the wisdom of trusting an agreement with countries that are home to corporations that so flagrantly union bust and lock out workers on U.S. soil: "Mitsui owns United Grain in Vancouver, Wash., that locked out members of ILWU Local 4 on February 27, and Marubeni owns Columbia Grain in Portland, which locked out members of ILWU Local 8 on May 4."

It was about 1:30 a.m. when Carol and I pulled up to the fleabag motel that Rick and Brett had snagged for our parking area that night. I would use a more formal description of the accommodations, but no other phrase sums up the place quite as well. Our stays in California had been at moderately priced decent motor lodges. Rick and Carol had stayed together in the hotel room those nights. If Brett complained about having to stay out in the camper, I never heard him. I didn't complain either; it didn't much matter to me where we slept, as long as it was quiet.

Rick had gotten it into his head that Brett and I were getting the short end of the stick by being stuck out in the camper every night since we'd left home. He decided that we'd get the room the night we stayed in Portland.

Before I went to the room, I was ready to pass on the offer. Fleabag motels generally look just as shady on the inside as they do on the outside. This place was no exception. But once we lugged our stuff upstairs and opened the door, I was certain Brett and I would not be staying in that room together.

Carol and I – a little more than a lot punchy by the time our drive up from San Jose had ended – laughed uproariously when we opened the door. We probably woke everyone sleeping in the rooms on either side of our tiny room. In the center of the dingy space, a single full-sized bed awaited us. I looked at her and said, "I'll send Rick up." Carol told me not to bother, that the bed was too small for Rick. So I helped her carry in the A's and tuck them in to sleep with their mom.

Then I went out to the parking lot and joined Rick, Brett and Sammi in the RV. Like I said, it didn't matter where I slept, especially not that night. I fell asleep about five minutes after my head hit the pillow.

The next morning we headed for Local 4 of the International Longshore and Warehouse Union (ILWU) hall. We had some great interviews and put together some shows with past and present officers of the various labor unions. The interviews painted an interesting picture of life for area workers since the mid 1930's. They explained 80 years of gains in workplace safety, wages, and benefits. All those interviews are available at the People's Tour website.

The real lessons of the trip to Portland and Washington came when we visited the docks. At both locations we interviewed articulate workers longing to get back to work. My very first impression of the "lazy" longshoremen holding out for fluffy benefits was "Really? These are the guys who don't want to work?" Firstly, I'd like to have met anyone willing to call one of these dockworkers "lazy" to his face. You didn't get to be that size and that strong by sitting on your duff avoiding hard work.

While we stood at the gate, replacement laborers – unaffectionately called scabs – would come through and pass the workers locked out of their jobs. The locked out workers would block the exit on the public driveway for a few minutes and try to initiate dialogue with the folks attempting to drive past them. Most of the questions involved why someone would take a job that would only get worse once the union was broken. No one responded to these attempts at conversation.

Rick and I tried to ask questions. I had a handheld voice recorder. We identified ourselves as members of the press. The replacement guys never said a word. They never even looked at us.

The locked out workers had nothing but time and they didn't share the scabs' reluctance to speak. They willingly and incredulously explained the injustice that Mitsui and Marubeni perpetrated on them and on the U.S. taxpayer. Clager Clabaugh, President of Local 4, explained that $275 million in public funds had made its way to the U.S. Port of Vancouver. Clabaugh pointed out that many of the workers sitting there, locked outside their workplace, had gone to Washington D.C. back in 2011 and testified to the U.S. Congress that investing in the north western ports would create job stability and growth in the region.

Once congress complied – having allocated and spent nearly one third of a billion dollars to subsidize these Japanese business interests – the longshoremen were out and the cheaper replacement workers were in their place.

Clabaugh looked exasperated when he explained that many of the replacement workers were visa workers from Guatemala. Clabaugh said, "Guest workers! In my wildest dreams, I never thought they'd bring in foreign labor."

Clabaugh's frustrations didn't end there. Foreign companies don't care about where the labor comes from, Clabaugh gets that, but they barred the longshoreman from mounting signs on boats to alert the ship pilots – folks who might have cared that they were crossing a picket line – that they were coming into a dock with locked out workers. The workers were put on notice of their "free speech zones" and not allowed to pass within 150 yards of a moving vessel.

When Local 4 took to the water with signs anyway, a federal court found them in contempt. Leal Sundet, ILWU coast Committeeman reportedly remarked that this ruling was, "yet another example of how the legal complex in this country protects foreign companies from American workers who resist the loss of good jobs."

Interviews like the ones we conducted in Portland and Vancouver belonged in a history book, but they were current events. Hard-working guys with mortgages, car payments and families had bargained in good faith and got the shaft from a foreign company headquartered thousands of miles away. Meanwhile, mid-western farmers rely on the ports to ship their grain. The lock-out had the potential to hurt hump-busting Americans all across the Midwest.

We hated getting back in the van after visiting both lock out sites. We all remarked that the longshoremen needed a whole lot more solidarity, support, and good press. We wondered if the American people would want their courts and congress persons coming down on the side of foreign corporations. But we had to get going. We had a little over a day to get to Salt Lake City, Utah.

Carol had taken the kids for the day. I can't imagine what she found to do with them. Rick, Brett and I piled into the RV to start driving and to put the show together. As we pulled onto route 84 we headed east for the first time in three weeks. Rick said to me, "Take my credit card and order those guys some pizza." I did a web search for pizza joints and sent both sets of picketers some pizza. When I got off the phone Rick muttered under his breath, "It's not much, but it's the least we can do."

Chapter 33 "Don't Mourn, Organize"

We drove from Portland, Oregon straight to Salt Lake City, Utah. That's a little shy of 800 miles and about twelve hours of driving. Since we'd added in the trip to the Pacific North West, we had no choice but to make a beeline to the bee hive state. We landed at the KOA on West North Temple. All of Salt Lake City is configured in relation to the Latter Day Saints' Temple. Salt Lake City is Utah's capitol as well as the spiritual center of the church more commonly referred to as Mormon.

The campground had everything the kids could've hoped for and it was easy for us to find when we got to town in the middle of the night. It was right next to the airport. If we'd needed it, the city's public transit system stopped there. Salt Lake City's got a nice network of streetcars. We had an early morning appointment with an historian, Pat Shea, at Sugar House Park. Because our day started early, the kids got shortchanged, once again, on the pool and playground. We got on the road as soon as everyone was up and dressed.

On mornings like that one, I shook my head in dismay at how wonderful those Smith kids were and are. Literally trapped in a car for twelve hours one day, only to be bedded down in a nice green space with basic family vacation amenities, and then moving on before they got a chance to really appreciate anything fun. If I'd been 4, 7, or 11, I can't imagine I'd have been so nice about it. The Smith kids were real troopers.

Luckily, our first appointment of the day brought us to a park. The panorama of mountains around Salt Lake City takes your breath away. Many people – kids and grown-ups – played in the park, against the magnificent backdrop of the Wasatch and Oquirrh Ranges. The Smith kids ran to join them.

The park where we stood was a very different place when the Utah State Prison stood there. In 1957 the prison was torn down. But it was what happened there in 1915 that put this trip to the park on our itinerary. On the 19th of November 1915, balladeer and labor organizer Joe Hill was executed by firing squad.

In 1984 *The Deseret News* interviewed a couple of the old prison guards from the Utah State Prison in Sugar House. These guys described a pretty nasty and dangerous place. Built prior to the Civil War, the seven-acre prison originally consisted of a couple of buildings for the guards to use and a big adobe wall. The prisoners were kept in holes in the ground with bars across the top. By the time Hill arrived, the "hole" was reserved for solitary confinement and prison barracks had been added to the compound. Still, there was no running water in the maximum-security building. The inmates had pails they used as a latrine that they emptied once a day.

Shea met us down at the park because he wanted us to see first hand how completely erased from existence the prison is today. Shea wants to change that. He's not so concerned about remembering the compound as he is about remembering what happened there. He especially wants folks to remember Joe Hill's execution.

As we'd learned at places like the old Ashe Building in New York City – where the Triangle Factory Fire took place – tributes to labor history are pretty rare and humble at best. Even at that tragic site where 146 workers died, only a small plaque remains. Shea's got an up hill battle fighting to put a marker for a convicted murderer in Sugar House Park.

It's not just that Joe Hill – tried, convicted, and sentenced to a death by means of his own choosing – probably didn't do the crime. Back in the day, most thinking people outside the Utah court system thought he got framed. President Wilson even interfered on Hill's behalf, although he demurred when it came to commuting Hill's sentence.

No, over the years governments have executed lots of innocent people. Monuments to these mistakes won't start springing up any time soon. But the reason Shea's up against it when he tries to commemorate Hill's execution is the same reason many people believe the government killed him 99 years ago. Joe Hill wrote the anthems of the working class.

Hill, an immigrant and a member of the working class, came to the United States in search of a better life but became instantly disenchanted by the plight of labor, especially immigrant labor. Hill joined the International Workers of the World (IWW) – better known as the Wobblies – and he wrote songs that resonated with both workers and organizers. Robert Weir and James Hanlan in their *Historical Encyclopedia of American Labor* dubbed Hill, "In the history of music and labor... *probably* the most famous writer of all time." The emphasis on probably is mine.

Hill's music – mostly written to tunes already popular and well known as hymns sung by the poor – would likely have gotten him noticed by the authorities eventually. But when he teamed up with the Wobblies – who were arguably the most radical of all the labor organizers – he hastened his notoriety and increased the size of the target on his back.

The Wobblies have been around since 1905. Their actual membership numbers have never matched their relative strength. The Wobblies tackled union organizing in an "all for one and one for all" manner that the other unions eschewed. In the early 20th century, their reputation as "too radical for most labor unions" earned the Wobblies and their folk heroes an undeserved reputation for being anti-government and – as the Bolsheviks rose to power and formed the Soviet Union – communist.

Throughout history the powerful have subjugated the powerless by keeping them apart. In the case of the American labor movement, the argument can be made that they kept themselves apart. Racism, sexism, and the reluctance of skilled laborers to unionize with unskilled labor, zapped potential from the power of organized labor and all workers in general. The Wobblies wanted to work together under one big tent. If they had managed to bind together millions of low-wage workers across the nation, they may well have been revolutionaries.

All the evidence against Hill at his trial was circumstantial and while he did little to help his case – some feel he wanted a martyr's death – he certainly resented Utah for executing him. One of Hill's last wishes was that he not be "found dead in Utah." His supporters took his ashes and scattered them all around the world.

Hill did not want to die in vain. He knew people sang his songs and in his final months he appreciated the love and support of thousands who wrote letters and attempted to intercede on his behalf. To these folks and his comrades in the movement he had one message, "Don't mourn, organize." A simple web search for that phrase yields an ironic profiteering on his words. One can buy everything from leather belts to coffee mugs to t-shirts with those words emblazoned on them.

The website Murderpedia lists Hill as a two-time murderer. Shea and countless others think he's a martyr to the cause of organized labor and human rights. They'd likely argue that the state of Utah belongs on a much longer list of murderers, and Hill's name should be removed. Because of this crime – the state-sponsored assassination of Joe Hill – Shea feels that the least today's Utah officials could do is put a marker to Joe Hill in Sugar House Park.

λ λλ

Chapter 34 Sammi's the Star

When we left the park we headed downtown. Salt Lake City's easy enough to navigate with all points marked off in increments radiating out from the Mormon Temple. According to their religion, God chose the site for the Temple. According to the Utah state website, the site of the capital was chosen by population density. Consequently, the 101-year-old capital and the Temple are right around the corner from each other.

After a quick trip to see these beautiful buildings and grab some lunch, our little band split up again. Carol took the A's and went to find something fun to do. We took Sammi and headed for the AFL-CIO.

Everywhere we went the folks we interviewed gave us their time, attention, and workspace. And they did so good-naturedly. But there was something extra special about the way they treated us in Utah. While Brett set up the equipment on the conference table in the office of AFL-CIO President Dale Cox, Cox and his assistant Judy Barnett treated us like royalty – and not just us – Sammi especially. Cox and Barnett both directed most of their attention and inquiry to Sammi. Instead of just being Rick's kid who ran errands and stayed quiet through hours of interviews as she had through our whole trip, Cox and Barnett treated her like she was the reason their organization existed.

Barnett, who doubles as Communications Director, showed Sammi photographs of child laborers. She spoke with Sammi about what it would have been like to be eleven years old in 1913 instead of 2013. When she finished showing Sammi around, Barnett sat Sammi at the head of the conference table with Rick and me on either side.

The AFL-CIO office in Utah was full of good news and great energy. And Barnett wanted to make sure we noticed that. Barnett told us that despite political losses nationally and anti-union propaganda, "It's not doom and gloom." She noted that 37 young union apprentices had just been sworn in and that the Utah legislature had made the following week "Safety Week." Barnett praised lawmakers like Utah Senator Karen Mayne who worked to pass, "not a union bill but a family bill." Barnett pointed out that when you advance the union agenda, you're helping the working family.

The swearing in of new union workers meant that young people had chosen to join a union and devote themselves to working together for a better life for all. Cox pointed out that federal and state projects can hire companies using union workers and pay up front for that on their bid, or they can go non-union and pay the price on health and human services to the low income. Cox also pointed out that the extra cost from injuries and do-overs when non-union shops get hired makes the project more expensive as well.

Cox explained that unions don't send workers to a site unless they're trained. Cox said unions have "the largest training program, outside the [U.S.] military, in the world." And they make the work place safer. You don't have to take Cox's word for it. There's a whole host of statistical data to support his claim. And you don't have to contact labor unions to get this intel; even the Alaska Center for Public Policy (ACPP) cites peer-reviewed studies proving Cox's claims. The ACPP site explains, "Union agreements often have sections in them that extend or at least reinforce job safety and health protections for workers. In addition, these agreements frequently outline structured ways that labor and management can address potential safety and health issues so that they are mitigated before they kill or injure a worker."

Cox knows that when businesses and agencies combine union safety measures with their better trained, more dependable labor force, it saves money and time on the job.

Cox and Barnett allowed us to use their offices all afternoon. We interviewed transportation workers (Amalgamated Transit Union) and the president of the Central Utah Federation of Labor. We spoke current events with these folks but when Wayne Holland Sr. walked in the door, the topic turned to history.

The largest man-made hole in the world is in Utah. It's a copper mine. It's more than a half-mile deep and two and a half miles wide. It's a scar on the earth so massive that it's now a National Historic Landmark. And it's part of the copper mining legacy in Utah. Copper mining lured the ill-fated Joe Hill to the state, and copper mining built and disappeared cities. Wayne Holland, Sr., had come to tell us about the city of Garfield.

Garfield – like many neighboring towns – was built to house the area miners. Work force housing, a company store, and eventually movie houses and schools were built to keep the workers near the mines. Holland told us that the "supervisors lived somewhere else." Probably somewhere that had regular shops and where they had a choice of doctors. Workers went to company doctors and dentists.

Holland, a retired steel worker, told us about the Kennecott Company's decision to sell the town of Garfield in 1955 in a private land deal. The homes didn't belong to the workers, so the residents got evicted and the houses were moved to neighboring towns. When the company deemed the town less valuable then the land was worth, Kennecott displaced the inhabitants and cleared the property for sale. Poor miners found that they'd become the 20th century's tribal peoples: No more necessary to the company owners than the Native Americans had been before them. It didn't matter how long a family had called Garfield home. The town was a construct of Kennecott, and Kennecott made it and them go away.

Sammi did a great job all along our trip, but it was really in Utah that she learned to be part of the process. She sat next to us at the table when we conducted our interviews and really learned from elders like Holland how much he and others respected the workers who built this country, as well as how much they respected her – a middle school student – for wanting to keep their stories alive.

We packed up our equipment and all the gifts given to us by the AFL-CIO and went outside to rejoin Carol and the kids. Sammi was beaming. Standing on the front steps of the union hall I asked, "Where to next?" Sammi piped up, "Colorado!" And off we went.

λ λ

Chapter 35   Cowboy Cuisine
ƛ ƛƛ

After our interviews ended with the union leaders, Sammi was right: we headed straight for Colorado via Wyoming. Most of the workday was gone, but we still had plenty of daylight to roll through the northwest. The best thing about driving through that part of the country is how far the horizon stretches. And the beauty and majesty can be seen fairly well from the highway. Every now and then we stopped to take pictures and catch our breath.

Rick and Carol stayed in pretty constant contact along the way. After a few hours they arranged to meet and stop for gas. Usually the roadside stops were all fast food joints. At times it seemed the Wild West had fewer national names and more local fare. We looked across the street from our gas station to a chrome and glass building with a big sign that read "Diner." Everyone's stomach growled and we decided to grab dinner there.

Inside it was your basic run-of-the-mill diner. The kitchen filled the back half of the building. In front of the cook's counter, a dining counter wound around the inside center of the dining room. Booths to accommodate four, six, or eight people lined the inside walls of the restaurant. We grabbed the booth for eight.

The diner served breakfast all day, three kinds of cheap American beer, and – wait for it – Chinese food. Our cook and wait staff appeared to be of Asian descent and while the interior was chrome and white linoleum all around, there were pretty red and gold tasseled decorations hanging from the knobs and light switches. Most of the patrons had ten-gallon cowboy hats and boots that matched.

Half of the Smith party ordered breakfast and the rest of us ordered Chinese food. The place filled up while we waited for our food and by the time we started eating we learned why. Our meals tasted yummy and despite the disparate décor and unexpected cultural experience, it turned out that the Wild West harbored some fine Asian cuisine.

I wanted to ask our hostess if her family had been in the U.S. long. Many of the Asian workers who came to the U.S. no doubt had four or five generations after them who are now living here. If tens of thousands of Chinese workers came to build the railroads backing the 19th century, then there should have been hundreds of thousands of their ethnic Chinese descendants in the west by now. Somehow, without these people knowing I was doing a book on the folks who built the U.S., it felt awkward to start asking them how long their families had been around the region. I decided just to relax and enjoy the stir-fry. So that's what I did. It was delicious.

After dinner we got back on the road and drove until a little after dark. Along the way, we passed markers that commemorated the pioneers and the settlers' wagons that went west. Not much – often nothing – was said at these sites about the Native Americans who had been removed from the region. It was striking as we crossed the vast expanse of the U.S. countryside that there's still so much sparsely populated terrain. If the descendants of Western Europe had to push west, there sure seemed to be enough room for everyone: the original inhabitants and the new ones. Removing the Indians couldn't have been about space. The Indian Wars, genocide, removal and relocation of the Natives came about because of racism and clearly not because of limited terrain or diminishing resources. Even today with more than 350 million people in the U.S., there's still plenty of room.

𓃭 𓃭 𓃭

Chapter 36 The American Nightmare

Author James Truslow Adams coined the phrase, "The American Dream," in 1931. His book, *The Epic of America*, describes it as "That dream of a land in which life should be better and richer and fuller for every man, with opportunity for each according to his ability or achievement."

No history of the middle class would be complete without mention of the people who were systematically denied the opportunity for better, richer, fuller lives. In fact, the centuries of U.S. history include people thrust into worse lives than those into which they were born. The enslaved Africans built the infrastructure for much of the U.S. on land ripped out from underneath the native tribes that had lived in North America for millennia.

Throughout the 17th, 18th and 19th centuries, the wealth class cashed in on the labor and property of the underclasses. When poor workers fought for and achieved a share of the wealth, they likewise benefitted from the stolen labor and land of those who went before them.

In a 2013 display, the History Colorado Center in Denver remembered the Sand Creek Massacre, one of the countless epic moments in U.S. history that removed the Natives from their land. Colorado State Historian and Director of Exhibits and Interpretation for the History Colorado Center, William Convery, knows that Sand Creek is an uncommon occurrence, not because butchering Natives was unique, but because handwritten eyewitness accounts resurfaced in 2000. Gruesome letters written by two soldiers in Colorado's 1st regiment detail the butchery they witnessed but felt powerless to stop.

Lieutenants Joseph Cramer and Silas Soule wrote to Maj. General Edward Wynkoop in protest of the massacre and in hopes that they might convince the U.S. Army not to promote Colonel John Chivington, the architect of the slaughter. During the attack Cramer and Soule both collected their troops away from the carnage and ordered them not to fire.

On November 29, 1864, within days of trading with the Arapaho Indians at Sand Creek, Chivington took 700 soldiers to the banks of the river and together the Colorado 1st and 3rd regiments – sans Cramer and Soule's men – killed approximately 200 Natives. These U.S. soldiers exterminated mostly women, children and elders. The National Park Service details the operation, "Using small arms and howitzer fire, the troops drove the people out of their camp. While many managed to escape the initial onslaught, others, particularly noncombatant women, children, and the elderly fled into and up the bottom of the dry streambed. The soldiers followed, shooting at them as they struggled through the sandy earth. At a point several hundred yards above the village, the women and children frantically excavated pits and trenches along either side of the streambed to protect themselves."

Once the women and children collected along the streambed, the howitzers were again trained on them and fired.

Gruesome details of the eight-hour slaughter recounted by Cramer and Soule so horrified their Washington higher-ups that hearings were convened to examine the details of the unprovoked attack on the friendly tribe. Even after Cheyenne Chief Black Kettle raised both the U.S. and white flags, the slaughter ensued.

Chivington and his men so violently savaged their victims that moms killed their children and then killed themselves rather than be tortured by the soldiers. After the butchery ended the soldiers doubled back and further mutilated the corpses, taking body parts for trophies. These trophies became evidence in the hearings held by the military and the U.S. Congress Joint Committee on the Conduct of War.

Chivington lied to the congressional committee convened to examine the massacre. Even with brave testimony by eyewitnesses like Soule – who was assassinated a few days after giving his testimony – Chivington and his men went unpunished.

Some soldiers went on to powerful positions in the military and other branches of the government. Jacob Downing participated in the massacre and later "provided legal counsel in the defense of Colonel Chivington during the military inquest." He went on to serve as probate judge over the Arapaho lands and amassed 2000 acres of property in the Denver area, property that – of course – once belonged to the Natives.

According to the National Park Service, in 1911, after Downing died, his widow donated one of the scalps he took at the Sand Creek Massacre to the Colorado Historical Society.

After Sand Creek the relationship between the tribal peoples and the U.S. expansionists continued to deteriorate. Eventually the Battle of Little Big Horn was fought as revenge for the Euro-Americans' assault on the native peoples of the desert southwest in general and Sand Creek in particular.

The North American Native Tribes never had a chance at "The American Dream." If anything, they were perceived as obstacles to the opportunity, freedom and wealth many professed as their impetus to immigrate to this new land.

The Sand Creek display at the Colorado History Center closed two months after opening because of protests by decedents of the Native Americans who survived the raid. The National Park Service website describes the Sand Creek massacre as something that happened in the "presence of two historically discordant cultures within a geographical area that both coveted for disparate reasons." The site goes on to say that it was, "an avoidable situation that resulted in tragedy."

The prevailing history knowledge deficit among Americans is a result of this sort of white wash. The Native People didn't "covet" the land. They lived on it for thousands of years.

And it's this sort of demurring of the facts that caused the survivors of the massacre to demand the History Colorado Center close the exhibit. Stephen Paulson in his Associated Press article quotes Dale Hamilton, a descendent of Chief Sand Hill a survivor of the inhuman attack. Paulson writes, "Tribal historians found some dates were wrong, excerpts from letters left out crucial details, and the exhibit attempted to explain American Indian-white settler conflicts as a 'collision of cultures,' said Hamilton, who lives in Concho, Okla., with Cheyenne and Southern Arapahoe tribes. 'This wasn't a clash of cultures,' he said. 'This was a straight-up massacre. All we are looking for is respect for our relatives who were murdered.'"

If Hamilton bristles at the use of the term "collision of cultures," one can only imagine what he feels when he reads the National Park webpage claiming "two discordant cultures… coveted" the same land.

Many theories exist for why the truth is sugar-coated when the stories to be told involve the U.S. Military and their various unfortunate victims. In the case of Native Americans, precedence has been set for reparations due descendants of the survivors. Perhaps it's just shame, or incredulity, or gentility that bars historians and laypersons from discussing the brutal carnage that has ensued under the cover of the Stars and Stripes.

But as long as the pretense is kept that brutal slaughters in Colorado, or Vietnam, or Iraq occur simply because cultures clash, there is no hope that justice will be served or the ruthless conduct will stop.

And if the sole motivation for rewriting history so that it is less egregious, less racist, less greedy, is so that 21st century U.S. tax payers won't be hit up for the cost of reparations, the afflicted are denied not only entre to the middle class, but the "dream of a land in which life should be better and richer and fuller for every man, with opportunity for each according to his ability or achievement" as well.

Chapter 37   Massacres R U$
᛬λ

Sitting next to Rick and interviewing William Convery, the Colorado State Historian, reminded me of a free association exercise. Rick rifled off catch phrases and insider comments about historic moments in Colorado labor history and Convery caught every wild pass and tossed the answers back with the correct reference point. About every five minutes I'd jump into the interview and make one of them explain what they were talking about for the rest of us in and out of radio land.

The History Colorado Center, where Convery works, had just closed the Sand Creek exhibit because the Native descendants of the massacre survivors didn't care for the soft-pedaling given to the events of November 29, 1864. Perhaps massacres in general are taken too lightly. When it comes to Colorado history, there's no shortage of massacres. Even current events are laced with slaughter. Could Colorado have become immune to their horror?

The night before we met with Convery I took a break from the People's Tour to have dinner with my niece, Casey LaMarche, and her fiancée, Cori. They picked me up at our Aurora campground. As we drove out of the dusty, dry, treeless park, I asked if they knew where the multiplex was. They did and we went there first.

Sitting in the car at the scene of the 2012 shootings that killed 12 and injured 58, my mind reeled as I watched people come and go from the movie theater. It shocked me that the theater had gone back to running films and selling popcorn. I didn't go inside, but from the outside there was no mention of the massacre. No memorial to the lost souls. Nada. Zip. Zilch. Nothing. When Rick and I joined Convery the next day, and he started talking about Colorado history, I got this feeling that massacres got processed and put away in the minds of Coloradoans and correspondingly in the minds of all Americans.

When the massacres get put away, the lessons get lost. In the time between the Century movie theater shootings and the People's Tour a year later, *USA Today* reported, "23 mass killings in 19 states have taken the lives of 126 people." In April of 2013 a *Washington Post/ABC News* poll revealed that 90% of Americans wanted expanded background checks for firearms sales and yet congress did nothing, just as congress did nothing after the Sand Creek Massacre. They held a few hearings, no one was punished and the military went back to killing Natives.

No one should be surprised that the descendants want the truth told. No one should be surprised that the descendants are outraged. No one should forget the origins of the United States. No one should forget the sacrifices forced on the nation's original inhabitants. No one should be watching movies at the Century movie theater like nothing ever happened.

Slaughter and its subsequent acceptance as "normal" paves the way for more carnage. Schools, museums and history books whitewashing or ignoring massacres just makes the next mass killing a whole lot easier for the killers.

Random 21st century killings seem senseless. Everyone asks why and nobody knows. Still, special interests – particularly the gun lobby – work diligently to make sure that the next mass shooting is possible. And they do so out of greed. More gun sales, more bullet sales, more fifty round clip sales, weapon manufacturers clean up after a murderous rampage.

In the case of Sand Creek, the reason for the massacre was just as senseless as the movie house shooting. Crazed bloodthirsty fiends– disguised as military men with ethics – tortured and murdered unsuspecting and unarmed innocents. But special interests – whether it was the railroad robber barons, the copper mine and coal mine owners, or just the westward expansionists – relied on preserving government policies that assured the killings would continue.

And just as the Natives were annihilated to take their land, subsequent massacre victims throughout 19th and 20th century Colorado history were slaughtered to steal their labor and to keep the workers who came after them in line.

Convery and Rick went back and forth talking about Columbine, Cripple Creek, and of course, Ludlow. Consistent with current trends, when folks familiar with relatively recent events think of Columbine, they think of a different massacre. But the shootings at Columbine High School in Littleton, Colorado on April 20, 1999, while horrifying, are not the first mass murders to take place under that name.

Just as Colorado had angry Natives who'd started out peaceful, it had angry workers who started out simply grateful for a job. The robber barons abused Colorado workers and eventually the workers struck for better wages, better working conditions, and a better way of life.

This story of struggle against oppression played out over and over again. As libcom.org explains it in an article written about the Columbine Mine Massacre, "For the fifty years prior to 1927, the struggles in the Colorado mines had been a flashpoint for labour relations throughout the mining industry and had been marked by many strikes, aborted uprisings and confrontations between miners and mine owners, and the state militia."

In our interviews with Convery, we examined three assaults on workers, the Columbine Mine Massacre's the most recent. Because of its modernity, photographs of the murdered miners are available at the University of Washington website. Looking at a photo of Rene Jacques' lifeless body laid out on his couch graphically demonstrates the brutality of the mine owners and the government agencies that did their bidding.

Even as far back as 1914, transcripts of correspondence between mine owner, John D. Rockefeller, Jr., the striking miners, and the federal mediators were preserved for modern history students to read and learn about the Ludlow Massacre. How Rockefeller could have missed the point as illustrated by the federal mediator boggles the mind. Ethelbert Stewart admonished Rockefeller with comments made in April of 1913, a year before Rockefeller's company, Colorado Fuel and Iron, entreated then Governor, Elias Ammons, to furnish National Guard troops who – along with company guards – murdered two women and eleven children.

> "Theoretically, perhaps, the case of having nothing to do in this world but work, ought to have made these men of many tongues, as happy and contented as the managers claim ... To have a house assigned you to live in ... to have a store furnished you by your employer where you are to buy of him such foodstuffs as he has, at a price he fixes ... to have churches, schools ... and public halls free for you to use for any purpose except to discuss politics, religion, trade-unionism or industrial conditions; in other words, to have everything handed down to you from the top; to be ... prohibited from having any thought, voice or care in anything in life but work, and to be assisted in this by gunmen whose function it was, principally, to see that you did not talk labor conditions with another man who might accidentally know your language -- this was the contented, happy, prosperous condition out of which this strike grew ... That men have rebelled grows out of the fact that they are men."

Perhaps Rockefeller and Ammons were mindful of the circumstances that had transpired ten years earlier – in 1904 – at Cripple Creek. There the striking miners – out gunned once Governor Peabody mobilized the National Guard – hired a thug, Harry Orchard, to blow up the train station. Orchard's bomb killed 13 company strikebreakers and public sentiment turned against the workers.

Over the decades, when miners killed workers, things went poorly for the union cause. But when the militia, National Guard, or company thugs killed miners, they got away with it.

Striking miners, under the leadership of Bill Hayward – the same man Joe Hill sent his "don't mourn, organize" telegram to just prior to his execution – petitioned the courts for justice, invoking their constitutional rights. The judge hearing their case responded, "To hell with the Constitution; we're not following the Constitution!" After these sorts of rulings, the miners sought even more radical leadership. They felt they had no other choice. Convery agreed, "Companies 100 years ago could basically use the National Guard as their mercenaries." Convery elaborated, "The National guard was getting two paychecks. One from the National Guard, the other from the mine owners."

Convery told us that the same Judge Bell who threw out the Constitution also remarked, "To hell with habeas corpus, I'll give them post mortems instead."

Labor journals like the *International Woodworker* printed first hand accounts of brutality against the workers. They detailed violent attacks by guards and National Guardsmen as well as violent attacks by miners against each other.

Convery emphasized the companies' practice of hiring foreign immigrants so that workers wouldn't be able to communicate, form alliances, and organize. Mine management took advantage of racism as well.

In a Wyoming diner I had toyed with the idea of asking our hosts if they were descended from the Chinese who came to the United States to build the railroads. Convery spoke of the Chinese Exclusion Act that not only eliminated Asian immigration but encouraged deportation and annihilation of the Chinese Americans who were here already. Because of this racist legislation the number of Chinese Americans in the U.S. was cut in half by the early part of the 20th century.

Three years after the Chinese Exclusion Act was passed, in 1885, in what is now Rock Springs, Wyoming, a riot broke out over wage differences between Chinese-American miners and Euro-American miners. The ethnically Chinese miners were – of course – paid less and therefore preferred by the Union Pacific Coal Company. When the fighting was through, 28 Chinese miners were dead and most of their homes had been burned.

When Rick and I started the interview with Convery, Rick quoted – as he often does on the show – Jay Gould. Gould is credited with saying, "I can hire one half the working class to kill the other half."

Studying Colorado history – whether it's the Native American massacres, or the working class massacres – bloodthirsty murder-for-hire has been pretty common for centuries.

Following our interview with Convery, we packed our things up and prepared to head east. Before we did though, we drove south a few hours hoping to get to the site of the Ludlow massacre. By the time we'd gone a hundred or so miles down the road, we realized we'd get there too late. Brett had hooked us up with a local community organizer, so we went to see him instead.

We chatted with retired steel worker, Al Becco. We asked him about Ludlow. We asked him about the women and children suffocating under their burning tents in holes they'd dug to escape the bullets fired by their own National Guard. Becco replied, "Ludlow made a lot of things easier [for me] in my lifetime."

Appreciating the price paid for all of us: Becco thinks that's one of the only things we can do now about all the carnage that went on before, on the plains and in the mine towns. The other thing Becco told us that we need to do – as we stood surrounded by his political signs and memorabilia mingled with the rest of his home décor – "We've got to keep bitchin'." Becco thinks it's too easy to let all that was gained through the sacrifices of the past slip away if we don't keep talking about what's at stake.

𝈎 𝈎𝈎

Chapter 38 Have You Seen What You're Driving?

We drove out of southern Colorado, none too soon. Colorado's got some breath-taking scenery, but the history is pretty daunting. I needed to decompress. We'd gotten as far south as Pueblo before we realized we'd be way too late to visit the Ludlow Massacre site. So we just turned east and headed for Kansas.

By this point we had more than 8000 miles under our wheels and I'd lost track of just about everything else and everybody else. I committed myself to keeping track of where I was and what I was doing. Carol and the A's had taken off for an adventure in Colorado but I had no idea where they'd gone or what they were doing.

Rick drove with Sammi up front in the passenger seat while Brett and I worked on the show in the back. He edited interviews and I logged my notes. Rick asked me to find a place to stay, so I started searching for campgrounds along route 70. We had no chance of getting all the way to Kansas City so I hunted for a place that would put some distance behind us, but allow us to get settled by midnight.

"Hey," I shouted to Rick, "Did you know we go right through Abilene?" He did. I told him that we'd be there in about seven hours and I really wanted to stay there. That made no sense to him. "Suit yourself," he said. "Why Abilene?" I told him that President Eisenhower's home and library were there. I said I would call first thing in the morning and see if we could hook up with the archivist like we had at Governor Bush's Presidential Library.

Rick didn't think we'd get much traction with so little notice. But in his usual "whatever trips your trigger" kind of way, he just said handed me the credit card and told me to get a place. The campground I found was a half-mile walk from the Eisenhower Library. I was psyched.

We hummed along through Kansas and Rick judiciously kept the RV going 75 miles per hour. That's the speed limit on that long flat road. Ike would no doubt have been proud of his highway system. 41,000 miles of interstate roads were built under his leadership through the Federal-Aid Highway Act of 1956. The president famously remarked that his new American highways would use "enough concrete to build six sidewalks to the moon."

RV travel changes the perspective of the traveler. The campers sit up high and the large windows allow better views and a lot more light to come into the cabin. When it's sunny, there's more sunlight. When it's dark out, more ambient street light gets into the living area. And when you're being chased by a police officer, there's way more blue light.

When the blue lights got close enough to fill the camper, Sammi screamed a little girl scream, popped off her seat belt, jumped out of the cockpit and ran to the back of the RV.

Rick slowed down along the side of the road and came to a stop on the shoulder. Sitting at the kitchen table I had a clear view of the Kansas Highway Patrolman.

Rick rolled down the window and the officer asked him, "Where were you?"

"Pueblo," Rick replied.

"Where are you going?" the officer asked.

"Abilene," Rick answered.

Brett and I looked at each other with pretty blank stares on our faces. We had no idea why we'd been pulled over and questioned.

The patrolman inquired further with several questions at once, "So, you have friends in Pueblo? Friends in Abilene, in Kansas? How many are in the RV?"

Rick said that we knew people in Pueblo but not Abilene, and that were four people in the RV. The officer walked back and looked in the windows at us. I was frantically taking notes – which is why I have the exact exchange written down.

The patrolman one again approached Rick's window and this time he asked for the registration. Rick got a little more loquacious at that point and told the young man that he had rented the RV. The officer asked, "Do you have the rental agreement?" Rick did and he handed it to him.

I sardonically wrote across the top of my note pad so that Brett could read it, "They must be looking for someone who stole an RV."

Finally the officer told Rick that his tail light was out and that he needed to get it fixed. I guess we looked like an unlikely family – or maybe it was because we were all wearing the same bright blue shirt that read *The People's Tour for America* with a giant solidarity fist on the front – but the officer asked what purpose we had traveling on the road. Rick explained that he was the host of a radio show.

Suddenly very interested, the patrolman asked, "What kind of radio show?" Rick told him it was a talk show. "What kind of talk radio show do you do?" Rick told him it was "labor based."

The officer seemed satisfied with that final answer and handed Rick back his paperwork. He told him to take it easy and, "slow down." Rick commented back with a confused tone, "But 75 is the speed limit." The patrolman had turned to walk away, but then he turned back and said, "Buddy, have you seen what you're driving?"

We got back on the road and after a few minutes Sammi climbed back into the front seat. About five minutes later we all started talking at once. We laughed, especially at the question, "Buddy, have you seen what you're driving?" Rick's an old Teamster; driving a 30-foot RV through Kansas at 75 mph was child's play.

Chapter 39 I Like Ike
ƛ ƛ

Of all the places we went that we didn't expect to end up, Abilene, Kansas was my favorite. The weather got hot early, the morning after we arrived. I walked downtown, scoping out the Eisenhower library and looking for a convenience store. I found a delightful little place with great coffee. I sat at the counter enjoying the luxury of so much ready-made and easily available caffeine. I had two cups. Then I slowly walked back to our campground. For the first time in a week or more, we weren't in a rush.

Before I'd left on my walk, I'd called the press contact for the library, Samantha Kenner, and she said she'd see if the Deputy Director of the Archives might have some time to talk with us later that day. As I returned to the RV, she called back and said that Tim Rives could see us after lunch.

Everyone got excited, especially the kids. We had about three hours to kill and the campground had a great little swimming pool. Sammi, Alex, Aly and I put on our suits and went to play in the pool. The old lady that ran the place let us use all her floating toys and pool chairs.

The easygoing morning gave me time to think about Eisenhower and compare him in my mind with his successors. I remembered a time when Ike – as an adoring nation called him – seemed conservative to me. But a lot had changed in the United States since then and a lot of presidents had left their mark on the nation's historical perspective.

Having a president is like having a baby. You really need to forget about the pain of the last experience before you can get too excited about having a new one. The pain of Pres. Eisenhower's time in office – more than 50 years ago – has faded into the past, so his great accomplishments really grab the spotlight now.

At his archives, we didn't focus on his conservatism. We pretty much ignored the McCarthy era, the red scare, or his ill-conceived cold war strategies in Asia. We didn't spend a lot of time talking about Pres. Eisenhower's negotiated peace in Korea, which – 60 years later – remains a drain on the U.S. military, the U.S. economy, and a potential threat to global peace. We didn't even talk about Vietnam and Pres. Eisenhower's insistence on separately recognizing both northern and southern leadership. There was no discussion of botched regime change in Iran, or Guatemala, or his increased emphasis on nuclear weaponry and the expanded role of the CIA.

Instead – just like gestational labor and delivery – we focused on the person that emerged, not the pain it took getting him to that point. I tried to remind myself of this as I stood in Eisenhower's boyhood home. It was really too late to blame him for his flaws, and a great time to celebrate his accomplishments.

This wasn't the first time I'd been at an Eisenhower residence. A Civil War buff, I'd been outside his retirement home in Gettysburg. I knew about as much about Dwight D. Eisenhower from that as I know about George W. Bush from living in Maine. I'd seen 43's summerhouse a dozen times. It's at Walker's Point in Kennebunkport. Eisenhower's childhood home – as well as his retirement place – appeared as though they'd have fit in the Walker's Point garage.

We walked through the Abilene house, which is completely intact, including the original furnishings. Ida Eisenhower's estate gave the home to the Eisenhower Foundation when she died. Ida and David raised Pres. Eisenhower and his six brothers using the salary David earned working 12 hours a day, seven days a week, as an engineer at the local creamery. In the years after her famous son served as president, Ida's neighborhood disappeared. Now, the home sits in the center of what has become the library compound. The one-time residential neighborhood now looks like a public park with few of the original buildings left.

Eisenhower's old grammar school was moved to the library grounds and houses the museum gift shop. It sits across the way from the Eisenhower meditation center where the President, his first lady, Mamie, and their son Doud Dwight are buried.

Doud's grave reminds visitors of the time from which the Eisenhowers came. Ike and Mamie's firstborn died in 1921 of scarlet fever. Eleven years after the three-year-old died, Alexander Flemming would construct Penicillin and save countless millions of children from dying a similar death.

Growing up, Ike's family didn't have much but his mom, Ida, loved music. In 1883 a family member of Ida's died and she inherited $1000, $600 of which she spent on a piano. That piano, covered with Ida's pictures of the Eisenhower boys, is on display in the presidential home on the campus of the presidential library.

These humble beginnings contrast markedly with Bush's wealthy entitled background. The dissimilarity is just one of the more glaring differences evidenced at their respective presidential libraries. 43's braggart display extolling his Harvard Master's degree in Business Administration (MBA) inadvertently emphasizes the difference in their respective family incomes. We learned from the historic interpreter at Ike's home that Eisenhower attended the United States Military Academy at West Point because "The Eisenhowers couldn't afford college educations. President Eisenhower wanted to go to West Point because it was free."

Historians can only speculate about how different the modern world would be if General Eisenhower had not pursued a military career. It's doubtful any contemplate even minor global differences had 43 not gotten an MBA.

The contrasts in the two presidential museums – like those of the two men's homes and educations – are stark. Ike's library showcases the table upon which the Invasion of Normandy was planned. 43's has an interactive game that attempts to explain away how tough his job was as the "decider."

One of Eisenhower's more famous quotations explains how he might have answered the same questions put before 43 if Ike had been the "decider" at the time – for example, whether he would have preemptively struck at Iraq – "Preemptive war was an invention of Hitler. Frankly, I would not even listen to anyone seriously that came and talked about such a thing."

And 43's words – for anyone who might forget – "As a matter of common sense and self-defense, America will act against any emerging threats before they are fully formed."

Fifty years before 43 "shocked" and "awed" the people of a sovereign nation, Ike rejected the concept that reigning death and disaster on a prospective foe – as well as your own soldiers – made any kind of sense. He certainly would not have labeled it common sense. "After my experience I have come to hate war. War settles nothing." Additionally, the assumption that an emerging threat was a fait accompli made no sense to the 34th president and he recommended, "When people speak to you about a preventive war, you tell them to go and fight it."

Millions of Americans took to the streets to tell 43 just that. These protests were absent from 43's museum. Also absent from the George W. Bush library were the shrines to 43's National Guard service in Alabama during the Vietnam War. Presuming he would have cared about the devastation caused by armed conflict, 43 didn't know what Ike knew about war because when war broke out, he turned from it and hid until his time in the military was finished.

The divergent philosophies of the Ike presidency and the 43 presidency might be a direct reflection of what it took to get them there. After World War II ended, General Eisenhower went on to become the first Chairman of the Joint Chiefs of

Staff and the first commander of the North Atlantic Treaty Organization (NATO). He received the republican nomination in August of 1952 but refused to start campaigning until after Labor Day.

43 held dinners to reward the donors who raised contributions totaling $100,000 to $200,000 each. His campaigns cost hundreds of millions of dollars and many have alleged that even after the campaign, his presidency consisted of doing the bidding of those big donors. While President Obama fundraising totals have since shattered 43's records, the same allegations of buying and selling influence are made. These assertions were not made of Ike, who publicly decried fundraising.

Oh, and one other difference between the two men also has to do with money. While there was donor recognition, there was no "freedom wall" in Ike's museum – unless you count the physical walls that hold the artifacts of a free society – but none of them had names of contributors on them. Eisenhower's family gave their home to his library. Special interests built Gov. Bush's library. We still don't know the size of the contributions required to land one's name on the "freedom wall."

Chapter 40 The Myth of Henry Ford
ʎ ʎʎ

It's no real surprise that Aldous Huxley, in his epic dystopian novel, *Brave New World*, made Henry Ford a deity. Thanks to greedy consumerists like Ford, Huxley predicted a future that swapped out voracity for benevolence: in a land where the ends invariably justified the means. Sadly, no one thinks of Huxley's 1932 cautionary tale after his or her own sophomore year in high school when the summer reading assignment has ended. Consequently Ford's legacy has become that of "American dream builder" instead of the more accurate "exploiter of humanity for his own selfish gain."

A 2012 *Forbes Magazine* article about industrialist Henry Ford and his infamous $5 a day wage debunks the notion that Ford gave his workers handsome wages so that they could afford to buy one of his cars.

Interestingly – but not surprisingly – the intent of the article is to trash the concept of increasing the minimum wage. For this they accurately portray Ford as a man who capitalized on the extremely low wages paid to workers at the time. In fact, Ford didn't have to be a decent employer. He could manipulate workers just by paying them more. Of course, if the minimum wage had been $5 at the time, Ford Motor Company's sweatshop jobs would have been no more attractive than any other employment and far less attractive than the vast majority of jobs.

Article author Tim Worstall finds the notion that Ford wanted all his workers to be able to buy Ford motorcars as laughable as the idea that aerospace manufacturers would look to their employees to make sales. Worstall writes, "It should be obvious that this story doesn't work: Boeing would most certainly be in trouble if they had to pay their workers sufficient to afford a new jetliner."

No, Worstall goes on to explain that Ford just wanted to be able to beat out the competition on labor and save a few bucks on the high cost of training workers who would inevitably tire of the working conditions in the Ford plant. Seems a Ford assembly worker cost about a hundred bucks to train and a $2.25 worker who packed up and moved on for greener pastures after a month and a half in the sweltering plant cost Henry Ford money. Pay the guys $5 a day and they'd think twice before giving up on the detestable job they had to do every day.

Most folks think they understand the work done by Ford employees in the early 20th century. Ford revolutionized auto-making with his state of the art assembly lines. He innovated in other ways that helped make his business profitable. We learned about the early practices employed by Ford Motor Company when we stopped to visit some of the retired workers who had put their time in at the Winchester Assembly Plant in Kansas City, Missouri. Winchester was the very first Ford assembly plant outside of Detroit.

The plant's huge! Founded in 1909, the plant grew until it housed 18.5 acres of assembly space under one roof. Local labor historian, Phil Brown, sat down with us during our People's Tour and outlined the history of the Winchester plant. He also gave us a copy of the history book he wrote on the subject. Brown's history book is a quick 35 page read that juxtaposes Henry Ford's greed against the way he neglected the needs of his workers.

Not a word of Brown's history disagrees with the 21st century *Forbes* opine that Henry Ford needed men who could work long enough to pay for their training. But after that, Brown goes further, pointing out that the workers would be worn out and easily discarded. Some men tried to push back against the lousy treatment. New men desperate for work readily replaced exhausted, injured, or assertive workers. A man with a big mouth for labor rights was as big a problem – or bigger – on the assembly line, as was a man who physically couldn't keep the pace.

Brown writes, "In January of 1914 Ford Motor Company Board of Directors met to discuss plans and policies for the next year... The directors dared Henry Ford to raise daily wages until they reached $5 a day." The board voted that half the profit they expected to make in 1915 should go to pay for the wage increase. The young company was already so profitable that $5 million was freed up for additional wages while $5 million more went straight to the company bottom line.

Worker availability was key to profitability. The Ford plant would shut down regularly. Bad wages in the local community and a depressed economy helped the Winchester plant operate. Whenever the plant shut down, the workers remained desperate to return. New models would require re-fitting the factory and during these times, workers could go for months without pay.

Employees didn't all make the full $5 a day, either. That was a sum they aspired to and even if they worked hard enough to make it, management often refused to pay the full amount based on the employees personal habits. If the company thought the worker behaved inappropriately on or off the clock, workers would be docked pay. Henry Ford's management team decided if the worker drank too much or lived in an unsavory manner. Wives couldn't work outside the home and a family couldn't have a male boarder or the Winchester employee was considered unfit and Ford lowered his wages.

A scrutinized home-life paled in comparison to the torturous working conditions at the plant. In its first few decades of operation, employees were abused by the working conditions at the plant. Men were not paid for a day's work. They were paid for 480 minutes working. If the conveyer stopped, the time clock stopped. If the plant shut down, the workers were released indefinitely. They didn't know when they'd get called back, so they just waited. If the conveyer didn't come back on they weren't compensated for the wait time. They had no sick pay. There was no ventilation, they got no toilet breaks and had to eat lunch while standing at their workstation. According to Brown, Ford didn't think 15 minutes was long enough to sit down and enjoy a meal so he provided no benches and insisted they eat where they stood along the assembly line.

Management constantly reminded the employees that somebody outside desperately wanted their job. Brown explains, "Often a new employee was taken to a window facing the park across the street from the plant and told; that there were plenty of men to take his place if he couldn't keep up the pace."

Workers who disliked the way they were treated often got dismissed for "fighting" with their supervisors. Once the workers were labeled combative and dismissed, they often left pretty bruised. Often the fired men were beaten bloody during the alleged altercation with management. These beatings – these fights allegedly picked by the abused worker – grew more common as workers attempted to organize.

Between 1909 and 1937 working conditions precipitated action. Had it not been for the Great Depression, workers might not have been so patient.

Eventually labor had to acknowledge the massive rip off they were experiencing. The workers had so little power over their own productivity that the line was sped up and additional cars were produced. The workers didn't know that they were actually making extra cars and subsequently the company stockpiled the surplus. With too many cars in stock, Ford used the excess inventory as an excuse to lay off workers. They were not rehired until the supply dwindled. For decades some workers suspected that they had been hurried into producing more vehicles than the company had agreed to pay them to make. Again Brown explains, "Line speed was set to run 536 units in 480 minutes. Some two hundred to three hundred extra units were produced each week and placed in an area known as a kitty. These units were later shipped to dealers which resulted in production being suspended for days, weeks, and sometimes months."

Nothing would get better for Winchester workers or any Ford plant workers until Henry Ford's opinion of the worker improved. And Henry Ford – not a man to change his mind – long contended that workers had no right to bargain for themselves or tell him how to run his company. Brown writes,

> "Henry Ford's policy on labor was that it was an expendable resource that could be used, and then disposed of, when it [sic] became ill or injured. There were no means of air circulation for lack of fans. No protective equipment was furnished to the men working in hazardous production areas, i.e. solder grinding and the paint department. No relief men were available to relieve the men for bathroom calls. The company's position was: if the men were too sick to work from lead poisoning or were injured on the job they were laid off and never recalled."

In the 1930's – thanks to the great depression – the U.S. was nowhere to be looking for a job. In 1937 – the year the Winchester workers fought back – 6.9 million people remained unemployed. In light of the workforce glut, the Winchester plant's deplorable conditions persisted and what Brown refers to as "The Ford Terror" tormented anyone who agitated for better wages and bargaining fairness. Ford had spies among the workers and Ford "thugs" physically abused men who attempted to organize the plant.

Still, on April 2, 1937, the Winchester Plant organizers called a sit down strike. Brown details how the strike happened: "Each key union member in each department pulled the fuses that ran the production lines. They announced to the workers that they were on a sit down strike. Of the 2176 hourly employees, seventy percent took part in the sit down."

Workers protected one another from company henchmen, shared what food they had, and the doors to the plant were welded shut. The following day an agreement was struck between UAW-CIO's Ed Hall and John Gillespie of Ford Motor Company. They verbally agreed that:

- "No worker would be fired for taking part in the sit down strike.
- Layoffs would be by plant wide seniority.
- Job security and [sic] working conditions would be corrected.
- Disputes that could not be [sic] settled within the department would be taken to the plant committee and the superintendent of the plant for settlement."

The workers left the plant victorious and conditions changed for the better after the strike. But the company wasn't done fighting. Henry Ford refused to acknowledge the post sit down strike agreement and he – instead – instituted a company union. Ford encourage workers to "organize" under company management and were expected to turn away from the UAW-CIO who had pushed back so effectively on their behalf.

When the Winchester Plant re-opened after the 1937 closure to refit for a new model, no one could get their job back unless they joined the company union, the Independent Union of Ford Workers (IUFW). Understandably they did not call it the Ford Union (FU), although – clearly – those initials would have been more appropriate.

Luckily for the workers and for working class rights, the Wagner Labor Relations Act had passed congress and been signed into law in the Fall of 1936. Brown describes that act, writing that it "gave any worker in the United States the right to belong to any legally defined union of his choosing without fear of discrimination by any company or company official." Of course – thankfully – the act applied to women as well. Many female factory workers toiled in other industries under equally bleak conditions.

Charges were levied against the Ford Motor Company. Over the course of the next four years, as workers fighting for their rights were locked out of their jobs, an intense legal battle ensued. Workers clashed with replacement workers and eventually many of the so-called scabs were convinced to join on the side of the UAW.

The Ford Motor Company finally lost to organized labor. Workers had safe and dependable jobs and the Ford Motor Company Winchester plant flourished.

The battle for workers' rights at Ford did not end with the wins in Kansas City. The People's tour would make one more stop at a site of worker protests against Ford Motor Company. Within a few days we'd visit the Ford Dearborn, Michigan location and add more details to the story of labor's struggle to make a selfish exploitative capitalist into a decent man. Because of labor's efforts – not in spite of them – Ford became an American manufacturing icon. As Huxley observed in 1932 – before organized labor forced Henry Ford to treat his workers humanely – hero status was something the robber baron, Henry Ford, would never have achieved on his own.

λ

Chapter 41 Fighting for Today's Low Wage Workers

As we left the union hall and headed downtown to sample a little Kansas City barbecue – we did, after all, have to put it up against Memphis and see how it faired – I glanced down at a pile of photocopied papers entitled, "Indoor Distribution Instructions."

I grabbed a flyer and read more closely. This paper had ten short guidelines on how to agitate for better pay and working conditions inside the world's largest employer, Wal*Mart.

In 2013, Forbes magazine rounded the number of Wal*Mart employees to 1.4 million in the United States alone. An MSNBC story the year before details a leaked memo enumerating the average worker's pay scale: "The document [PDF], first obtained by the *Huffington Post*, shows that Walmart workers can earn a base pay as low as $8.00, and earn wage increases in increments as low as 20 or 40 cents. *As a result, a 'solid performer' who starts at Walmart as a cart pusher making $8 an hour and receives one promotion, about the average rate, can expect to make $10.60 after working at the company for 6 years.*"

A million or so workers earning ten bucks an hour certainly accounts for low prices at the power retailer. Still, low wages aren't necessary for low prices. CEO Michael Duke makes more in an hour than one of his new employees will make in a year. Duke's compensation (I can not bring myself to call them earnings) is $35 million each year: that's $16,826.92 per hour, and that was way back in 2010. I didn't have the stomach to dig long enough on the internet for more recent totals.

All this cheap skating – I'll call it Henry Fording – of how Wal*Mart treats its millions of employees puts a real drag on the U.S. taxpayer. In April of 2014, *Forbes Magazine* staff writer, Clare O'Connor, reported "Walmart workers cost taxpayers $6.2 billion in public assistance." And yeah, that's billion with a "b." If you're wondering how much that is per underpaid Wal*Mart employee, it's an average of $4415 per worker that taxpayers pay to subsidize Wal*Mart's low wages and inadequate benefits.

Just like the Kansas City organizers made Ford Motor Company a better company and a better corporate citizen, the union members who volunteer to distribute information inside the mega-business are now attempting to improve the conditions and impact that Wal*Mart has on their community.

The flyer I picked up was pretty straightforward and filled with common sense recommendations like "don't disrupt commerce" and "don't interrupt an associate when they are waiting on a customer." I was surprised that the organizers are not trespassing unless a member of management with appropriate authority tells them they are. After all, Wal*Mart makes itself a public place so that consumer can go in the store and browse whether or not they make purchases.

The flyer states, "You are not 'soliciting' under federal labor law simply by talking to workers and asking them to accept leaflets or other items." And, "you are not trespassing unless a manager with the appropriate authority orders you to leave and you refuse. If you leave when ordered, you have not trespassed. Violating a company's no-solicitation or no-distribution policy is NOT the same as violating trespassing laws. In almost every state, it is NOT trespassing in a retail store open to the public… If a manager only says you are violating a company policy, you are NOT violating trespassing law." Upper case emphasis was theirs, not mine.

That's because Wal*Mart doesn't make the nation's laws, at least not all of them, and at least not yet.

⚲ ⚲ ⚲

Chapter 42 "You Got Spunk. I Hate Spunk."
λ λλ

Ed Asner walked into his Kansas City, Kansas, June 29, 2013 press conference remarking to the reporters who had assembled waiting for him, "I'm late, don't punish me with bad words."

With that comment and every word after, the audience was spellbound. The actor – perhaps best known for his role as Lou Grant in the television series "The Mary Tyler Moore Show" – grew up in Kansas City, graduating from Wyandott High School in 1947. Members of the Wyandott High School football team waited patiently for their turn to speak to the aging alum.

Asner – a 1940's star of Wyandott's football team – took one look at one of the muscular young men assembled and blurted, "My skin turns bruised just looking at him."

Asner chuckled about how much larger and stronger the kids on the team had become over the decades, but that wasn't the only change they'd made. In the decades since Asner played football, the high school desegregated and the teams now consisted of kids Asner had never been allowed to play with or against: black kids. Asner didn't shy away from the area's segregationist past. He explained that black schools didn't play white schools when he was a kid.

Asner thought that while this was wrong, his hometown was still "a gentle place to grow up." In a country fueled by racial hatred where blacks might be lynched for offending white folks, his upbringing was different. "In Kansas there was discrimination, but there wasn't hatred."

Still, Asner doesn't defend any of it. He said in Wyandott he was "one of six Jews and there were maybe three Greeks." He explained that his family came out of the packinghouses, worked for the railroads, and certain beliefs were ingrained in him. He spoke of black housekeepers and said that he loved them "in his own way and vice versa." Asner looked at the young black athletes and said, "I feel guilty about the prejudice. How a Jew can feel prejudiced is the stupidest thing."

Asner returned to Kansas City to perform "FDR," the one-man show he's been performing since 2010. It's a benefit for the local chapter of the United Way. He also came to speak – as he often does – about weighty issues. His own upbringing is one of those issues. Asner explained, "I don't spit on my memories. In a way we're born into families and we've got to love that family. Cain and Abel exist all through history. From our initial family we have to extend it all over." Looking at the Wyandott players he continued, "You do it with your football team. We have to keep expanding that brotherhood. I had a great football coach. We had a quarterback who was a racist. My coach would have had his ass whipped if he had heard him."

Asner told the young men that he believed that society came from a broad base of different types of people and that things needed to be learned, generations like his had to build on what they had and that these young men needed to develop the way he had after he'd been exposed to his coach. Asner explained, "If we keep taking good steps we get a pyramid." But time had passed, his level of the pyramid was put in place and now, "It's not up to me. It's up to you."

He saluted the young athletes and their coach who brought them to see him. He spoke to the press about many things but he directed a few fundamental thoughts to the team. He called them his lessons from high school.

Firstly, from playing football: "Excess weight, when applied properly, can produce a dividend. It can be a good lever."

Then Asner went on to more general lessons of high school:

- There are a lot of pretty girls in the world and you can't have them all.
- Brotherhood comes from strange places. A lot of which, you wouldn't expect.
- I learned to love.
- I loved my football coach.
- I loved my journalism professor.
- I had two best friends. I will always cherish the memory of those two guys.
- I learned I wasn't such a bad guy.

For the non-Wyandott family he had a broader message, although it was a message that was no doubt shaped by the things he learned in school.

Asner proclaimed, "There is no free press. It wasn't free when I did Lou Grant and there is no free press now." Asner blames censorship and the Reagan Administration for the cancellation of his award winning *Mary Tyler Moore Show* spinoff, *Lou Grant*. "I bleed for all reporters who try to write and tell the truth and the establishment for which they work doesn't support them."

He called honest reporters "sacrificial victims to progress." He said that they "try and write the truth and too often get knocked down. The press belongs to the man who owns one."

Asner also condemned the attacks on organized labor. Asner served as president of the Screen Actors Guild from 1981 to 1985. During the June press conference, Asner called the attacks on labor "horrendous." He explained the insidious nature of the anti-union movement and its focus on the exception rather than the rule, "The non-union man becomes fascinated by the crookedness of a union and doesn't understand what a good union does or has done for him. Take away the unions and you have a dictatorship. We practically have that now."

Asner believes the message people get is too controlled by the profiteers. "This is a capitalist country. In every other [capitalist] country you have papers that represent many thoughts. Here, progressive accomplishments never get entrenched."

Lastly, Asner spoke of his support for the United Way. In 2012 Asner had been honorary chair of the local affiliate. "The United Way is a way of expressing brotherhood." He wished more tax dollars were spent the way the United Way spends money. "The government squanders trillions on the military and they don't need it." The causes the United Way supports need that money.

Asner closed with what he feels proudest about when he thinks of the United States. "It's the people it creates. It creates monsters too, but it creates the labor organizers, the teachers who give their own, the ministers and clergy, the social workers. It's the little people in America who believe in the myth of America and try to embody it."

That's why he loved *The Mary Tyler Moore Show*. Asner said it was a show "about the cities that people fly over." It was Mary Tyler Moore's vision that created the program. Because, as Asner's character pointed out in one episode, Mary Tyler Moore had "spunk." Asner's Lou chastised Mary for it chiding, "You got spunk. I hate spunk." But the real life Ed Asner doesn't hate spunk, he embodies it.

λ

Chapter 43 There Aren't Enough People Exposing the Truth
♪♫

People we'd touched base with ahead of time worked diligently to host us around the country. They worked to set up interviews and make sure we could produce at least three hours of radio about their issues or geographical region and – when they could – they'd hook us up with the historians we needed. Folks did a great job everywhere we went. But of all our local guides, Judy Ancel, Director of The Institute for Labor Studies (ILS) at the University of Missouri-Kansas City, blew us all away.

Her astounding success at hooking us up with everything we needed in a systematic fashion had to come from her own years of telling stories that need to be told. See, Ancel – probably more than anyone – understood our needs. When not teaching college students about domestic and international labor issues, Ancel co-hosts her own radio program, the "Heartland Labor Forum."

Because everything was so perfectly scheduled, because she arranged for interview space, because she mapped out our succession of events geographically to match them chronologically so we didn't have too much backtracking to do, when Ancel hooked us up with interviews AND showed us her favorite barbecue restaurant we felt pretty lucky. But after we got home and I started researching the information she shared with us about the Kansas City garment district, it became glaringly apparent just how lucky we were to have her as our guide. Without her, there simply wouldn't have been a story.

I went to the website for the Kansas City Garment Industry Museum. Clicking on the "history" icon, I found three short paragraphs explaining that the "manufacture of coats, suits, dresses, hats, and children's wear started on the upper floors of the wholesale dry goods buildings in the early 1920s."

It also boasts, "1 out of every 7 women in the U.S. purchased a garment designed and made in Kansas City. The garment manufacturing industry was the second largest employer of any industry in Kansas City." That's pretty impressive because the site also mentioned that in its hey day, it employed more than 4,000 people.

Oh, and the site also pointed out that there's a lovely park with a big needle sticking a few dozen feet into the air to commemorate the long gone garment industry. That's it!

To be fair, we didn't go in the museum, so perhaps it's more informative than the website. But, had it not been for Ancel taking the time to tour with us the five or so square blocks that made up the garment district, we would have had no sense – from the museum's history webpage or from the now gentrified region – of what it was like to work making America's clothes and what we've lost since the industry vanished.

We met Ancel on a pristine street between two beautiful brick buildings. Ancel explained that the garment district had been transformed from manufacturing hub to a region hosting nightclubs, studios, and chic loft living space.

Gone was the whir of machinery, the worker clogged factories, the largely immigrant labor force, and the International Lady Garment Workers Union (ILGWU) which organized the industry.

Ancel explained to us that clothing manufacturing in the area actually began in the 19th century – decades before the 1920's. Kansas City's clothiers made Lee Jeans, uniforms for both world wars, men's, women's and children's everyday clothing, as well as fine coats and expertly tailored suits.

Ancel explained that the workers had to organize because the employers were already organized against them. Ancel told us, "Bosses always unionize first." If a worker left one employer in the garment district for poor working conditions they could be pretty sure they wouldn't find better conditions somewhere else. The bosses banded together, making sure they all offered the same raw deal.

Even though the region had mostly unskilled immigrant labor, the mid-western garment industry competed favorably with the highly skilled garment manufacturing facilities in New York City or Chicago by implementing the "section system" which was a kind of assembly line. Missouri garment workers "specialized" in one aspect of piecing clothing items together. One woman might put collars on, while another attached sleeves. And they worked at this one piece of the garment all day long. This piecing system didn't just provide a way to employ unskilled labor; it also provided a way to pay the workers. The "piece rate" resulted in lower wages for garment workers and would cause many of the disputes between labor and management.

Kansas City's garment workers – mostly women – didn't get real union representation until after the Great Depression. In the mid-to-late 1930's, the workers went out on strike for better wages and better working conditions. Because the craft unions remained segregated until after World War II, management would often try to pit black and white workers against each other. Ancel pointed out that while Missouri didn't join the Confederacy during the Civil War, it was, nonetheless, a slave state. Missouri carried that heritage of racism forward through much of the 20th century.

Ancel's job of tracing labor history in the area is easier than in many other regions. Ancel has lots of hard data from a highly organized industry. Unlike most of the mining and agriculture worker data, garment worker records remain and carefully detail how low wages were, how insecure jobs were, and how easy it was to get fired. The very nature of piecework guaranteed that the worker could be readily replaced. Ancel believes the garment workers were successfully organized because of the pressures World War II put on the region's employers. With men leaving for the war and women filling their positions in the region's other factories – benefitting from the higher wages the men had won over the years – the garment industry owners had to do better by their workers in order to compete for laborers. Rosie the Riveter didn't just fill her brother's shoes; she pulled her working sisters' work place standards up as well.

In the 1970's as the garment industry began to wink out of existence in Kansas City, Ancel said, "There was a lot of blaming the unions." Ancel – an educator and historian – wanted to know the truth. She began interviewing retired owners of the garment factories. They told her that it wasn't the unions' fault.

Ancel explained how her research indicated that the dawn of huge power-retailers demanded mass production on a scale unprecedented in U.S. garment working history. New mega outlets sprung up all across the nation. These giant chain stores – all selling the exact same garment – drove the small specialty clothing and department stores out of existence.

Ancel believes that U.S. manufacturers could have refitted to supply the massive demand had it not been for government complicity in offshoring jobs and factories. Ancel points to subsidies and legal protections that make it impossible for local manufacturing to come back. "Small business today is truly an endangered species," Ancel explained, "Unless we have some major major changes in who runs this country, I don't see that kind of local market system coming back here."

The off-shored factories that now manufacture nearly all the clothes purchased in the United States are – for the most part – using labor practices illegal in the United States. The literature available through the Alliance for American Manufacturing – a think tank promoting a return to American-made products as an engine for economic reform – argues that no garment should be sold in the United States if it's constructed in a way that endangers the lives or health of the workers and/or destroys the environment.

Manufacturing in nations without worker protections, environmental protections, and with unfair currency manipulation has conspired to bring U.S. manufacturing to its lowest level in two centuries.

But in Kansas City, they do have a giant needle in a park to remind us what we've lost.

Chapter 44 "The Buck Stops Here"
🚲 🚲🚲

As we headed out of Kansas City, Rick pulled another of his "presto change-o let's make everybody happy" moves and brought Brett, Alex and me over to the Harry S Truman Presidential Library and Museum in Independence, Missouri. We only had about an hour to spend, so we didn't call ahead and we didn't try to arrange interviews with any archivists or curators.

Pres. Truman's Library was the first of twelve built according to the Presidential Libraries Act of 1955. The president and his first lady, Bess, are buried there. So too are their daughter, Margaret, and her husband, Clifton Daniel.

Pres. Truman lived 19 years after leaving the White House. Following the library's completion, Pres. Truman worked from an office in a building across from the exhibit galleries. No other president has done this.

Because Pres. Truman was just down the hall from his artifacts and documents, when he wanted to, he provided eyewitness testimony to visitors. He especially enjoyed visiting with school children. One famous anecdote involved the President admonishing a history professor to "go home and read his books before trying to interview him again."

🚲

When Franklin Delano Roosevelt died suddenly in office, Chief Justice Harlan Fiske Stone hastily inaugurated then Vice President Truman in the White House Cabinet Room. It was April 12, 1945 and Pres. Truman inherited a world in complete chaos. Though the long bloody war in Europe was coming to a close – Germany surrendered on May 7th – the war in Asia promised to rage indefinitely.

Pres. Truman's America had unique, one of a kind, nuclear capabilities and he resolved almost instantly to use them to end World War II. Years later, the President discussed this decision in his farewell address to the nation, "The war against Japan was still going on. I made the decision that the atomic bomb had to be used to end it. I made that decision in the conviction it would save hundreds of thousands of lives--Japanese as well as American. Japan surrendered..."

All told, 51 million souls were lost in World War II, and all across Europe and Asia cities, economies, and lives had been destroyed. Life in the United States had changed dramatically. More women than ever were working outside the home. Soldiers came home to find little available employment as the country struggled to absorb them back into homes and jobs that had grown accustomed to their absence.

It's hard to imagine a president coming to power with more challenges and fewer options. The momentum and trajectory of decisions made by his predecessors must have made Truman feel as though he'd woken up at the rodeo: already riding a bull.

Even though we couldn't stay long at the library, it didn't take more than a few exhibits to explain that rebuilding something would be much harder than destroying it had been. And rebuilding was the task that lay ahead of Pres. Truman from August of 1945 until he handed the keys to the White House to Dwight D. Eisenhower in 1953. Years of neglect had left the chief executive's home in Washington D.C. riddled with rot and exhibiting slapdash additions and fixes from years before, so even the White House – as well as the western world – Pres. Eisenhower inherited, had been rebuilt by Pres. Truman.

We left the museum and Rick set the navigation on his iPhone to take us from Independence straight to St. Louis.

After acknowledging the human cost of World War II and the subsequent millions killed in the Cold War – and still more in Iraq and Afghanistan – it would be flippant and inaccurate to describe our ride later that day through St. Louis, Missouri as though it were a war zone. But I wasn't thinking so literally at the time of our drive and those were my thoughts when we got lost and tried to find our way through forsaken city blocks.

The People's Tour had an appointment with Teamsters Joint Council 13. We'd already traveled 8000 or so miles pretty flawlessly using the GPS mechanisms on our phones. But that day the directions wound us through parts of St. Louis I don't know that I could ever find again. Over the last two decades witnessing and reporting on poverty, I have never seen such devastation in the United States. The third world neighborhoods I've experienced compare in destitution, but not in prior splendor. There were entire city blocks without a visible pane of glass remaining in the buildings. And unlike rural poverty, with fallen down shacks peppering the landscape, these buildings were standing right together, just a few feet apart, and the desolation went on for miles.

In Pres. Truman's final speech as President of the United States, he appropriately mentioned the Marshall Plan – the historic rebuild of Western Europe by the United States – as a great achievement. 21st century America needs a Marshall Plan. If ever a city needed a post-war rebuild, it was St. Louis, which clearly had become a major casualty in the war on the middle class.

The U.S. Department of Labor statistics shows St. Louis as a city with a steadily declining work force. The U.S. Census Bureau has corresponding population out-migration and the crime rate is alarmingly high. Reversing these trends would require a man or woman with Pres. Truman's capacity to rebuild at least as resolutely as he had rebuilt the White House.

When Truman served as president, he commuted most of the time from a house across the street from the White House. Since leaving office, Pres. Truman's self-exile to rebuild the presidential mansion, has been all but forgotten because of other more memorable events – the atomic bombing of Japan and the war in Korea to name two. And much like the post Iraq War rebuild in the Middle East consumed resources needed at home, rebuilding domestic infrastructure might have gotten less of Pres. Truman's attention, if he'd been less of a president.

Rebuilding the United States is undoubtedly less dynamic and headline grabbing than restoring the foreign lands our weapons have helped destroy. But if St. Louis can be used as an example, it is at least as vital and therefore as important. The argument can be made that resources pulled from domestic needs fund the wars. The impoverished in the U.S., therefore, are victims of the wars as well. Incidentally, this victimization is a reality later presidents have chosen to ignore, even though it's been so for more than half a century. In fact, Pres. Truman's successor made that argument only a few months after taking office: "Every gun that is made, every warship launched, every rocket fired, signifies in the final sense a theft from those who hunger and are not fed, those who are cold and are not clothed."

President Eisenhower went on with a laundry list of infrastructure possibilities – every one of them an item sorely needed in 2013 St. Louis. "The cost of one modern heavy bomber is this: a modern brick school in more than 30 cities. It is two electric power plants, each serving a town of 60,000 population. It is two fine, fully equipped hospitals. It is some fifty miles of concrete pavement. We pay for a single fighter with a half-million bushels of wheat. We pay for a single destroyer with new homes that could have housed more than 8,000 people."

Not a single president to come after Pres. Truman, *The Great Rebuilder*, or Pres. Eisenhower, *The Great Priority-Setter*, swapped out weapons for domestic needs. Not even Lyndon Johnson's "War on Poverty" scrapped the military for the sake of the homeland.

After driving slack-jawed through town and reprogramming the coordinates of our destination, we eventually found our way to our rendezvous at the union hall. There we interviewed Eastern Missouri Retirees club President Ron Gushleff and Roy Gillespie from the Joint Council 13 Human Rights Commission. These interviews are archived with all the others at the People's Tour website and remain available through the Rick Smith Show.

Ed Finkelstein from the *St. Louis Labor Tribune* sat at the mic with us as well, and then turned the tables on us by interviewing Rick about his show and asking what turned Rick onto the idea of telling the true story of an American middle class. Rick explained that he wanted his kids to know the real history of the U.S. and what made it great. Rick said that he'd waited long enough for school books and the media to get the story right, so he'd decided to just go all Harry Truman on the topic. For Rick Smith, when it came to teaching his kids the truth, he'd determined that, "The buck stops here."

⁂

Chapter 45 Miners Died: Worker's Comp Was Born
λ

Very early on the morning of July 1st, Ray Tutaj met us at the Cherry Library. He stood in front of the scale model he'd painstakingly built and explained what caused the Cherry Mine Disaster. Because of his work – an exact duplicate in 1/87 scale – we could look straight through the miniature and understand how the unthinkable actually happened 104 years earlier under an Illinois prairie.

By November 13, 1909, the underground mine had been operating for more than a week without electricity. The Chicago, Milwaukee, and St. Paul Railroad opened the mine in 1906. Railroads needed a great deal of coal, and owning a coal mine – eliminating the middleman – made rail operations far more profitable.

The town of Cherry basically existed to support the mine. Miners lived in shacks along the roads leading away from the opening. The State Bank of Cherry – also founded in 1906 by 19 shareholders with $25,000 – remained an important part of the town long after the mine closed in 1935.

Unlike mines dug into the sides of mountains with tunnel openings into which and from whence coal wagons would pass, the mines under a prairie resembled ant farms. They even sported cone shaped piles of rubble like the soil piles made by tunneling ants. Workers brought up from the veins – not just coal – but the slag, rocks and dirt that they harvested as well. Miners weren't paid to mine dirt, so mountainous slag piles formed near the mineshafts as the worthless byproducts of coal mining were discarded.

Coal mines required quite a bit of infrastructure. An engine house and boiler house with huge smoke stacks provided the power needed to raise and lower cages used to haul men and apparatus up and down the 500 foot long equipment shaft. Once out of the ground the coal carts and miners were further hoisted to the top of a sorting building known as the *tipple*. The tipple was built over a rail yard. Railcars would pass underneath the sorting area so the workers could *tip* their carts and fill the train cars beneath them. Other cars would be used to haul the slag off to the slag pile.

The 9-foot by 4-foot cages, used to bring the miners and their carts up and down the supply shaft, had floors with the same narrow gauge rail tracks as the mine passageways. Mules pulled coal and hay carts along the miles of underground tracks. Two cages rode up and down this supply shaft simultaneously: when one cage came up the shaft, the other went down the shaft.

The Cherry Mine had a second shaft – several hundred feet away – used for ventilation. An enormous fan blew air down the ventilation shaft to improve the air quality for the miners and the mules. Next to the ventilation shaft was a third smaller escape shaft. Both egresses contained ladders that workers could use to climb in and out of the mine. All of the mine infrastructure was made of wood.

The Cherry Mine tunneled through three diagonal coal seams. Three mine channels ran perpendicular to the ventilation, transport, and escape shafts cutting through the seams and allowing the men to harvest the coal. The men did not work alone. Coal carts weigh too much for men to push around. Mules lived in the mines and worked alongside the men. Rather than bring the mules up and down when needed, the company stabled them underground. Some mules rested while others worked. Each of the mule stables had ample hay to feed the animals for days at a time with additional carts of hay positioned throughout the mine.

Young boys also worked in the mines. The children would tend to the mules as well as operate mine doors, which would be opened and closed as the miners went through the underground maze. These *trappers* – as the boys were known – used the doors' opening and closing to create airflow. The children made sure that air changed direction, ventilating the various tunnels within which the men worked.

All the supports in the mine were built of wood. Shafts were lined with wood, stairs supports and rungs were wooden, and wooden cogs held tunnel ceilings in place, bracing corners and openings that held canvas doors. These were the doors the children opened and closed.

Tutaj's model allowed us to look at this operation as a cross section. He pointed at the places he described, making it infinitely easier to understand what happened. Tutaj pointed to the intersection of the ventilation shaft and the middle tunnel, 315 feet below the surface. Because the mine's electrical system stopped functioning, the miners went back to working with kerosene torches for light. One of these torches – located right by the escape hatch – dripped onto a hay cart that Tutaj explained, "had been pushed by a younger miner." The child – working as a trapper ventilating the area – had moved the cart out of his way.

Tutaj said that before long, "A spark from the torch ignited the kerosene-saturated hay." But, Tutaj added, the men didn't react to the fire right away, "Fires happen often in mines. Guys didn't get paid to put out fires. They thought they'd let someone else take care of it."

But the location of the fire worked against the miners. The hay cart, so close to the mine's freshest supply of oxygen, quickly ignited the timbers all around it. The ventilation fan blew the flames outward into surrounding parts of the mine. The workers operating the fan increased the pressure hoping to blow the fire out. Instead it just blew the fire down the long wood-lined passageways.

Tutaj said that the men realize they'd misjudged how the fire responded and reversed the fan to pull smoke out of the mine. Another grave mistake was made as the reversed fan direction pulled the fire up the ventilation and escape hatches and, "burned up the wooden steps."

Finally the frantic operators of the fan simply shut it off entirely. By this time, coal in the mine had begun to burn. Starved for oxygen, it created fumes known by the miners as *black damp*. The black damp would stifle and eventually extinguish the fire, but not until it had used up all the available oxygen. The miners that survived the fire would die quickly once the black damp filled their lungs.

While poor decision-making and panic consumed the men working over the ventilation and escape hatches, the mine manager, John Bundy, organized rescue crews to ride in the cages of the utility shaft down to the mine and save workers. Twelve courageous men rode up and down the supply shaft six times hauling survivors to the surface. They would not live through their seventh attempt. After their final descent into the mine, all the men who had gone down were brought back to the top burning alive. None survived this final rescue attempt.

The mine owners – fearful that all their natural resource would burn – ordered the mine sealed. The people of Cherry grew angry. They had loved ones in the mines and with the mineshafts closed; they'd be buried, possibly alive.

Concerned that the townspeople might get violent, the railroad company appealed to Illinois Governor Charles S. Deneen, who mobilized the National Guard. All the while, hundreds of miners trapped below the town perished. Many of these doomed men took the time to write love notes and good-byes. These notes are on display at the small library in Cherry where we met Tutaj and examined his model.

All the farewell letters deserve mention, but George Eddy's is unique in that it comes from a member of a rescue crew and not one of the original miners originally trapped underground. "Dear Wife and Children I write these few lines to you and I think it will be for the last time. I have tried to get out twice but was driven back, there seems to be no hope for us, I come down this shaft yesterday to help save mens (sic) lives. I hope the men I got out were saved."

In addition to the hundreds of survivors who escaped the day the fire broke out, 21 men survived eight days trapped in the mines. When they realized how hopeless rescue had become, they went as far back in the mine tunnels as possible and barricaded themselves in so that the black damp would not contaminate their air. After four days they made a small hole in the barricade and one by one they took turns trying to find a way out. On the eighth day, a few of these desperate men crossed paths with the clean up crew that had been sent into the mine to remove dead bodies.

The mine owners intended to re-open the mine. Collecting the dead was an essential step to restarting their operation. The clean up crew never expected to find living men. Tutaj attributes their survival to "luck and coincidence" because it would have been so easy for the clean up crew to miss them over and over again until they perished from hunger or thirst.

If the Chicago, Milwaukee, and St. Paul railroad had repaired the broken lighting system in the mine, the Cherry Mine Fire would never have happened. Prior to this disaster, few laws held owners liable for injuries or illnesses caused in or by the workplace. The Illinois Labor History Society credits the Cherry Mine Disaster and its 259 dead miners for changing that. "In 1911, Illinois passed its first workers' compensation law. The passage of that law can be directly tied to a disaster in the tiny village of Cherry, Illinois."

Still, 104 years later, in May of 2014, a mining disaster in Soma, Turkey, claimed the lives of 282 miners. Death tolls for the mine fire could exceed 400. Turkish Prime Minister Recep Tayyip Erdogan explained in his remarks to a stunned and grieving coal town, "Such things happen." In his unconscionable remarks, he referenced disasters that took place in the United States as proof that such disasters are unavoidable.

No matter how many scale models are built, there'll be no explaining how the unthinkable is still happening anywhere on earth.

Chapter 46 "Working Men to Arms"
λ λ

On May 3, 1886, locked-out workers stood in protest outside the McCormick Reaper Factory. Strike breakers – replacement workers better known to the workers as "scabs" – left the building after their shift ended and a fight broke out between these scabs and the men on the picket line. The Chicago police responded, attacking the striking workers with clubs and guns. Several of the locked-out men and their companions were killed.

August Spies witnessed the murders and wrote a circular entitled, "Working Men to Arms." Spies (pronounced "spees") edited the *Arbeiter Zeitung*, a publication of the Socialist Publishing Society. Spies had been invited to speak at a rally around the corner from McCormick Reaper and had no intention of participating in the strike, had no prior knowledge that trouble might arise, and certainly hadn't expected to witness the violent events at the factory picket line.

From around the corner, Spies heard gunshots and ran in the direction of the sound. At that time, he became an unintended witness to police brutality and state sanctioned murder. Spies, the journalist – having observed what he believed to be an unprovoked massacre – felt compelled to write an account of what he saw. Spies, the labor activist, felt likewise compelled to call upon his brothers in the working class community to rally against the slaughter of innocent protesters.

Spies would later testify in court, explaining what he saw at the McCormick Reaper Factory, "I saw a policemen [sic] run after the people who were flying, who were fleeing, who were running away, and firing at them. Well, as a matter of course my blood was boiling, and I think in that moment I could have done almost anything, seeing men, women and children fired upon, people who were not armed fired upon by policemen."

The evening of May 3rd – after returning to his office – Spies wrote a news story for the paper. His title "Working Men to Arms" was later changed to "Revenge! Working Men to Arms." Spies could not say how the term "revenge" was inserted into the title of the piece he wrote. Although many speculate that pressmen at the paper interjected the word.

Spies did testify, however, that when he wrote the report he "was very indignant."

While 2500 copies of the circular were printed although Spies believed that at least half were never circulated. According to his own account, Spies' only goal in writing the story and distributing it was to let people know what had happened at McCormick Reaper and exactly how the protesters were killed. He did not intend to incite a riot or give the police anymore excuse to kill civilians.

Spies went on to describe his emotions following the McCormick massacre. "I was excited. I knew positively by the experiences that I have had in the past that this butchery of the people out there was done for the express purpose of defeating the eight hour movement in this city."

The above quotes by Spies came from his trial. He and seven other men were tried for events that would occur May 4th – the day after Spies wrote his famous "Working Men to Arms" article.

May 4th, at a rally in a part of Chicago known as the "hay market," a bomb exploded in the center of a police formation, killing one officer and setting off a riot resulting in the deaths of several more. Dozens of policemen were injured with similar casualty counts for civilians as well. No one was ever put on trial for the civilian deaths or the officers killed with bullets. The prevailing theory is that the police were killed by friendly fire. Policemen firing into the crowd after the explosion literally killed each other and helpless civilians. The police were the ones with the guns, and therefore must have been responsible for the deaths of their colleagues and the people they were sworn to protect.

After the bomb explosion and subsequent riot, circulars were found on the ground that invited people to be at the hay market and hear Spies and others speak. The circulars – according to Spies' sworn testimony – were different from the ones he had approved the night before the incident at the hay market.

Spies testified that he was unwilling to speak at any rally that called workers to engage in violence. The flyers found on the ground contained the line, "Workingmen arm yourselves and appear in full force?" Spies insisted that this belligerent language did not appear in the circular he approved. Indeed, a second circular was found as well. The second, not as widely circulated, fits the description Spies gave on the witness stand.

Spies was tried along with seven accused co-conspirators: Albert Parsons, Samuel Fielden, Michael Schwab, Oscar Neebe, George Engel, Adolph Fischer and Louis Lingg. Spies testified that he looked for Parsons at the event but couldn't find him. That's because Parsons wasn't there. He had a prior speaking engagement at a different rally. A rally Parsons did, in fact, attend. The fact that Parsons never went to the hay market on May 4th did not stop a corrupt court from finding him guilty and sentencing him to death.

Every aspect of their trial was crooked. The judge allowed broad leeway on the part of the prosecution and limited the defense unfairly. A special jury was selected in defiance of protocol. A friend of one of the police officers served on the jury. The case against the eight defendants flouted the law. The trial miscarried justice so egregiously that seven years later Illinois Governor John Atgeld pardoned all of the defendants. Sadly, only three lived long enough to realize their freedom.

A transcript of the governor's pardon details the allegations made at the time, that the trial was unfair. The governor agreed. According to the governor's statement which accompanied his action, these are the five reasons Gov. Atgeld invalidated the convictions and issued his pardon.

"FIRST - That the jury which tried the case
was a packed jury selected to convict.
SECOND - That according to the law as laid down by the
supreme court [sic], both prior to and again since the trial
of this case, the jurors, according to their own answers, were
not competent jurors and the trial was therefore not a legal trial.
THIRD - That the defendants were not proven to be
guilty of the crime charged in the indictment.
FOURTH - That as to the defendant Neebe, the state's attorney
had declared at the close of the evidence that there was no case
against him, and yet he has been kept in prison all these years.
FIFTH - That the trial judge was either so prejudiced against the
defendants, or else so determined to win the applause of a certain
class in the community that he could not and did not grant a
fair trial."

The "certain class" of which the judge sought the applause was – of course – the robber baron class who wished to crush labor organizing in general, and the socialist/anarchist movements in particular.

With a judge, prosecution, and jury so tainted, the convictions of eight men, the executions of four, and the suspicious death of one, the Haymarket Massacre stands as the defining moment of the labor movement.

In 1881, an International Socialist movement officially began. Elected officials and political parties with deliberate agendas knitted themselves together with their shared goal of advocating for the common man.

In 1889 – just three years after the Haymarket Massacre and two years after the executions of the Haymarket Martyrs, as these events and people came to be known – the Second International Congress was held. May 1st was designated as International Workers Day in honor of the Chicago events. Today more than 80 countries celebrate International Workers Day.

On the People's Tour, we stopped at the Waldheim Cemetery where the executed martyrs Parsons, Spies, Fischer, and Engel are buried. Larry Spivack, President of the Illinois Labor History Society, met us at the graveyard. He showed us the monument built to commemorate the courage of the heroes of the 19th century labor movement and explains that they're all buried there now. Where once a few labor leaders were buried there are now dozens. With the help of their families and admirers, after they passed, the graveyard has become the gathering place of people who fought for justice and found their final resting place together. These graves hold the remains of victims of a morally bankrupt justice system and are now a part of the National Registry of Historic Places. But for Spivack that's simply not enough. He doesn't want a forgotten marker. He wants a vibrant labor movement. For Spivack, it's important that the true nature of corporate culture be understood and remembered long into the 21st century.

When corporations fight against decent wages, decent working conditions, worker safety, and environmental protections, and then manipulate government agencies and the halls of justice, democracy is dead.

There's a website that actually tells you – day by day – who was executed where and why. It's titled – not surprisingly – executedtoday.com. On November 11th it describes the execution of the Haymarket Martyrs: "On this date in 1887, the Chicago political machine hanged four at Cook County Jail to defend civilization from the eight-hour day."

For decades, the government and the Chicago police tried to defend their actions against protesters agitating for change. But after a while, even the statue built to honor the policemen killed at Haymarket had to be moved to police headquarters to stop people from defacing it and, at times, destroying it entirely.

The most famous statement oft quoted from the Haymarket martyrs, Spies delivered as he stood on the gallows. "The time will come when our silence will be more powerful than the voices you strangle today." And while that brief statement is profound, these brave working class heroes had a lot more to say in defense of themselves, their fellow workers, and their actions as socialists and anarchists.

Because we have the space here in Daddy, What's the Middle Class?, it seems only fitting that a few more of their words should be remembered.

Please take the time and let these men's thoughts settle in your consciousness and then perhaps stir you to action so that we may forever have a middle class.

Oscar Neebe – the only man not sentenced to death – regretted his sentence of 15 years. Seeing as all the men were innocent, Neebe thought, that all the men should have the same fate, even if that meant they all died as martyrs. Here are a few excerpts from Neebe's written work "The Crimes I Have Committed." Note: Grinnell is the prosecutor from the trial.

"I have been in the labor movement since 1875. I have seen how the police have trodden on the Constitution of this country, and crushed the labor organizations. I have seen from year to year how they were trodden down, where they were shot down, where they were "driven into their holes like rats," as Mr. Grinnell said to the jury. But they will come out! Remember that within three years before the beginning of the French Revolution, when laws had been stretched like rubber, that the rubber stretched too long, and broke—a result which cost a good many state's attorneys at that time their necks, and a good many honorable men their necks.

"We socialists hope such times may never come again; we do everything in our power to prevent it by reducing the hours of labor and increasing wages. But you capitalists won't allow this to be done. You use your power to perpetuate a system by which you may make your money for yourselves and keep the wage-workers poor. You make them ignorant and miserable, and you are responsible for it. You won't let the toilers live a decent life."

Louis Lingg, condemned to death along with the other four, died in his cell. For more than a hundred years it has been assumed and reported that he took his own life rather than allow the state to kill him. Larry Spivack strongly rejects this notion and explained to us that it seems implausible that he would have allowed his friends to face the gallows alone. Spivack believes Lingg was assassinated in his cell.

During his trial, Lingg was allowed to address the court. The following excerpt is from the speech he made. Note: Schaack was the lead investigator of the Haymarket bombing.

"It is not murder, however, of which you have convicted me. The judge has stated that much only this morning in his resume of the case, and Grinnell has repeatedly asserted that we were being tried not for murder, but for anarchy, so the condemnation is—that I am an anarchist!

"What is anarchy? ... The state's attorney, however, has not given you that information. He has merely criticized and condemned, not the doctrines of anarchy, but our methods of giving them practical effect, and even here he has maintained a discreet silence as to the fact that those methods were forced upon us by the brutality of the police. Grinnell's own proffered remedy for our grievances is the ballot and combination of trades unions, and Ingham has even avowed the desirability of a six-hour movement! But the fact is, that at every attempt to wield the ballot, at every endeavor to combine the efforts of workingmen, you have displayed the brutal violence of the police club, and this is why I have recommended rude force, to combat the ruder force of the police...

"You have charged me with despising 'law and order.' What does your 'law and order' amount to? Its representatives are the police, and they have thieves in their ranks. Here sits Captain Schaack. He has himself admitted to me that my hat and books have been stolen from him in his office—stolen by policemen...

"Grinnell had the pitiful courage here in the courtroom, where I could not defend myself, to call me a coward! The scoundrel! A fellow who has leagued himself with a parcel of base, hireling knaves, to bring me to the gallows. Why? For no earthly reason save a contemptible selfishness—a desire to 'rise in the world"—to 'make money,' forsooth.

"This wretch—who, by means of the perjuries of other wretches is going to murder seven men—is the fellow who calls me 'coward'! And yet you blame me for despising such 'defenders of the law' such unspeakable hypocrites!

"Anarchy means no domination or authority of one man over another, yet you call that 'disorder.' A system which advocates no such 'order' as shall require the services of rogues and thieves to defend it you call 'disorder.'

"The Judge himself was forced to admit that the state's attorney had not been able to connect me with the bomb throwing. The latter knows how to get around it, however. He charges me with being a 'conspirator.' How does he prove it? Simply by declaring the International Working People's Association to be a 'conspiracy.' I was a member of that body, so he has the charge securely fastened on me. Excellent! Nothing is too difficult for the genius of a state's attorney!...

"I protest against the conviction, against the decision of the court. I do not recognize your law, jumbled together as it is by the nobodies of bygone centuries, and I do not recognize the decision of the court...

"...let me assure you I die happy on the gallows, so confident am I that the hundreds and thousands to whom I have spoken will remember my words; and when you shall have hanged us, then—mark my words—they will do the bomb throwing! In this hope do I say to you: I despise you. I despise your order, your laws, your force-propped authority. Hang me for it!"

And lastly, Albert Parsons wrote a final letter to his wife Lucy. Lucy's buried with her husband at the memorial to his heroism and to her lifetime of activism in his place after he was murdered by the state of Illinois. Here are some of his final words to Lucy.

"My Darling Wife:

"Our verdict this morning cheers the hearts of tyrants throughout the world, and the result will be celebrated by King Capital... Nevertheless, our doom to death is the handwriting on the wall, foretelling the downfall of hate, malice, hypocrisy, judicial murder, oppression, and the domination of man over his fellowman. The oppressed of earth are writhing in their legal chains...

"There was no evidence that any one of the eight doomed men knew of, or advised, or abetted the Haymarket tragedy. But what does that matter? The privileged class demands a victim, and we are offered a sacrifice to appease the hungry yells of an infuriated mob of millionaires who will be contented with nothing less than our lives. Monopoly triumphs! Labor in chains ascends the scaffold for having dared to cry out for liberty and right!

"You I bequeath to the people, a woman of the people. I have one request to make of you: Commit no rash act to yourself when I am gone, but take up the great cause of Socialism where I am compelled to lay it down.

"My children—well, their father had better die in the endeavor to secure their liberty and happiness than live contented in a society which condemns nine-tenths of its children to a life of wage-slavery and poverty. Bless them; I love them unspeakably, my poor helpless little ones.

"Ah, wife, living or dead, we are as one. For you my affection is everlasting. For the people, humanity. I cry out again and again in the doomed victim's cell: Liberty! Justice! Equality!"

ℷ ℷ ℷ

Chapter 47 The Teamsters
λ

"I may have many faults, but being wrong ain't one of them."
~Jimmy Hoffa

We pulled into Detroit in separate cars. That was pretty common for Carol and the kids but for me it was a switch. Except for when I was driving Carol, I was in the RV. But we were getting really close to where one of my kids lived and Carol and Rick generously lent me the van so I could go visit.

Carol climbed into the RV with the men and the kids. It had been my job to ride along with Rick and work on the radio show while taking notes for this book. I think when Carol hopped in and I hopped out, that must've been as close as the trip was going to be to a vacation for them. For that last month or so, we'd all worked pretty much every waking hour of every day of every week. The work we did never really felt like a job. That might have been because there's probably no other job in the world like the one we all had: one with a radio crew that takes off with a young family and tours the country.

Another reason it felt so un-work-like was because the Smiths treated me *like their own* and as though I was actually a part of this very unique family holiday. The People's Tour was really a cross between Howard Zinn's *People's History of the United States* and National Lampoon's *Vacation*.

Before we made our quick stops in Chicago and Cherry, we went to Mt. Olive, Illinois, to pay our respects at the grave of the esteemed labor leader, Mother Jones. She's buried there with some of the laborers she'd devoted her adult life to defending.

We'd finished in Chicago, and so I split off from the rest of the crew and headed for Indianapolis, Indiana, where my son, John – who had only recently gotten out of the Peace Corps – had just started at Marian University's graduate school. Carol and Rick knew I'd love to see him. Only a few hours away, I'd thought about renting a car to zip down Route 65. But thanks to the Smiths, I didn't have to spend the time or the money.

The next morning I drove to meet them in Detroit. Rick and Brett had scheduled interviews at the Teamsters headquarters. I pulled up along side the office building for Local 299. Looking up at the center window of the yellow brick building, I felt much the same way I did when I stared into the window a few weeks earlier at the schoolbook depository in Dallas. That was one famous window. I couldn't see into the second floor office, but I didn't need to: Jimmy Hoffa hadn't sat at his desk in decades.

The RV sat parked in the lot to the left of the building. I walked to the side entrance and knocked. Carol opened the door and at different levels along the height of the door, little Smith heads popped out with a chorus of, "Hi, Miss Pat!"

Carol explained that Brett and Rick were inside taping the interviews we'd need to produce at least two shows. I turned to go in and join them but Carol told me to wait, that I'd need her to help me. The building had some real security barriers so she and the kids escorted me inside to find the guys.

If Jimmy Hoffa had come on the People's Tour with us, he'd have been 100 years old. Born, Valentine's Day, 1913, James Riddle Hoffa – the son of a coal miner – rose to a level of prominence unrivaled in American history. As well known as other American icons, no other U.S. superstar built his or her name exclusively by advocating for a guild of workers.

The International Brotherhood of Teamsters supported the People's Tour like no other union in the nation. Perhaps they'd have supported the promotional efforts of any former Teamster, but considering Jimmy Hoffa's history, it makes sense that the Teamsters wanted a national story told. Jimmy Hoffa went to unparalleled lengths to unite every local in the nation. By coordinating 450,000 truck drivers, he also brought together their 44,000 employers. Jimmy Hoffa embraced the extra work and additional benefit his *big-picture* perspective lent to his efforts. Similarly, his son, James P. Hoffa, went out of his way to help us.

James P. Hoffa – current Teamsters' President – endorsed our trip. Teamsters contacts all along the way had put us in touch with other labor leaders of every stripe. We met in Teamsters halls. We wound our way around the country on roads made safe because of laws the Teamsters lobbied for and got passed. With only two days left to our trip, we stood outside the office of the most famous labor leader of the 20th century. *Encyclopedia Britannica* calls the International

Brotherhood of Teamsters, Chauffeurs, Warehousemen and Helpers of America "the largest private-sector labour union in the United States." In 1950 more than a million people belonged to the union.

The Teamsters have a storytelling legacy. Begun in 1903, Teamster leadership has invested in literature about their mammoth successes over the years.

Some of the volumes available – along with a top notch on-line presence at their website – *TEAMSTERS: Snapshots in Time; 100 years of Teamsters History: A Strong Legacy; A Powerful Future, James R. Hoffa Remembered; "They All Went Up": The Story of the National Master Freight Agreement*; and many others helped me understand the tough battles waged on behalf of the workers from the time of horse drawn carriages right up through the locals bargaining to get a fair deal for airline pilots.

Even though obstacles threaten membership and organizing – like the ones in Tennessee where Teamsters fight against *right to work* laws – the Teamsters stayed together. In Memphis, we met workers who were basically job sharing to keep more of them employed.

As various state legislatures and the U.S. Congress destabilize the legal footing upon which workplace democracy rests, locals struggle to increase membership and get workers busy advocating for their own needs and the needs of others.

Rick asked virtually everyone we interviewed how to get younger union workers involved and how to get them to agitate among their non-union colleagues. To a person they responded, "education." Retired workers and labor leaders agreed that young workers don't know what they have or how hard it was to get it or how easily it could be lost.

The Teamsters don't just talk about their history. They publish their own historic literature and – of course – they went on the hook promoting the People's Tour. When the tour ended and I began doing the research for *Daddy, What's the Middle Class?* I was grateful for every one of the books our Teamsters hosts offered us. And I was glad I took them, even if it made my bag almost too heavy to carry.

What I ended up learning was that while Hoffa – to quote his son James P. Hoffa – "brought more Americans into the middle class than anyone in our nation's history," only served as general president for 14 years, the Teamsters had a lot of history before and after him that they hold dear.

If humans drive it, the Teamsters represent them. Because labor unions elect their leadership and bargain collectively, battles on behalf of the workers are battles by the workers. The story of labor unions is a story of one worker sticking up for another worker. The story of union destruction is a story of powerful influence interfering with that alliance.

Whether prostitutes working as strike breakers go after female workers, mine owners hire the private thugs to burn out camps, or corporate attorneys write the legislation that undermines collective bargaining, individual workers have had to remain loyal to each other in order to fight back. Workers have had their heads cracked open – Jimmy Hoffa among them – fighting for workplace democracy. The Teamsters documented many of these conflicts. In the beginning of each history book, President James P. Hoffa invites the reader to learn more. "A cardinal rule for the labor movement – and for life in general – is that one must study the past in order to better prepare for the future."

James P. Hoffa reminds readers, "The Teamsters story is a story of the North American worker – a story of struggle and sacrifice, heartbreaking setbacks and enormous accomplishments. As you browse through the pages of this book, we invite you to share in the celebration of our union's heritage – and join us as we learn from our proud legacy and build a powerful future."

Chapter 48 Detroit Destroyed

Teamsters Central Region Training Coordinator, Shawn Ellis, took us on a ride through Downtown Detroit and over to the United Auto Workers (UAW) Local 600 hall. Ellis walked quietly and respectfully into the auditorium and pointed to the stage, "Shhh," he said, "Take a good look. A lot of history took place here." Ellis' words were striking in their understatement. What had transpired in the Detroit labor movement directly caused the growth of Detroit as a city and the growth of the city's middle class.

The labor hall was bustling and several guys asked us if they could help us. When Ellis explained that he was a member of the Teamsters bringing a radio show in to see some of the historic photos and artifacts of the UAW labor movement, we pretty much had free access to the whole hall.

Ellis wanted us to see the photos of the strikes and the strikebreakers, the riots and the riot police, the labor leaders and the management bosses who locked horns at the Ford Rouge Plant. He thought he'd put these pictures in our heads before we actually went over there and saw the way things look now.

When we got over to Henry Ford's dream plant, it appeared to have changed less than any of the other landmarks we'd seen in the Motor City. Detroit is decaying and much of the city shows signs of rot. Even though they produce trucks there, the Rouge Plant is a third of its original size with a tenth of its labor force and it just looked abandoned.

A few weeks after we left Detroit, in July of 2013, state-appointed city emergency manager, Kevyn Orr, decided to take the city into bankruptcy. That enabled Detroit to pay her city employees because she'd stop paying her creditors. This solution might stave off immediate problems stemming from $14 billion in debt and a 2013 shortfall of nearly $400 million more, but it promised little in the way of good news for city employees and retirees who will likely receive cents on the dollar for their pension plans.

In 1948 the UAW launched their "Too Old to Work, Too Young to Die" campaign. The union that brought tens of thousands of Detroit citizens into the middle class would eventually secure that elder autoworkers wouldn't lose their middle class existence just because they could no longer work. Additionally, a decent retirement package insured that – after decades on the job – workers wouldn't have to fear old age.

Detroit's decline is blamed on many factors. In the mid 20th century, 1.8 million people lived in the nation's fourth largest city. *The British Daily Mail* says depopulation began when urbanites fled for the outskirts in the 1950's, "But like many American cities, Detroit's fall began late that decade as developers starting building suburbs. Then came the 1967 riots that accelerated the number of white residents who moved to the cities north of Eight Mile Road, considered the region's racial dividing line." Intense competition in the auto industry from both Japan – in 1957 the first Japanese cars were imported into the U.S. – and Europe, caused massive injury to U.S. auto manufacturing. These intrusions into American manufacturing, coupled with factory worker mobility and income that allowed them to join the suburban flight, meant cities like Detroit didn't stand a chance as the 20th century drew to a close. When the stock market crashed in October of 2008, much of the American automotive manufacturing supply chain winked out of existence.

On our way to the UAW hall, Ellis made a quick stop at the *Labor Legacy Landmark*. Created by David Barr and Italian born artist, Sergio DeGiusti, the 63-foot arch stands in the main plaza of the Blue Cross Blue Shield building. More welcome than Di Modica's Wall Street gift, *Charging Bull*, the arch pays tribute to the contributions of the worker. Stone markers around the base bear inscriptions – as does the arch itself – that remind visitors of what organized labor has earned and what might be lost. One inscription reads, "We want more school houses and less jails... more justice and less revenge. – Samuel Gompers."

The artwork is across Lake Michigan from – and is visible to – observers in Canada. Several other statues with a message share the waterfront. One sculpture commemorates the Underground Railroad, which as a system of hiding places and safe havens used to ferry enslaved blacks out of the slave states and eventually to Canada. Another statue commemorates Samuel de Champlain, the colonial explorer who first charted the region for the French.

It's pretty remarkable how all that history was condensed in one place. It has become a site honoring the evolution out of oppression. The story begins with the natives who had their land ripped from underneath them and continues with the black Africans who were transported and lost every semblance of their humanity, as they became mere possessions of the ruling class. But then the tide turns when the worker – who through workplace democracy and inspired agitation – won a fair wage and gained entre to earned comfort.

It's ironic – to say the least – that this all happened in a city that has forfeited its contract with its citizens. Thousands of Detroit street lamps have burned out and the alleyways have become dark forbidding places. Ellis told us it that it can take hours for the police to respond when called. And, at times, emergency vehicles don't come at all.

Ten thousand abandoned houses have been torn down and tens of thousands more wait to be razed. Detroit is a city of abandoned and dilapidated housing and yet the United States Department of Education estimates that Michigan has nearly 40,000 homeless school children. No one has a plan to match empty homes with homeless families.

Detroit was once the land of promise for aspiring members of the middle class. Now, so much of Detroit has been destroyed that those promises of decent wages, a decent education, and a decent retirement, may go unkept forever.

λ λλ

Chapter 49   Put Ford on Trial
λ λλ

There's a saying running round the 21st century social media: "I'll believe corporations are people when Texas executes one." Former Secretary of Labor for the Clinton Administration, Robert Reich, chided the use of this phrase. He feels it trivializes the impact of corporate personhood by making a joke of it. And it does nothing to address what really needs to happen when illegality, injury and/or death result from actions performed with the approval – tacit or deliberate – of corporate management.

Riech – now a professor at the University of Public Policy at Berkley – opposes holding corporations responsible for felonies. He doesn't believe corporations can be responsible. Reich denies that justice was done when British Petroleum (BP) "plead guilty to 14 criminal counts, including manslaughter, and agreed to pay $4 billion over the next five years." Reich believes that corporations shouldn't be considered human when it comes to campaign contributions, voting rights, or criminal activity. And when citizens buy into the notion that corporations can be responsible for murdering workers, customers, innocent bystanders, or entire ecosystems, people are likewise acknowledging the same corporate personhood that empowers them to speak in elections.

Reich writes, "It defies logic to make BP itself the criminal. Corporations aren't people. They can't know right from wrong. They're incapable of criminal intent. They have no brains. They're legal fictions — pieces of paper filed away in a vault in some bank. Holding corporations criminally liable reinforces the same fallacy that gave us *Citizen's United v. the Federal Election Commission*, in which five justices decided corporations are people under the First Amendment and therefore can spend unlimited amounts on an election."

If corporations like BP don't bear the responsibility when their oil rigs blow up and kill workers, then who does? Why, the people in charge, of course. People – not paper – killed the BP workers, and people should be held responsible. Reich explains, "The people responsible for BP's deaths... were the executives who turned a blind eye to safety while in pursuit of their own rising stock options, and who conspired with oil-services giant Halliburton to cut corners on deep water drilling when they knew damn well they were taking risks for the sake of fatter profits. They're the ones who should be punished."

And what's the consequence of allowing the corporation to pay a fine instead of holding the humans in charge responsible? Reich continues, "Failure to punish them simply invites more of the same kind of criminal negligence by executives more interested in lining their pockets than protecting their workers and the environment."

Assuming Reich is right – and he is – then we really need to look at *Citizen's United v. the Federal Elections Commission* the other way around. *Citizen's United* wasn't a fight by corporations to have unfettered control over the outcome of U.S. elections, at least not entirely. *Citizen's United* implicitly cast in stone the notion that no human has ever been responsible for the abuses that labor, bystanders, or the environment have endured at or around the workplace. When the boiler exploded at the Ford Rouge plant on February 1st of 1999, somebody or somebodies should have been charged with murder.

It's not just that corporate executives shirk responsibility for killing workers in their factories. When corporate personhood shifts real responsibility from the people in charge to their legal construct, it also allows negligent bottom-line driven directors and trustees to walk away unscathed when their faulty products kill their customers.

A May 16, 2014, *New York Times* article used personifying language to discusses the National Highway Traffic Safety Administration's penalty levied on General Motors when the corporate decision-makers delayed the recall of faulty ignition switches. "G.M. will pay a $35 million penalty — the maximum allowed and the largest ever imposed on an automaker — and will be required to make wide-ranging changes to its safety practices that will be supervised by the government, another first for an automaker."

Anthony Foxx, the U.S. Secretary of Transportation, likewise spoke as though the corporation literally was capable of acting independently and was made of something far more physically capable than a typed-up collection of legal protections. *The New York Times* quotes Foxx, "What G.M. did was break the law."

If any member of any labor movement injured any officer of any corporation – and some have tried over the years to do so – the individual would have been charged, tried, and, there's little doubt, convicted. The Haymarket Massacre and subsequent trials exemplify this reality. While one man died in the explosion at Chicago's hay market, four were executed. Six men died at the 1999 explosion of the Ford Rouge plant, and Ford Motor Company paid $7 million dollars to the state of Michigan and the UAW. $1.5 million was a penalty to the Michigan Occupational, Safety and Healthy Agency. The rest went to fund scholarship programs, health clinics – for the treatment of burns, a ghastly reminder of how the six men died and the injuries of the other 14 – and increased safety measures.

No personal responsibility attached to the disaster. And though Bill Ford commented that February 1, 1999 was the worst day of his life, being sentenced to a decade in prison for ignoring safety violations might have given that day a good run for its money. As Reich pointed out, corporate personhood shielded BP executives –just as it did Bill Ford and Bill Ford's great-grandfather – from any real consequences of their actions or inaction.

When Teamster Shawn Ellis took us to the Rouge plant – Henry Ford's crown jewel of production and greed – we discussed the Battle of the Overpass. Henry Ford's hired security guards and strikebreakers attacked labor organizers attempting to leaflet the walkway that ran over the road to the plant. Ford's thugs injured men and women alike.

Every level of American history would have been different if corporations – as well as government entities – had not shielded the individuals making these decisions from direct and well-earned consequences.

If Henry Ford had been held personally responsible for every work place injury that was not a legitimate accident, if police officers and troops doing the bidding of politicians and corporate executives were likewise responsible for the injuries and deaths they cause, the middle class wouldn't have had such bloody beginnings. And middle class gains wouldn't be so prone to collapse.

In Dearborn, Michigan, Henry Ford built a factory capable of eliminating most suppliers so that his corporation could own all the profits. When we visited in 2013, it had become a shell of what it used to be, so it was difficult to picture the expansive complex filled with men and women who were literally taking a beating from goons hired to ensure Ford's supremacy over the worker.

But I did try to imagine what American history would have been like if Henry Ford, his cronies and his successors had been sent to prison for work place injuries caused by their greed.

Chapter 50   Ball-Busting "Patriots" Offshore the Middle Class

λ

Rick, Brett and I said goodbye to Carol and the kids. It was the 3rd of July and our last stop, Toledo, Ohio, was only a few hours away from the Smith family Independence Day bash. Carol and the kids didn't need to hang around anymore. We'd meet up one last time, on the evening of July 4th – after the hamburgers and potato salad had been consumed – and we'd all headed back to Carlisle. On July 4th 2013, the People's Tour would end.

If we hadn't all been so tired I think we'd have taken the split up a lot worse. I know I would have squeezed the kids for a long time if I'd really thought about it. My time spent with Sammi, Alex and Aly were some of the best times of the trip. Sure, they acted like little kids. But to some extent we all did. Perhaps that's why we got along so well.

Now that we'd officially separated from the family, the Toledo trip felt a whole lot more like work. The weather had turned hot and we were working up a steam trying to get everything finished. We ran around completing interviews that had been set up for us at the International Brotherhood of Teamsters Local 20 offices.

Mario Vargas was one of the folks waiting patiently to speak to us. Vargas organizes workers for the Farm Labor Organizing Committee. We'd seen bent-backed workers all across the United States harvesting America's food. But we had to come all the way to Toledo to interview someone who represented the only production jobs in the U.S. that can't be outsourced.

Vargas represents both documented and undocumented workers. Employers fearful of running afoul of the law, but too greedy to pay their share of federal, state or local withholdings, pay some undocumented workers completely underhandedly: in cash or through third parties. Still, most employers pay their guest workers using a system the Internal Revenue Service (IRS) created for folks without social security numbers. The argument can be made that employers who pay guest workers really have no way of proving whether or not the worker has permission from the federal government to be in the U.S.. All the employer knows for sure is that they're complying with IRS guidelines for non-U.S. citizens.

Perhaps that's why – in February of 2014 – the Obama administration reduced penalties on businesses that hire workers illegally. Or perhaps it's just because business has always been more important than the people.

At any rate, these guest workers – documented or not – receive a paycheck after taxes have been withheld by their employer. The accounting for this withholding goes through the IRS and is categorized by means of an Individual Taxpayer Identification Number (ITIN).

Undocumented workers pay taxes, but usually cannot use services available through government agencies, even though their taxes pay for these services for others. Undocumented workers forfeit their tax refunds and Social Security payments as well.

If these guest workers are agricultural workers, then Vargas represents them. Agricultural workers have fewer protections then other workers. Because of a provision in the Department of Labor regulations ironically titled the *Fair Labor Standards Act*, minimum wages and overtime protections do not apply for most agricultural workers. Children can be found in the fields next to their parents: children who would be much to young to work in any other kind of manufacturing everywhere else in the country.

Vargas shared stories of his own childhood in the fields as well as the stories of the people he represents. Vargas' comments and all the interviews from the People's Tour are available through the website www.peoplestourforamerica.com

We wrapped up our interviews in the union hall and headed out to sight see around Toledo with our last interviewee, Timothy Messer-Krause. Messer-Krause is a history professor and the Chair of the Department of Ethnic Studies at Bowling Green University.

Touring Toledo with Messer-Krause was like tooling along the ocean floor with Robert Ballard. Whether Ballard takes you to the scene of the Titanic or the Bismarck, you know two things: it'll be fascinating and it'll be tragic.

We piled in Messer-Krause's car and he took us to empty lots, superfund clean-up sites, and an occasional but damned rare factory still employing Ohioans.

We saw the rusting hulls of industry that mark the place where the middle class took on water and started to sink. Consequently, Toledo's population, like that of Detroit and so many other former manufacturing hubs, has dwindled.

In the 2012 presidential race, Republican candidate Mitt Romney tried to score points for his campaign. He used a Toledo in shambles to make his point when he announced that Jeep would be moving its production facilities to China. Gov. Romney neglected to mention the 50,000 factories offshored during the last republican president's tenure and how these losses impacted the nation in general but Toledo in particular.

Also absent from Gov. Romney's remarks was any reference to what the 2009 Stimulus Plan and subsequent economic recovery had done for re-shoring jobs since the country began rebuilding after the stock market crashed in 2008. In May of 2014, the Toledo plant Gov. Romney mentioned, wasn't just making Jeeps in Toledo, it had added 1000 jobs.

The addition of new jobs and the radical outmigration of the area's work force population has given Toledo its lowest unemployment rate in ten years. The negative population growth has also left houses, schools, and entire neighborhoods empty and rife with urban decay.

The booming and busting of the banking and housing markets in the region is the topic of *Banksters, Bosses and Smart Money*, a great book on how the American people got ripped off by land speculators in cahoots with the banks and how communities were duped into building and paying for the infrastructure that big business needs. Professor Messer-Krause, our tour guide, wrote *Banksters, Bosses and Smart Money*.

And while we enjoyed our trip with the region's foremost authority on labor history and banking, Rick just couldn't relax. Rick had been sputtering and preoccupied this badly only once before on our trip. It was when we stood on the Golden Gate Bridge and stared over at the San Francisco-Oakland Bay Bridge. Rick just couldn't enjoy the view. He kept muttering about Chinese steel.

The eastern span of the original San Francisco-Oakland Bay Bridge, begun in 1933 and completed three years later, was replaced in 2013 by what the California Department of Transportation website calls, "a state-of-the-art marvel to behold." Rick calls it a "Chinese bridge."

In an effort to save money, the new bridge sections opened to the driving, cycling, and walking public in 2013, were built in China of Chinese-made materials. To a big picture guy like Rick, that seemed mightily foolish, considering all the extra jobs and economic growth the region would have enjoyed had U.S. labor and materials been used. But since the sections have been put into place, it's clear that while jobs were outsourced, corruption was not.

According to results published following a 2013 California Senate inquiry, thousands of weld cracks were detected during the construction phase of the bridge. Instead of repairing or replacing the problems, supervisors fired the individuals who detected the cracks. The report goes on to state, "Bridge officials rejected warnings in 2008 that suspect anchor rods for the suspension span were not adequately tested; some of those rods snapped last year."

It is unclear how expensive the required fixes to the shoddy San Francisco-Oakland Bay Bridge will be. Time will tell if outsourcing the bridge saved any money at all.

Anyway, here we were in Toledo, and Rick had that same look in his eye. Rick wanted Messer-Krause to take us to the Glass Pavilion at the Toledo Museum of Art. You guessed it. The 360 panels – each weighing more than 1300 pounds – came from China. A 2010 *Wall Street Journal* (WSJ) report quotes Bruce Tsin of the Avic Sanxin Company, of Shenzen, who says his company got the job "Because of its willingness to invest in technology necessary for complex glass, including a $500,000 piece of equipment." Tsin concluded, according to the WSJ, "U.S. companies… are too cautious, preferring standardized processes and 'easy money.'"

Rick's not new to the outsourcing game. He knows that China has been seizing opportunities to corner the global manufacturing market at an unprecedented rate. It's the irony of the glass pavilion in America's glass city that really got Rick's goat. In 1900 Toledo had more than 100 glassmakers. And the owner of one of the largest manufacturers, Edward Drummond Libbey, endowed the Toledo Museum of Art.

Libbey died in 1925, long before he saw the *City of Glass* fade into the past. Were he alive today, he might feel the way 17th century Native Americans would, should they look for any of their heritage anywhere but in a museum.

After we finished our tour, we climbed back into the RV and headed to Cleveland to wave a few Chinese-made flags and celebrate 'independence.' The 4th of July never seemed more absurd.

The People's Tour for America was ending on such a melancholy note.

Still, as ironic as the Toledo Glass Pavilion's "made in China" label was, it seemed even more contemptuous that the corporate "patriots" who build the Freedom Tower on the site of the World Trade Center disaster back in New York – a block from where the People's Tour began just one month before – used Chinese glass as well.

It's like Abraham Lincoln said,

> "**America will never be destroyed from the outside.
> If we falter or lose our freedoms,
> it will be because we destroyed ourselves.**"

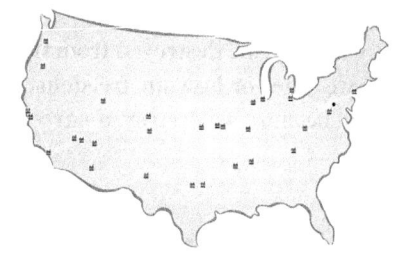

Epilogue

by Rick Smith

I hope you enjoyed riding shotgun as we traveled across this big, beautiful country. We had an amazing adventure, visiting a few of the many important places in American Labor history, meeting some very interesting people (good, bad, and ugly - appearance excluded), and feasting on tasty local cuisine.

Whether it was "Friends of Coal" with side arms trying to run us off or the most gracious of retirees inviting us into their homes for tea and cookies, The People's Tour for America had a little bit of everything.

I asked to write this chapter as a kind of post-trip analysis of the why, what for, where, and when. Pat LaMarche has done an amazing job of documenting this trip's day-to-day movement while peppering our movements with heartwarming and interesting stories and sharing actual historical information. To Pat, and The Rick Smith Show producer Brett, thank you for your hard work and commitment to this giant-sized project that can only be described a Herculean lift performed by dedicated lovers and fighters of the struggle.

I have been asked numerous times: Why this project? Why put my wife and kids, my show (including Pat and producer Brett), and myself through 30 days crammed into a 28' rolling hotbox through the South and Southwest in June? At least it wasn't July! The simple truth is, The People's Tour for America was the result of several moments of fatherly frustration with what my children were seeing in the media, were being taught, or, more to the point, were not being taught, in school, and what they were being fed by society as a whole.

On television, one of what could be a million examples was the History Channel's series, The Men Who Built America. This was a series that successfully glorified the robber barons of yesterday while simultaneously minimizing the hard work, skill, and dedication of those workers whose hands, blood, sweat, and lives actually built the country brick by brick and produced the enormous wealth of the gilded class.

To be fair, you cannot blame the History Channel for its sloppy wet kiss designed to pander to the ego of today's class of uber-wealthy elite. Our corporate-controlled, for-profit media culture is all about money. Concepts such as truth, reality, justice, and fairness seem to fall to the wayside when cold, hard cash is waved under the noses of corporatists. They can't help it. It's who they are. So, the People's Tour was about teaching my children, bringing a realistic view of who really built the nation to the radio airwaves, and enjoying the research of unearthing who workers were (are), where they came from, and what battles were fought (still fighting) because it is my belief that my children may have to fight the same battles again in their lives.

In school, the history of workers and the struggles they encountered have been eviscerated from history books and classroom curriculum. What is still allowed in the classroom has been sanitized, sterilized, and reinvented. From Rosa Parks, who my daughter said "was just tired," to Martin Luther King, who she thought "gave a good speech," I wanted this tour to be about digging deeper and expanding how my children, my listeners, and, to a large extent, how I, think about our collective past. I believe we have succeeded in opening eyes, softening hearts, and steeling spines. The old saying about those who do not learn from history being doomed to repeat the events of the past is true. The wealth class of our nation understands it all too well, which is why Labor Education has been under constant attack for the last thirty years.

All across the nation, Labor Education Centers have been defunded, dismantled, and discarded, and labor's history is in the process of being rewritten. The Labor Education Center at Indiana University of Pennsylvania (IUP) once had a thriving, brilliantly-staffed, well-resourced institution, explicitly dedicated to educating future generations of workers about the struggles of their parents and grandparents in creating a middle class economy, an active electorate, and educated citizens. Unfortunately, this institution that opened in 1976 and was dedicated to learning, research, and training, was defunded and shut down in 2010. Their extensive archives were dismantled and destroyed, and the brilliant staff was dislocated.

IUP's situation is not unique. These centers, along with colleges and universities that offer Labor Studies programs, are under heavy attack. As union density continues to drop and available dollars dwindle, it is a perfect storm that is destroying labor's past, harming the present, and handcuffing the future.

One of the most egregious examples of attacks on Labor Studies programs is being waged in Michigan by the likes of the heavily funded Mackinac Center for Public Policy. In 2011, the Mackinac Center for Public Policy filed an open records request with labor-studies centers at Michigan State University, the University of Michigan at Ann Arbor, and Wayne State University for emails of all employees and contractors where emails contained either the name of Wisconsin Governor Scott Walker, the state of Wisconsin, the Wisconsin capitol of Madison, or MSNBC television host Rachael Maddow, as well as "any other e-mails dealing with the collective-bargaining situation in Wisconsin." Why? Intimidation and harassment!

The wealth class understands the importance of history. Look at the February 2011 uprising in Madison, WI. It is my belief, and that of many other more learned scholars, that the uprising occurred because of Wisconsin's legal mandate that school children have at least a semester of Labor History. So on February 11, 2011, when the Associated Press article titled "Walker Says National Guard is Prepared for Possible Unrest" hit the stands, those college students who lead the uprising harkened back to governors of the past who called out the National Guard and shot workers in the streets.

Across the nation there has been a thirst for change, a demand for justice, and action to close the growing chasm between the producers and the takers.

Corporate media has done an outstanding job of rewriting reality. Fast food workers across the nation who are in the streets demanding a life-sustaining wage of $15 an hour and the right to join a union are mocked as greedy by the corporate-controlled for-profit media at a time when the CEO of McDonald's is taking in more than $9,200 per hour and has an ironclad contract.

Retail workers from sea to shining sea are taking their fight for decent wages, hours, and conditions to the streets as they struggle to make ends meet while producing enormous amounts of wealth for the takers sitting in corporate boardrooms, for institutional investors, and for birth lottery winners like the Walton heirs. The handful of Walton family heirs sits atop a fortune that is greater than that of the bottom 40%-45% of Americans COMBINED while our media complains the workers who actually produced that wealth are underserving because the "market" won't bear the costs. Laughable, I know.

But they have the megaphone and an overwhelming amount of power and resources. Since the Great Bush Recession of 2007, society has reinforced the "at least you have a job" frame to keep workers, whose wages have been declining, benefits have been disappearing, and conditions have been worsening, quiet, and in a weird Stockholm Syndrome way, appreciative.

I am a very fortunate man. Good health, a wonderful family, a vocation I enjoy, the list could stretch on for pages with those things for which I feel immensely fortunate and grateful. One of the things for which I am most grateful, beyond health and family, is that I have yet to, and, hopefully never will, have to look into my children's eyes and know they are hungry and I cannot feed them, know they are cold and I cannot warm them, know they are sick and I cannot get them medical care, know they are scared and I cannot protect them. Many of these things I myself experienced growing up in a poverty-riddled housing project.

Too many Americans are not as fortunate. Poverty, homelessness, and hopelessness have all increased in recent years. I often think back to the days of my childhood when I would find my mother crying, usually at the end of the month, because the cupboards were bare and she had no money, or I was shivering and the heat had been turned off. I remember those days vividly and am eternally grateful that my children will never find their mother as I would often find mine.

You see, the 1970's were unfriendly times for a desperate single mother. Jobs for women were inflexible or unstable, or were temporary service-based jobs with low pay, no benefits and no security. There were a number of times where I had fallen ill and my mother lost her job because there was no one available to care for me. This left my mother and me often bouncing between work and welfare. Sadly, the same situation is all too common today.

I often think back to my childhood. In my neighborhood the only people who ever got out of the projects--aside from death or jail--were athletes who were good enough to get scholarships, young men who signed up to fight in Vietnam, or workers who got good paying union jobs at the auto plants, feeder plants that surrounded the auto industry, or warehouses.

As a kid growing up:

- A union job meant decent wages that would put food on the table for the entire month.
- A union job meant some measure of stability.
- A union job meant some measure of security and allayed the daily fear of being fired unjustly.
- A union job meant health security in the event of illness.
- A union job meant opportunity.

In short, a union job meant a path to the Norman Rockwell white picket fenced, mom at home baking apple pie, the American Middle Class portrayed on television's Leave it to Beaver and The Andy Griffith Show. A union job was the golden ticket to a better future. A union job was the ladder out of poverty that we all sought. And you know what? It still is.

My grandparent's generation understood the simple truth that there is power in numbers.

This project, this People's Tour for America, was predominately about exploring Labor's past and breathing life into to the stories of the men, women, and children who fought, bled, and died in the battle to win an eight hour work day, the struggle for a forty hour workweek, the end of child labor, the beginning of an education, safe working conditions, and simple dignity.

This book tells some of those stories but it is also a call to action. None of the victories of the past came to fruition without solidarity and struggle, nor can those that have been won be maintained without a constant vigilance. As we look at the numerous attacks on workers and their families in virtually every state across the nation, we are reminded that our cherished "middle class" is but one generation from extinction.

In states like Mississippi, where, according to the Bureau of Labor Statistics' January 2014 report, union density at an anemic 3.7, well below the national average, the Mississippi legislature passed and the Governor signed three extremely restrictive pieces of legislation to snuff it out entirely. One law bans workers from boycotting or protesting companies that choose to harass and intimidate their workers, another makes mass picketing illegal, and the third bans Project Labor Agreements (PLA's). Mississippi is but one of twenty-one states to propose or enact legislation banning these agreements between workers and contractors, putting right wing corporate ideology ahead of right wing free market ideology. Why? Power and control.

The same moneyed interests that push for an end to PLA's are the reason a large number of the twenty-six remaining non right-to-work states have seen legislation introduced into their legislatures. Mitt Romney, the 2012 Republican Presidential candidate, promised if he were President, ours would be a Right-to-Work nation.

The best response to the right wing, Right-to-Work scheme was stated more than 50 years ago by Dr. Martin Luther King, Jr: "In our glorious fight for civil rights, we must guard against being fooled by false slogans, such as 'right to work.' It is a law to rob us of our civil rights and job rights. Its purpose is to destroy labor unions and the freedom of collective bargaining by which unions have improved wages and working conditions of everyone.

Wherever these laws have been passed, wages are lower, job opportunities are fewer, and civil rights almost don't exist. We do not intend to let them do this to us. We demand this fraud be stopped. Our weapon is our vote."

We must stand steadfast and united on the founding principles of liberty and justice for all, knowing the coming struggle for equality for all will not be easy, but it is a fight worth waging for the benefit of future generations, my children.

To steal a line from Thomas Payne, "if trouble must come, let it come in my time." So let this People's Tour for America, as well as those other projects currently in the planning stage for the future, serve as a road map for how you will teach your kids the truth about their own history. And then teach your kids to stand up for themselves and their peers.

Let the characters we met, who shared our journey and were featured in our broadcasts, show you the way to make that same kind of difference in your own community. Get involved. Vote for people who will defend workers and their wages and benefits. That way, none of us will have to answer the question, "*Daddy, What's the Middle Class?*"

Thank you to my wife.

Mere words do not suffice when describing my affection and gratitude for choosing me, and sticking around after this tour. And thank you to Samantha, Alex, and Alyssa for being the most adorable and cool kids on the road.
You are my reason for waking up each morning.

Special thanks to our People's Tour for America sponsors

Alliance for American Manufacturing
   (AAM) americanmanufacturing.org

American Federation of State County Municipal Employees
   (AFSCME) AFSCME.org

Amalgamated Transit Union
   (ATU) ATU.org

International Brotherhood of Electrical Workers
   (IBEW) IBEW.org

International Brotherhood of Teamsters
   (IBT) Teamsters.org

International Longshore and Warehouse Union
   (ILWU) ILWU.org

United Steel Workers
   (USW) USW.org

Appendix

Introduction

http://www.netrootsnation.org/event/netroots-nation-2013/

http://www.historynet.com/the-men-who-built-america-a-preview.html

http://www.history.com/topics/cornelius-vanderbilt

http://www.pbs.org/wgbh/amex/carnegie/peopleevents/pande01.html

http://www.nydailynews.com/new-york/fraunces-tavern-frequented-george-washington-reopens-unique-renovations-article-1.148537

Chapter One

http://chargingbull.com

http://www.vanityfair.com/business/features/2010/11/financial-crisis-excerpt-201011

http://www.marketwatch.com/story/big-banks-conspiracy-is-destroying-america-2013-08-07

http://www.philly.com/philly/blogs/attytood/The-one-picture-that-tells-you-everything-.html

http://digitalcommons.iwu.edu/cgi/viewcontent.cgi?article=1105&context=rev

Chapter Two

http://lawcha.org/wordpress/annualmeeting/nyc2013/

http://www.aflcio.org/Blog/In-The-States/Union-Members-Help-During-and-After-Superstorm-Sandy

Chapter Three

http://www.ilr.cornell.edu/trianglefire/primary/survivorInterviews/MaryDomskyAbrams.html

http://www.ilr.cornell.edu/trianglefire/primary/survivorInterviews/SarahDworetz.html

http://www.ilr.cornell.edu/trianglefire/primary/survivorInterviews/RoseHauser.html

http://www.ilr.cornell.edu/trianglefire/primary/survivorInterviews/JosephFlecher.html

http://law2.umkc.edu/faculty/projects/ftrials/triangle/trianglevictims2.html

Chapter 4

http://www.nlrb.gov/who-we-are/board

http://www.salon.com/2013/01/09/jack_lews_union_busting_past/

Chapter 5

http://articles.washingtonpost.com/2013-09-07/world/41853173_1_bangladesh-garment-labor-studies-rana-plaza

http://www.aflcio.org/Blog/Global-Action/Walmart-Gap-Refuse-to-Sign-Bangladesh-Safety-Pact

http://www.rferl.org/content/article/1054882.html

http://www.outsidethebeltway.com/critics_call_radio_hosts_trip_propaganda_mission/

http://mediamatters.org/research/2013/03/19/where-are-the-medias-iraq-war-boosters-10-years/193117

http://www.talkers.com/tag/united-nations/

http://www.conservativechannel.net

Chapter 6

http://www.huffingtonpost.com/pat-lamarche/ancient-rome-had-unions-t_b_3417491.html

Chapter 7

http://www.americaslibrary.gov/jb/civil/jb_civil_wv_1.html

http://www.wvculture.org/history/statehood/statehood07.html

http://www.encyclopediavirginia.org/Martinsburg_Virginia_During_the_Civil_War#start_entry

http://avalon.law.yale.edu/19th_century/lincoln2.asp

Douglass, Fredrick. My Bondage My Freedom. Barnes & Noble Classics. New York. 2005.

http://www.academia.edu/457545/The_invention_of_infant_mortality

Chapter 8

http://corporate.walmart.com/frequently-asked-questions

http://www.forbes.com/forbes-400/

Shogan, Robert. The Battle of Blair Mountain, The Story of America's Largest Labor Uprising. Basic Books. New York.

http://www.politifact.com/personalities/rush-limbaugh/

http://mediamatters.org/blog/2012/03/08/limbaughs-advertisers-sponsored-these-10-attack/184833

Chapter 9

http://www.friendsofcoal.org/2007081612/latest-news/about.html

http://www.bloomberg.com/news/2013-05-29/patriot-coal-wins-approval-to-cut-retiree-pensions-benefits-1-.html

Chapter 10

http://www.stltoday.com/business/local/umwa-peabody-patriot-announce-settlement/article_fb253c2b-b149-51db-b8d1-001d488c9b02.html

http://www.wvgazette.com/News/201309100025

Shogan, Robert. The Battle of Blair Mountain, The Story of America's Largest Labor Uprising. Basic Books. New York.

http://www.apwu.org/laborhistory/10-4_blairmountain/10-4_blair mountain.htm

http://www.npr.org/2011/03/05/134203550/coal-reignites-a-mighty-battle-of-labor-history

Chapter 11

http://www.bestplaces.net/religion/city/tennessee/knoxville

http://www.areavibes.com/knoxville-tn/employment/

Chapter 12

http://highlandercenter.org

http://www.usatoday.com/story/news/nation/2013/08/14/civil-rights-training-school/2657801/

Chapter 13

http://www.teamster.org/content/james-p-hoffa

http://www.unionfacts.com/union/teamsters

http://www.huffingtonpost.com/pat-lamarche/ancient-rome-had-unions-t_b_3417491.html

http://www.memphistravel.com/beale-street-beal-street

http://bcnn1wp.wordpress.com/2012/08/25/remembering_robert_r_church_sr_family_of_americas_first_black_millionaire_led_racial_advances/

http://www.dailymail.co.uk/tvshowbiz/article-1021569/Great-Balls-Scandal-How-Jerry-Lee-Lewis-marriage-13-year-old-wrecked-career.html

http://www.memphismagazine.com/Blogs/Memphis-Stew/April-2013/Heres-a-Sneak-Peak-at-Jerry-Lee-Lewis-Cafe-Honky-Memphis-Centric-MenuTonk/

http://mlk-kpp01.stanford.edu/index.php/encyclopedia/encyclopedia/enc_memphis_sanitation_workers_strike_1968/

Chapter 14

http://www.archives.gov/education/lessons/memphis-v-mlk/

http://vi.uh.edu/pages/buzzmat/tafthartley.html

http://ctj.org/ctjreports/2013/09/fedex_paid_42_federal_tax_rate_over_5_years.php#.Ul4uvLTcFUQ

Chapter 16

http://www.uscourts.gov/educational-resources/get-involved/federal-court-activities/brown-board-education-re-enactment/history.aspx

http://www.history.com/topics/central-high-school-integration

http://www.nps.gov/chsc/index.htm

Chapter 17

http://legal-dictionary.thefreedictionary.com/Right-to-Work+Laws

http://www.arkansasafl-cio.org/index.cfm?action=cat&categoryID=356 7f869-0ffe-4231-9d3c-06ecc0c02b66

www.peoplestouforamerica.com

http://fuelfix.com/blog/2013/08/02/in-wake-of-canadian-disaster-u-s-issues-emergency-rules-for-trains/

http://www.teamster.org/content/brotherhood-locomotive-engineers-and-trainmen-denounce-one-person-train-operations-rail

http://www.daas.ar.gov/profilar.html

Chapter 18

http://www.census.gov/prod/2012pubs/acsbr11-05.pdf

http://dfw.cbslocal.com/2013/09/17/texas-has-highest-uninsured-rate-high-poverty/

http://texaspolitics.laits.utexas.edu/12_2_0.html

http://www2.ljworld.com/news/2012/dec/27/couples-life-road-hits-pothole/

http://www.texasento.net/prob.htm

Chapter 19

http://www.bushcenter.org/sites/default/files/2013%20Bush%20Center%20Membership%20Levels.pdf

http://www.archives.gov/presidential-libraries/about/history.html

http://www.archives.gov/presidential-libraries/laws/1978-act.html

http://www.huffingtonpost.com/2011/11/14/colorado-no-child-left-behind_n_1093383.html

Brown, Don. America is Under Attack. Roaring Brook Press. New York. 2011.

http://www.telegram.com/article/20130719/NEWS/130719733/1052&template=MOBILE

http://m.sodahead.com/united-states/texas-becomes-42nd-state-to-dump-bushs-no-child-left-behind-agrees-to-comply-with-key-obama-edu/question-3962647/

http://www.washingtonpost.com/wp-srv/politics/campaigns/wh2000/stories/bush073099.htm

http://www.theguardian.com/world/2008/oct/04/usa.internationalaidanddevelopment

http://articles.chicagotribune.com/2013-04-26/news/chi-retired-justice-oconnor-bush-v-gore-stirred-up-the-public-20130426_1_bush-v-retired-justice-o-connor-high-court

Chapter 20

http://www.trishgriffin.com/listings.php?page=1

http://www.dailykos.com/story/2013/10/11/1246469/-Fertilizer-plant-that-leveled-Texas-town-OSHA-suggests-a-measly-118-300-fine#

http://www.washingtonpost.com/wp-srv/special/national/west-texas-fertilizer-explosion-map/

https://www.osha.gov/pls/imis/establishment.inspection_detail?id=1911015

http://www.usatoday.com/story/news/nation/2013/04/25/firefighters-killed-fertilizer-blast-texas/2112825/

http://www.star-telegram.com/2013/04/22/4795158/more-inspections-wouldnt-have.html#storylink=cpy

http://www.usatoday.com/story/news/nation/2013/08/02/fema-approves-aid-for-texas/2613611/

http://www.fema.gov/news-release/2013/10/07/federal-disaster-assistance-tops-16-million-west-texas

Chapter 21

http://www.census.gov/hhes/www/income/data/statemedian/

http://www.aauw.org/files/2013/09/New-Mexico-Pay-Gap-2013.pdf

Chapter 22

http://www.azcentral.com/news/articles/20131002sheriff-arpaio-racial-profile-lawsuit-ruling.html

http://www.alre.org/uploads/ASU%20ALRE%20Presentation.pdf

http://www.nytimes.com/2011/08/03/opinion/reagan-vs-patco-the-strike-that-busted-unions.html?_r=0

Chapter 23

http://www.bobspixels.com/kaibab.org/powell/powexp.htm

http://www.nps.gov/grca/forteachers/upload/GeoArticle-2.pdf

"Territorial Times" Grand Canyon Railway. Volume XLI. Williams, Arizona.

http://www.thetrain.com/lodging/rv-park/

http://www.ucc.org/justice/public-education/philip-anshutz.html

Chapter 24

http://cprr.org/Museum/Chinese.html

http://ocp.hul.harvard.edu/immigration/railroads.html

http://www.britannica.com/EBchecked/topic/102543/Central-Pacific-Railroad

http://npshistory.com/nature_notes/grca/vol7-5c.htm

Zinn, Howard. A People's History of the United States. Harper Perennial Modern Classics. New York, New York. 1999

http://www.nps.gov/grca/parkmgmt/upload/2013-park-profile.pdf

Chapter 25

http://florenceks.com/text/local/local_hh-fred-harvey.htm

http://florenceks.com/text/local/local_hh-girls.htm

http://www.jstor.org/discover/10.2307/2119448?uid=3739800&uid=2&uid=4&uid=3739256&sid=21103017317943

http://www.westegg.com/inflation/

http://www.bloomberg.com/news/2013-04-25/waitresses-stuck-at-2-13-hourly-minimum-for-22-years.html

http://www.msnbc.com/all/walmart-collecting-food-donations-workers

Chapter 26

http://npdp.stanford.edu/node/63

http://www.cnn.com/2009/POLITICS/06/02/tillman.mcchrystal.hearing/

http://usatoday30.usatoday.com/news/nation/2010-10-18-hooverbypass18_ST_N.htm

http://travelnevada.com/destinations/hoover-dam/fun-facts/

http://highestbridges.com/wiki/index.php?title=Mike_O%27Callaghan-Pat_Tilman_Memorial_Bridge

http://www.hooverdamtourcompany.com/stats.html

Construction of Hoover Dam. Department of the Interior, Bureau of Reclamation. KC Publications. Wickenburg, Arizona. 1976.

http://www.thepeoplehistory.com/1933.html

Chapter 27

http://www.wunderground.com/history/airport/KLAS/2013/6/19/Custom-History.html

http://www.reviewjournal.com/news/report-nevada-prisons-have-sufficient-space-inmates

http://elkodaily.com/news/opinion/commentary-nevada-must-be-made-whole/article_ef0c23e4-bdaf-11e2-aa4f-001a4bcf887a.html

Chapter 28

http://www.usatoday.com/story/money/business/2013/10/05/most-dangerousstates/2925679/

http://www.newrepublic.com/article/80316/relationship-poverty-crime-rates-economic-conditions

http://www.reviewjournal.com/news/education/number-nevada-children-living-poverty-climbs

http://nymag.com/news/features/tide-detergent-drugs-2013-1/

Chapter 29

http://articles.latimes.com/2013/nov/15/local/la-me-hangtown-haven-20131116

http://www.usnews.com/news/articles/2013/10/25/number-of-homeless-students-has-soared-since-the-recession-began

http://calwaterwars.com

http://perush.cjs.ucla.edu/index.php/volume-2/jewish-urban-history-in-comparative-perspective-jewish-buenos-aires-and-jewish-los-angeles/4-caroline-luce-socialism-radicalism-and-the-jewish-labor-movement-in-los-angeles-history-and-historiography

http://www.jewishlabor.org

http://jobs.aol.com/articles/2011/06/02/ups-vs-fedex-which-pays-best/

http://money.cnn.com/magazines/fortune/fortune500/2012/full_list/

Chapter 30

http://www.nationalnursesunited.org/press/entry/nurses-to-host-golden-gate-bridge-march-june-20-call-to-stop-keystone-xl-pi/

Chapter 31

http://www.motherjones.com/tom-philpott/2011/09/california-agriculture-too-productive-our-own-good

http://www.crater.lake.national-park.com/info.htm

http://www.nps.gov/crla/planyourvisit/brochures.htm

http://www.nps.gov/history/history/online_books/crla1/rimdrive1.htm

http://www.craterlakelodges.com/find-us/frequently-asked-questions/

Chapter 32

http://www.longshoreshippingnews.com/2013/10/members-of-congress-ask-u-s-trade-representative-to-help-resolve-dispute-during-tpp-negotiations-with-japan/

http://www.pcworld.com/article/2070760/documents-leaked-again-amid-secret-trade-negotiations.html

http://www.longshoreshippingnews.com/2013/11/federal-judge-cites-ilwu-for-contempt-of-court/

Chapter 33

http://news.google.com/newspapers?nid=336&dat=19840125&id=vZg_AAAAIBAJ&sjid=EIMDAAAAIBAJ&pg=5270,3376428

Hanlin, James, Weir, Robert, Editors. Historical Encyclopedia of American Labor. Greenwood Press. Westport, Connecticut. 2004.

Zinn, Howard. A People's History of the United States. Harper Perennial Modern Classics. New York, New York. 1999.

http://historytogo.utah.gov/people/joehill.html

http://murderpedia.org/index.htm

Chapter 34

http://karenmayne.com/category/senate-2/

http://acpp.info/2009/07/29/research-shows-union-jobs-are-safer/

http://webecoist.momtastic.com/2009/09/10/massive-man-made-and-natural-holes/

http://historytogo.utah.gov/utah_chapters/mining_and_railroads/coppermining.html

Chapter 36

http://home.nps.gov/sand/historyculture/index.htm

http://www.colorado.edu/csilw/sandcreekltrs.htm

http://www.denverpost.com/news/ci_23959631/history-colorado-center-closes-sand-creek-massacre-display

http://www.sott.net/article/255391-Sand-Creek-Massacre-descendants-seek-justice-148-years-later

Chapter 37

http://www.usatoday.com/story/news/nation/2013/07/15/mass-killings-after-aurora/2512501/

http://www.washingtonpost.com/page/2010-2019/Washington-Post/2013/03/12/National-Politics/Polling/question_10030.xml

http://www.csmonitor.com/USA/DC-Decoder/2012/0725/Why-gun-sales-spike-after-mass-shootings-It-s-not-what-you-might-think

http://libcom.org/history/1927-colorado-miners-strike-and-columbine-mine-massacre

http://content.lib.washington.edu/cdm4/item_viewer.php?CISOROOT=/social&CISOPTR=3020&CISOBOX=1&REC=9

http://www.pbs.org/wgbh/americanexperience/features/primary-resources/rockefellers-ludlow/

http://www.history.com/this-day-in-history/colorado-governor-sends-militia-to-cripple-creek

http://books.google.com/books?id=yXYrAAAAYAAJ&pg=PA474&lpg=PA474&dq=habeas+corpus+i'll+give+them+post+mortems&source=bl&ots=5hJe9pLQVL&sig=HdfG-tJv00vEoODNpaBfhJcilSs&hl=en&sa=X&ei=QQzpUsvuGIXLsATQw4CIBA&ved=0CCcQ6AEwAA#v=onepage&q&f=false

Chapter 38

http://www.history.com/topics/interstate-highway-system

http://millercenter.org/president/eisenhower/essays/biography/5

Chapter 39

http://en.thinkexist.com

http://www.washingtonpost.com/wp-dyn/articles/A29142-2004May15.html

Chapter 40

http://www.forbes.com/sites/timworstall/2012/03/04/the-story-of-henry-fords-5-a-day-wages-its-not-what-you-think/

http://www.kchistory.org/cdm4/item_viewer.php?CISOROOT=/Local&CISOPTR=40843&CISOBOX=1&REC=1

http://brookesnews.com/100103obama1937.html

UAW Local 249 and Ford Motor Company. Brown, Phil. Kansas City, Missouri.

Chapter 41

http://www.forbes.com/sites/realspin/2013/11/27/why-do-1-4-million-americans-work-at-walmart-with-many-more-trying-to/

http://www.msnbc.com/the-ed-show/leaked-document-shows-what-walmart-really-pay

http://abcnews.go.com/Business/walmart-ceo-pay-hour-workers-year/story?id=11067470

http://www.forbes.com/sites/clareoconnor/2014/04/15/report-walmart-workers-cost-taxpayers-6-2-billion-in-public-assistance/

Chapter 42

http://www.shmoop.com/brave-new-world/ford-symbol.html

http://www.biography.com/people/ed-asner-259339#the-mary-tyler-moore-show&awesm=~oCgALgpCDVs7Kz

http://www.starpulse.com/Actors/Asner,_Ed/Biography/

http://www.sagaftra.org/edward-asner

Chapter 43

http://cas.umkc.edu/labor-ed/staff.htm

http://www.kkfi.org/program/heartland-labor-forum/

http://www.kcgarmentmuseum.org/history/

http://www.garmentdistrictkc.com/index.cfm?page=events

Remaking America. McCormack, Richard, Editor. The Alliance for American Manufacturing. 2013.

Chapter 44

http://www.trumanlibrary.org

http://millercenter.org/president/truman/essays/biography/6

http://trumanlibrary.org/calendar/viewpapers.php?pid=2059

http://www.bls.gov/eag/eag.mo_stlouis_msa.htm

http://quickfacts.census.gov/qfd/states/29/29510.html

http://www.city-data.com/crime/crime-St.-Louis-Missouri.html

http://www.teamsterslocal618.org/?zone=/unionactive/view_article.cfm&HomeID=296312

Chapter 45

http://www.statebankofcherry.com/history.html

The Cherry Mine Disaster. Kotecki, Jason. Stout, Steve. Utica, Illinois. 1999.

http://dig.lib.niu.edu/ISHS/ishs-1979february/ishs-1979february57.pdf

http://guitarjourney.tripod.com/cherrycoalminedisaster/id4.html

http://www.illinoislaborhistory.org/articles/131-we-owe-them-a-great-debt-cherry-mine-centennial.html

http://www.thedailybeast.com/articles/2014/05/15/after-100s-of-miners-die-turkey-s-prime-minister-says-this-happens.html

Chapter 46

http://www.iww.org/branches/US/CA/lagmb/lit/haymarket.shtml

http://law2.umkc.edu/faculty/projects/ftrials/haymarket/spiestestimony.html

http://www.chicagohistory.org/hadc/intro.html

http://law2.umkc.edu/faculty/projects/ftrials/haymarket/pardon.html#REASONS_FOR_PARDONING

http://www.pukmedia.com/EN/EN_Direje.aspx?Jimare=20173

http://www.executedtoday.com/2008/11/11/1887-parsons-spies-fischer-engel-haymarket-martyrs/

http://www.britannica.com/EBchecked/topic/257829/Haymarket-Riot

http://historymatters.gmu.edu/d/47

http://historymatters.gmu.edu/d/45

http://historymatters.gmu.edu/d/46

Chapter 47

http://teamsterair.org/professions/pilots

100 Years of Teamsters History. Delancey Publishing Company. Alexandria, Virginia. 2003.

TEAMSTERS Snapshot in Time. Peake Delancey Publishing, Inc. Hyattsville, Maryland. 2010.

James R. Hoffa REMEMBERED. Peake Delancey Publishing, Inc. Hyattsville, Maryland. 2013.

Life in the Teamsters. "They All Went Up": The Story of the National Master Freight Agreement. Mack, Bob. Peake Delancey Publishing, Inc. Hyattsville, Maryland. 2012.

http://www.britannica.com/EBchecked/topic/585238/Teamsters-Union

http://www.princeton.edu/~achaney/tmve/wiki100k/docs/Taft–Hartley_Act.html

Chapter 48

http://www.dailymail.co.uk/news/article-2371191/Aretha-Franklin-leads-cries-Detroit-feet-filed-bankruptcy.html

http://www.investopedia.com/articles/pf/12/auto-industry.asp

http://www.thedetroiter.com/site/laborpage.html

http://mea.org/michigan-facing-growing-number-homeless-children

Chapter 49

http://robertreich.org/post/35848994755

http://www.nytimes.com/2014/05/17/business/us-fines-general-motors-35-million-for-lapses-on-ignition-switch-defect.html?_r=0

http://www.michigan.gov/documents/CIS_WSH_minwsf99_27783_7.pdf

http://labornotes.org/1999/03/ford-rouge-blast-was-corporate-cost-cutting-blame?language=en

http://www.thehenryford.org/rouge/historyofrouge3.aspx

http://www.hfmgv.org/exhibits/fmc/battle.asp

Chapter 50

http://www.aecf.org/upload/publicationfiles/fes3622h337.pdf

http://www.oig.dhs.gov/assets/Mgmt/2014/OIG_14-33_Feb14.pdf

http://www.allpar.com/corporate/factories/toledo.html

http://www.businessweek.com/articles/2014-03-14/the-jeep-plant-mitt-romney-said-was-moving-to-china-is-hiring-1-000-workers-in-ohio

http://www.americanprogress.org/issues/labor/news/2012/07/09/11898/5-facts-about-overseas-outsourcing/

http://www.toledoblade.com/Economy/2014/05/21/April-s-jobless-rates-at-lowest-in-over-10-years.html

http://baybridgeinfo.org/visit-bridge

http://online.wsj.com/news/articles/SB10001424052748703428604575418680197041878